Critical Muslim 20

PostWest

Editor: Ziauddin Sardar

Deputy Editors: Hassan Mahamdallie, Samia Rahman, Shanon Shah

Senior Editors: Syed Nomanul Haq, Aamer Hussein, Ehsan Masood, Ebrahim Moosa

Publisher: Michael Dwyer

Managing Editor (Hurst Publishers): Daisy Leitch

Cover Design: Fatima Jamadar

Associate Editors: Tahir Abbas, Alev Adil, Nazry Bahrawi, Merryl Wyn Davies, Abdelwahhab El-Affendi, Marilyn Hacker, Nader Hashemi, Jeremy Henzell-Thomas, Vinay Lal, Iftikhar Malik, Boyd Tonkin

International Advisory Board: Karen Armstrong, William Dalrymple, Anwar Ibrahim, Robert Irwin, Bruce Lawrence, Ashis Nandy, Ruth Padel, Bhikhu Parekh, Barnaby Rogerson, Malise Ruthven

Critical Muslim is published quarterly by C. Hurst & Co. (Publishers) Ltd. on behalf of and in conjunction with Critical Muslim Ltd. and the Muslim Institute, London. *Critical Muslim* acknowledges the support of the Aziz Foundation, London.

All correspondence to Muslim Institute, CAN Mezzanine, 49-51 East Road, London N1 6AH, United Kingdom

e-mail for editorial: editorial@criticalmuslim.com

The editors do not necessarily agree with the opinions expressed by the contributors. We reserve the right to make such editorial changes as may be necessary to make submissions to *Critical Muslim* suitable for publication.

C. Hurst & Co (Publishers) Ltd.,41 Great Russell Street, London WC1B 3PL

ISBN: 978-1-84904-675-6 ISSN: 2048-8475

To subscribe or place an order by credit/debit card or cheque (pounds sterling only) please contact Kathleen May at the Hurst address above or e-mail kathleen@hurstpub.co.uk

Tel: 020 7255 2201

A one year subscription, inclusive of postage (four issues), costs £50 (UK), £65 (Europe) and £75 (rest of the world).

A Cataloguing-in-Publication data record for this book is available from the British Library

IIIT Publications

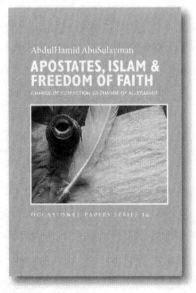

HALAL FOOD FOUNDATION

Halal Is Much More Than Food

The Halal Food Foundation (HFF) is a registered charity that aims to make the concept of halal more accessible and mainstream. We want people to know that halal does not just pertain to food – halal is a lifestyle.

The Foundation pursues its goals through downloadable resources, events, social networking, school visits, pursuing and funding scientific research on issues of food and health, and its monthly newsletter. We work for the community and aim at the gradual formation of a consumer association. We aim to educate and inform; and are fast becoming the first port of call on queries about halal issues. We do not talk at people, we listen to them.

If you have any queries, comments, ideas, or would just like to voice your opinion - please get in contact with us.

Halal Food Foundation

109 Fulham Palace Road,
Hammersmith, London, W6 8JA
Charity number: 1139457
Website: www.halalfoodfoundation.co.uk
E-mail: info@halalfoodfoundation.co.uk

 @HFF_UK

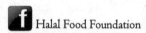 Halal Food Foundation

Critical Muslim

Subscribe to Critical Muslim

Now in its fifth year in print, Hurst is pleased to announce that *Critical Muslim* is also available online. Users can access the site for just £3.30 per month – or for those with a print subscription it is included as part of the package. In return, you'll get access to everything in the series (including our entire archive), and a clean, accessible reading experience for desktop computers and handheld devices — entirely free of advertising.

Full subscription

The print edition of *Critical Muslim* is published quarterly in January, April, July and October. As a subscriber to the print edition, you'll receive new issues directly to your door, as well as full access to our digital archive.

United Kingdom £50/year
Europe £65/year
Rest of the World £75/year

Digital Only

Immediate online access to *Critical Muslim*

Browse the full *Critical Muslim* archive

Cancel any time

£3.30 per month

CM20

October–December 2016

CONTENTS

POSTWEST

ARTS AND LETTERS

REVIEWS

ET CETERA

Ana Maria Pacheco, *Shadows of the Wanderer* (detail)

POSTWEST

INTRODUCTION
THE LAST POST

Shanon Shah

You know the story. Prince Hamlet grieves the untimely and mysterious death of his father and resents Claudius, his uncle, for marrying his mother and taking over the kingdom of Denmark with dictatorial glee. But then one day, Hamlet is visited by the ghost of his father who names Claudius as his killer and demands vengeance. Beset by indecision, torn by grief, and vexed by his troubled relationships with his mother, Gertrude, and potential girlfriend, Ophelia, Hamlet eventually hatches an elaborate plan to expose and punish Claudius. In this most archetypal of Shakespeare's tragedies, all hell breaks loose. People die spectacularly bloody deaths to end a morality tale about deception, betrayal and the abuse of power.

Surely the moral and aesthetic appeal of this story is universal — transcending time, place and culture. At least that's what the Oxford-trained American anthropologist Laura Bohannan decided to demonstrate during her fieldwork among the Tiv in Nigeria in the mid-twentieth century. During a lull in her research, Bohannan began to despair as the Tiv villagers held daily booze-soaked storytelling sessions while waiting for the swamp waters to subside before resuming with their farming. On their part, the villagers could not understand why Bohannan did not join in and preferred to pore over her notes and academic tomes. The elders soon challenged her to do some storytelling of her own, which prompted a lightbulb moment — why not share the story of Hamlet? Surely these villagers, with their proud oral traditions, would be dazzled by this most celebrated of stories by England's most beloved playwright of all time?

Every story hinges on a problem or a challenge that the protagonist has to overcome. So wouldn't the death of Hamlet's father and the marriage of his dastardly uncle to his mother be enough to produce a crackerjack plot? Not for the Tiv elders. They applauded Claudius. 'In our country also,' they said, 'the younger brother marries the elder brother's widow and becomes the father of his children. Now, if your uncle, who married your widowed mother, is your father's full brother, then he will be a real father to you.' So for them it was a good thing that Claudius took charge of the country and married Gertrude! Just like that, the central moral conflict in *Hamlet* was turned on its head and became a straightforward virtue.

Bohannan was stunned and things continued going downhill. The Tiv quibbled about almost every element of the story. They were especially stumped by 'ghost' as a concept. Surely Bohannan meant that what Hamlet saw was an omen sent by a witch? No, Bohannan explained, it was a ghost – 'someone who is dead but who walks around and can talk, and people can hear him and see him but not touch him'.

The Tiv objected. 'One can touch zombies.'

Bohannan tried again. 'A "ghost" is the dead man's shadow.'

Again the Tiv objected. 'Dead man cast no shadows.'

'They do in my country,' Bohannan snapped. Despite their incredulous smirks the Tiv villagers begged Bohannan to continue.

At the end of the session, the villagers said they had thoroughly enjoyed *Hamlet* but gently reminded Bohannan of the 'errors' she made in telling it. They invited her to tell more stories but they would 'instruct' her in their 'true meaning' so that she could impart her newly found wisdom to her own elders when she returned home.

This anecdote is taken from Bohannan's much-anthologised short article, 'Shakespeare in the Bush'. On one level, it is a cautionary tale about how meanings can get lost in translation and how our perceptions and expectations are shaped by our different perspectives. But it also questions the assumptions that some people make about universality – 'Surely Shakespeare transcends all boundaries?' – and how these assumptions come to exist in the first place. It is a delightful reversal – it is the Tiv villagers who relentlessly challenge Bohannan's cherished beliefs about a major work by a white, male, English playwright from the sixteenth century. Personally, it's also a bit of a revenge fantasy in response to every privileged, white – yes, I'll go there now – Westerner who has ever told me that the Qur'an (or Islamic art or anything else perceived as 'Islamic' and therefore 'non-Western') is boring, incoherent or irrational compared to the Bible, Shakespeare or, I don't know, Michelangelo. But I'll come back to that later.

At this point, it is worth noting that 2016 marks the 400th anniversary of the death of William Shakespeare. There have been numerous celebrations of his lasting contributions to the English language and literature, 'Western culture' and, indeed, the world. Do you know what kept Nelson Mandela going throughout those horrible years of incarceration on Robben Island? *The Collected Works of William Shakespeare*. Mandela — Nobel Peace laureate, son of a Xhosa chief and anti-apartheid hero, whose mother tongue was not even English. That sort of thing.

Shakespeare is interesting like that. Apart from being feted as a literary legend, he is celebrated for his enduring influence on Western culture *and* world civilisation. He is big in China, India, the Arab World and Latin America, with his plays adapted to address local audiences and circumstances. In many Arab countries, for example, *Othello* has morphed into an analysis of Orientalism or a tragedy about gender violence. When this happens, though, can we say that these works exert their influence because of Shakespeare's status as a Western genius, or have they been transformed into something else? When Hamlet is played as a Che Guevara-type revolutionary in an Arabic adaptation, is this still Shakespeare as we know him or is it Shakespeare gone post-West?

In essence, post-West is an idea which suggests that something has been reconfigured. But exactly what that 'something' is must be investigated further to conclude satisfactorily that it has indeed been reconfigured or perhaps undermined.

This is not the first time the word 'post' has been attached to a concept to contend that a paradigm shift of sorts has occurred. There's the 'postcolonial' — the idea that the world as we know it still grapples with the legacies of colonialism and imperialism. 'Postmodernism', initially describing trends within twentieth century Western architecture and visual art, refers to the broader intellectual movements that critique taken-for-granted wisdom in various disciplines, including philosophy, history, linguistics and literature. It suggests that 'grand narratives', which provide meaning and sense of direction, are dead. Now there's even the notion of the 'post-secular' — the proposition that the decline of religion has been reversed, or that religion was never on its way out in the first place.

Each of these concepts has its strengths as well as its own problems. Postcolonial criticisms can veer into simplistic and dangerous 'blame the

West' arguments which play into the hands of former colonies with their own home-grown, post-independence authoritarian governments, from Zimbabwe to the Caribbean. Postmodern theories have been criticised for being circular, jargon heavy and disconnected from the real world. In the subtitle of his masterly deconstruction *Postmodernism and the Other*, Ziauddin Sardar described it as 'the new imperialism of western culture'. Post-secular perspectives about the resurgence of religion (or that religion never receded to begin with) can often overstate the case – can we really claim that the West is already 'post-secular'? And often, concepts such as these contain unexamined assumptions about the parent ideas they are meant to depart from. What exactly is 'secular' or 'modern'?

This does not mean that these concepts are useless. If they are fuzzy, then they force us to reckon with this fuzziness and to investigate if or how the picture can be made clearer. Yes, intellectual sloppiness produces sloppy concepts but intellectual rigour can result in sharper analyses that helpfully explain underexplored or hitherto confusing aspects of life. So exploratory or inchoate concepts such as 'post-West' – along with the 'postcolonial', 'postmodern' and 'post-secular' – can be what the French anthropologist Claude Levi-Strauss once referred to as *bon à penser*, or 'good to think with'.

But who on Earth decided which parts of our spherical planet could and would be designated as the 'West'? Deciding on North and South is pretty straightforward, but for a planet revolving around a north-south axis surely notions of west and east can only be relative? Yet something called the 'West' does exist in our imaginations and it is not merely a geographical area – it is understood as a civilisation with its own self-understanding and superior outlook, distinguishable from the non-Western world. How did this idea of the 'West' come to take on these meanings in the first place? This complex question is deftly tackled in Jasper M. Trautsch's essay, 'The Concept of the "West"'.

Trautsch clarifies that contemporary notions of the West actually contain two distinct conceptual origins. The first was the concept of the 'Occident', referring to a 'cultural community' in Western and Central Europe, which was developed at the turn of the sixteenth century and 'found its imaginary Other in the (Muslim) "Orient"'. 'Western civilisation', however, emerged as a concept only in the nineteenth century to divide the European continent into two political groupings – the liberal 'West' and the autocratic

'East'. It was only in the twentieth century that both concepts merged to inform the idea of the 'West' as a political bloc of liberal democracies *and* a cultural community with a shared historical and religious identity.

As Trautsch demonstrates, concepts that seem stable and eternal can be inconsistent and deeply contested. It is worth being reminded that in the early days, the United States of America was also considered Occidental Europe's Other (albeit to its west, with Russia being its eastern Other). The positioning of the US as a paragon of the West is thus a relatively recent phenomenon. And Germany, anchor of the European Union, was once considered to be neither here nor there in terms of its Western credentials. In fact, the First World War was portrayed in France and Britain as an epic battle between 'Western civilisation' and 'German barbarism'.

If the idea of the West contains these significant ambiguities and inconsistencies, then what of the 'East'? In her essay, 'Where is the East?', Amrita Ghosh argues that Benjamin Disraeli's famous uttering, 'the East is a career', 'still becomes the best possible answer to analyse' the term's 'discursive multiplicity'. For the British, the East properly came into existence beginning with the exploits of the East India Company and soon encompassed faraway China and Japan. With imperial expansion, however, came confusion. As Ghosh points out, India was sometimes lumped together geographically with Ethiopia, which was variously placed in Africa or Asia. Britain's growing influence in the Indian subcontinent also elevated the geopolitical importance of the journey eastward, hence the invention of the 'Middle East'. In 1948, the United Nations defined the Middle East to be spread across three continents – Africa, Asia and Europe – and including Afghanistan, Iran, Iraq, Syria, Lebanon, Turkey, Saudi Arabia, Yemen, Egypt, Ethiopia, and Greece. Yet, as recently as 2004, the administration of George W. Bush adopted the term to refer to the region extending from Morocco to Pakistan – talk about an expanding midsection!

Beyond the spatial, the concept 'East' is laden with other paradoxes. Like the concept of the 'West', it defines an imagined topography through particular values, aesthetics and ways of being. The East was invariably portrayed in the West as exotic, mystical and primitive. The quality of exoticism could range from the benevolent in reference to China and Japan to backward in reference to India and violent and irrational in reference to the Middle East. And in colonialist or imperialist portrayals, rarely was the

East ever cast as the West's equal in politics, culture or economic advancement.

How the West came to dominate the East is well described by Roger van Zwanenberg. In his essay, 'The Struggle for World Power', van Zwanenberg narrates the story of Western imperialism with a focus on monopolistic European trading companies. From this perspective, the rise of the West and its domination over the East was driven primarily by economics and gradually became embroiled with military and political interests. These tangible aspects of colonialism were 'bolstered by the idea that Western man had a superior civilisation and was part of a superior race – non-European peoples of "colour" were considered inferior'.

In van Zwanenberg's Marxist analysis, the peoples who were colonised fought bitterly against Western domination but it was always an uphill battle. They were up against a system propped up by a monumental slave trade and rapid technological advancements. European colonialism sowed the seeds of its own destruction, however, by exacerbating nationalist intra-European tensions which led to the First and Second World Wars. And this, van Zwanenberg argues, is what led to the US eventually bursting onto the scene as the new global-cum-imperial power. Far from being a beacon of freedom and democracy, he contends, the US continues to manipulate international trade and exploit the world's resources to prop up Western domination. In response to those who might argue that advancements in digital communication will nurture more democratic alternatives, van Zwanenberg contends that monopoly companies actually control vast information networks so that they can bypass national governments and public scrutiny. 'Then and now,' he insists, 'monopoly power posed and continues to pose a major threat to people's aspirations for a truly representative and participatory democracy.'

Small wonder, then, as Gordon Blaine Steffey argues 'an obituary of the West is untimely and as deliriously naïve as prophecy'. In 'PostWest Anxieties', Steffey argues that the post-West, 'like the West wherein it first draws breath', is a bit of a shapeshifter. It changes before your very eyes the moment you think you've grasped what it looks like. Like the West, the post-West is a bit of a mythical creature, too – 'there is no object to which it must or could correspond'. How the picture of the post-West takes shape depends very much on how different people see the West – as 'lost, transformed, overcome, dispensable, usable, or redeemable in its projection'. Visions of the post-West can thus be apocalyptic. They can signal decay and destruction, becoming a warning of how the West is presently digging its own grave – for example in being too relaxed about immigration. Or post-West visions can be utopian, of a world imbued with wisdom originally inspired in and by the West. As circular or paradoxical as this might sound, in both sets of visions the post-West is a Western construct. It emerges out of the same 'sociopolitical paradigm' that succours dominant conceptions of the West. For Steffey, the way to overcome global power imbalances is not by celebrating the coming of the so-called post-West, but through mutual learning and listening between the West and its Others.

However, this kind of mutual learning and listening is easier said than done. Especially if one discovers that one is a bit of a shapeshifter, too. When I was seven, I said something that amused the mother of one of my classmates. It was after the last bell had rung, and all the boys were waiting for their parents or school buses to pick them up and go home. I was chattering away to my friend in Penang Hokkien, a local variant of the Hokkien Chinese dialect spoken in northwest Malaysia. My friend's mother was confused that I, a Malay-looking boy, was speaking to her son in fluent-but-strange Hokkien. She did not know that I am mixed race, and that members of my extended family speak Punjabi, Tamil, Malay, and various dialects of Chinese, including Hokkien, Hakka and Mandarin. So, in Hokkien she asked a typically Malaysian question, 'What *are* you, exactly?' I had to think about it and eventually answered, in Hokkien as well, 'I'm English.' (The Hokkien expression I used, 'ang moh', is an epithet which actually means 'red hair' and generally refers to white Europeans.) When my mother arrived, the two mothers started talking and both ended up bursting into tears of laughter about my quip.

In hindsight, this category confusion was perfectly understandable. My extended family is multi-ethnic, multi-religious and multi-lingual, but my own immediate family primarily speaks English. My parents perpetuated this confusion when they referred to American television shows like *Little House on the Prairie* and *The Incredible Hulk* as 'English programmes'. But this was also understandable since they were using language to distinguish the various programmes on television – we also watched 'Malay', 'Chinese', 'Hindustani' and 'Tamil' shows sometimes. These technicalities – which were undoubtedly linked to the legacies of British colonialism – profoundly shaped my self-perception. The Malaysian education system shook me up, though – I was soon forced to accept that I was not 'English' and it also became impossible to claim multiple ethnic backgrounds. I was officially Malay and that was that. And at that stage in my life this felt a bit disappointing, to be honest. Laura Ingalls Wilder and Dr David Bruce Banner were not Malay. The kids in my favourite Enid Blyton and Roald Dahl stories were not Malay. And Shakespeare was definitely not Malay.

In fact, I was so entranced by Anglocentric Euro-American literature, music and television that it took ages to even realise that there were hardly any racial Others – and certainly no Muslims – in these cultural universes I wanted to belong to. The more I became aware of this, the more it seemed to lend credence to the anti-Western rhetoric espoused by some of my Islamic Studies instructors in school. Still, as a kid who had Abba, the Famous Five and Mary Poppins hardwired into his subconscious, I could not be fully convinced that white people were bad. Instead, life became a struggle between my Muslim, 'Malay' and 'Western' selves. East was East and West was West – never could the twain meet. It did not get any easier when I went to university in Australia, where the virulent anti-Semitism, anti-Western rhetoric, misogyny and homophobia I encountered in the Muslim prayer room was matched only by the Islamophobia and racism outside. I felt torn and even at war with myself at times. Discovering Ziauddin Sardar's *Introducing Muhammad* was therefore a bit of a lifeline – it showed me that there was another way to think about Islam, science and Western civilisation. It also made me even more incensed with all the bigots – anti-Western and anti-Muslim – I'd ever encountered in my life for withholding this information from me.

In this way, the concept of 'post-West' is *bon à penser* on multiple levels, not least the level of personal experience and identity. My experiences are the product of the meeting of the so-called East and West and yet they are also constantly threatened by the collision between the two. Perhaps the political scientist Samuel Huntington was right up to a point in that civilisations can and do clash – but only if we want them to. They can also enrich each other if we let them. Sadly, this mutual enrichment remains unrealised and even appears impossible in so many national environments now, especially with countries that are meant to step in as new post-Western superpowers.

We need only consider Russia, likened in Julia Sveshnikova's essay to 'a vulgar, clumsy bear that everybody wants to avoid'. Even that description might be too kind. In the EU and the US, the mass media largely portray its president Vladimir Putin as a kind of over-the-top Bond villain. And it's not hard to see why – Putin's leadership has coincided with the increasing harassment of human rights activists and independent journalists and the suspicious deaths of political opponents, alongside the annexation of Crimea and military incursions into Eastern Ukraine and Syria. Sveshnikova argues, however, that whilst Putin and his allies might claim to be standing up to the West and resisting US domination, their words and deeds are symptomatic of an existential-like insecurity on a national level. She contends that ever since the collapse of the Soviet Union, Russian leaders have tried unsuccessfully to forge a viable, positive national identity. This political failure has laid the ground for the emergence of an aggressive Slavophile nationalism which thrives on sticking it to the West.

To develop more nuanced insights, Sveshnikova looks at the complicated and contradictory ways that Islam has formed part of Russian identity from the pre-Soviet era to the present. The picture is somewhat surprising – the kind of manipulation and surveillance that Islam is subjected to under the guise of counterterrorism in Russia is not comparable to what happens in the US and Western Europe. Although Muslims form a minority, Islam has been part of the Russian national landscape from pre-modern times. In the first millennium A.D., Vladimir Sviatoslavovich the Great, the ruler of Kievan Rus', allegedly almost made Islam the official religion but ditched the idea because the religion forbade the consumption of alcohol. In 2003, Putin even declared Russia 'an Islamic country' and in 2005 it joined the Organisation of Islamic Conference (OIC), albeit with observer status. That would simply not happen in the US or any EU member state (which technically still includes Britain but not for long). In relation to this, Russian intervention in the Middle East does not actually unite Russia's Muslims in opposition to Putin – the range of their political attitudes seems to reflect that of the wider population. But while there are possibilities for the emergence of a positive, multi-layered Russian identity, this is constantly stunted by the state's disastrous economic mismanagement, internal political repression and international sabre rattling.

China seems to be far more adept at balancing these different elements in its quest for power, albeit precariously, as argued by Jalal Afhim in his essay. As Afhim puts it, China's 'no enemies' policy might not result in a post-West but it is certainly reshaping the world. For instance, China is reaching out to its neighbours with promises of economic aid without political interference and supports an independent Palestinian state. This contrasts markedly with the political conditions that form part of many US aid schemes and the US's steadfast pro-Israel stance in the Middle East. Yet alongside this promising global picture, there are serious concerns about China's internal management of human rights, democracy and the status of minorities, especially in Xinjiang and Tibet.

As with Sveshnikova, Afhim focuses on China's management of its Muslim population to analyse its evolving geopolitical position, especially in light of a potential rebalancing of relationships between the Middle East, the US and China. China's domestic policies appear alarmingly anti-Muslim, particularly towards its restive Uyghur population, yet its national landscape – like Russia's – has been shaped by the presence of Islam for more than a millennium. Afhim observes that throughout the eight years he lived there, he did not once see 'a single film, television programme, or advertisement which featured a Chinese Muslim character'. Ignorance about Islam is also widespread. At the same time, it is hard to accuse the Chinese authorities of singling out Muslims since the Communist republic is officially secular, after all. Afhim suggests instead that Han-Uyghur tensions are driven by a strong desire by the Uyghur to defend their cultural and political autonomy, which happens to include the right to practise Islam. Other Muslim groups such as the Hui have succumbed to greater degrees of acculturation and are therefore not seen by state authorities as a problem. Nevertheless, Afhim cautions that there are younger Hui who are ambivalent, feeling that they can neither fulfil the aspirations of older Hui nor fully belong in mainstream Chinese society. The problem with rebellious young Uyghur is more serious, with increasing numbers reported to be joining armed militias like Jabhat al-Nusra in Syria. So the future of China as a post-Western superpower depends significantly upon how it solves its internal Muslim puzzle.

China and Russia are not the only challengers to the prevailing world order. They form only half of the BRIC label – one of the more popular acronyms coined to describe the rise of non-traditional powers. Yet the

BRIC label is flawed – Russia and China technically are established powers. They have both been permanent UN Security Council members with veto power since 1945. They are both nuclear powers as recognised under the Non-Proliferation Treaty. If there was a post-West race of sorts, China and Russia would already have a head start compared to Brazil and India. So we now need to pay attention to how Brazil and India can try to shift the balance of global power.

Brazil's shining moment could have been the 2016 Olympics in Rio de Janeiro, but this was overshadowed by a protracted and bitter political crisis in the wake of President Dilma Roussef's impeachment. In a year that should have bolstered national pride, the political stability and democratic consolidation of the decades following military rule unravelled dramatically. This was not the same Brazil of 2009, which proudly greeted the announcement that the 2016 Games would be awarded to Rio. Back then, President Luiz Inacio 'Lula' da Silva proclaimed, 'now we are going to show the world we can be a great country.' In hindsight, that pronouncement was pure hubris – the country's colossal political crisis has been accompanied by a massive corruption scandal and a deep recession.

What about India, then? India, as Shiv Visvanathan argues in his lyrical essay, is on the verge of being thwarted by 'sheer mediocrity'. In a letter written from the future, Visvanathan reflects on what could happen to India after Prime Minister Narendra Modi has been voted out of power circa 2020. Post-premiership Modi, in this scenario, did try to convert India into a superpower while he was in government but only managed to raise it to secondariness. He pumped money and resources into science and technology but ignored the importance of the humanities and social sciences. He eschewed opportunities for India to become a pioneer in the fight against climate change. He erased India's intrinsic Muslim heritage by demonising Pakistan, distorting Islam and further marginalising India's Muslim minority while promoting an aggressive Hindutva identity. He chose to resent Nepal's transition from Hindu kingdom to democracy instead of leveraging upon it to forge more cooperative relations with the wider South Asian region. Visvanathan's is as much a post-West as it is a post-Modi narrative – a cautionary tale for an India that is missing opportunity after opportunity to change its destiny.

To be fair, post-independence India's founding leaders also grappled with questions of national identity and global positioning. Jawaharlal Nehru had his own dilemmas about whether he belonged to the East or to the West, an ambivalence expressed politically in his founding and leadership of the Non-Aligned Movement. Yet at the beginning of the twenty-first century, leaders such as former Foreign Minister Jaswant Singh of the Bharatiya Janata Party described the history of India's ambivalent foreign relations with the US as 'fifty wasted years'. It almost appears that for India to rise above secondariness, it will first have to shake off second guesses, premature regret and political sectarianism. As sketched by Visvanathan, India's predicament could well be captured by the beginning of Hamlet's famous soliloquy:

> To be or not to be – that is the question:
> Whether 'tis nobler in the mind to suffer
> The slings and arrows of outrageous fortune,
> Or to take arms against a sea of troubles,
> And, by opposing, end them.

It seems one BRIC country, China, provides even a tentative possibility for a post-West alternative. Does this mean that the West – with all the problems that the term contains – is here to stay? Only if it does not self-destruct, is one way to answer the question. The year 2016 has already seen multiple shockwaves reverberating throughout the US and the EU – the string of terror attacks by supporters or sympathisers of the so-called Islamic State in Paris, Nice, Brussels and other European cities; the biggest mass shooting in US history at Pulse, the lesbian, gay, bisexual and transgender club in Orlando by another IS sympathiser; the murder of the British Labour Parliamentarian Jo Cox by a man with Far Right sympathies; the British referendum vote to leave the EU; growing anger about police violence against African American men and the backlash against the fatal shooting of three police officers in Baton Rouge; and the confirmation of Donald Trump as the Republican presidential candidate – a man who wants to see his political rival Hilary Clinton sorted by his gun-toting followers, ban Muslim immigration and build a wall to stop the alleged flow of Mexican 'illegal immigrants'. Taken cumulatively, maybe these are signs that the West is going to hell in a handbasket after all. And that's only a partial list.

So is the West, as Jim Dator claims, dead? Not hitting a plateau, not in decline, but dead already. By this, Dator does not mean that China or India or some other superpower or civilisation has replaced the West. China wants nothing but to become 'America on steroids' and India has been struck by the 'lethal combination of two fundamentalisms: neoliberal economics and nationalistic Hinduism'. The BRIC countries and other transnational configurations are dead, too. It's all kaput because of what Dator calls the 'Unholy Trinity': '1) the end of cheap and abundant energy; 2) the swift rise of environmental challenges beyond any hope of prevention; and 3) the grotesquely unfair and unsustainable global neoliberal economic system'. But for Dator, all this is a sign of hope, not despair. 'What a wonderful opportunity for creativity and hope lies before us!' he writes. 'The need for true, cooperative, and radical creativity has never been greater.' It is up to us to stop whinging and to construct 'the new normality', otherwise our futures will be colonised yet again as they have been before. This is certainly one way to look at things. At its best, it is a liberating, empowering vision, but there is also a risk that it could be read as over-ambitious prophecy. What Dator actually wants is to motivate us to work towards a post-West world of peace, inclusiveness, justice and wisdom; and thus usher viable and prosperous futures for all.

However, we ought to take the narratives of decline and fall with a healthy dose of scepticism, as Boyd Tonkin argues. There is definitely something going on in the world now, Tonkin suggests, but different people interpret that something differently, depending on their perspective. It's a bit like Bohannan and the Tiv squabbling about Hamlet. So, as Tonkin points out, we now have books about why China already rules the world and why it will not, and about why the West still rules and why it soon will not. With all these narratives of rise and fall or civilisational growth and decay, Tonkin encourages us to ask, 'whose "West", and whose "East"?' For we must always remember that 'West' and 'East' are historical, cultural and political constructs and that their meanings continue to be constructed by different people for different ideological ends. And it is imperative to distinguish between the constructions that are acts of the powerful and constructions by the powerless who are speaking truth to power.

Perhaps 'post-West' can be a starting point for new avenues of self-reflection, as explored by Andrew Brown in his essay, 'Is liberal democracy a religion of peace?' Brown deconstructs the idea of liberal democracy – so often trumpeted as a Western achievement and ideal – and traces its partially religious roots, specifically within Christianity and Islam. While contemporary ideals of liberal democracy emerged from secularised understandings of human dignity in religions like Christianity and Islam, they are still implemented inconsistently, partially, and sometimes even violently by self-professed liberal democratic states. More importantly, Brown points out that the impulse by Western powers to spread liberal democracy throughout the world shares uncomfortable similarities with the civilising mission of European colonialism in a previous era. Back then, as with now, 'the spread of peace and order – and their later maintenance – become a process that is itself neither orderly nor peaceable'. For proof, we need look no further than the moral justifications by US and British leaders for military intervention in Iraq in 2003 and the ensuing, horrific consequences for the invaders and the invaded.

For Brown, this does not mean throwing out the baby with the bathwater – liberal democracy remains a sound ideal and the impulse to reform society for the better is not something to be dismissed. Brown gives the example of slavery – it is always wrong and it is right to resist it. Yet resistance to slavery has also seen its own internal contradictions and violent tendencies. This does not diminish the higher ideals of opposition to slavery. Brown argues that perhaps what happens is that the 'expansion of sympathy' has the paradoxical effect of 'narrowing our tolerance'. We expect the people whom we accept into our moral universe to keep within its acceptable boundaries of conduct. Welcome can therefore turn into intolerance towards those who flout or seek to destroy our moral rules – this can manifest itself in anti-Western jihad in some contexts or in politicised counter-terrorism measures specifically targeting so-called jihadism in others.

So post-West as a concept remains speculative and it obscures as much as it explains. However, it is not the concept itself but its slipperiness that can open our minds to new ways of thinking. Scepticism about 'post-West' should therefore also entail scepticism about what is the 'West' and the 'East' in the first place. The essays in this issue of *Critical Muslim* tackle these questions from geo-political, epistemological, philosophical and personal perspectives. Implicitly or explicitly, they caution against any kind of smugness or self-satisfaction when we do inevitably slip into talking about the West, the East or the post-West. And implicitly or explicitly, they acknowledge that global politics, economics and cultural expressions are currently dominated by something called the 'West'. But they engage with 'post-West' as an idea to address these concerns afresh.

It is reminiscent of the way Bohannan was forced to look at Hamlet anew after engaging with the Tiv elders. In that instance, it did not mean that the Tiv ended up with the upper hand – Bohannan's telling of Hamlet occurred within a particular social setting with its own power dynamics, after all. The people who challenged her were mostly the village elders and villagers who knew that they were intervening in the presence of their leaders. Might Bohannan have encountered different responses, for example, if she had related the story in confidence only to the younger Tiv men and women? Perhaps they would still be puzzled about several plot points, but might they have identified more closely with Hamlet's youthful rebellion? And might the elders have reacted differently if they were told the story by a white man? What if they were told it by an African American man who had never set foot in Nigeria before? These questions indicate that there is much to interrogate about big assumptions and grand narratives – e.g. 'Shakespeare is universal' or 'the West is best/awful/still powerful/in decline' – from the perspective of people's lived experiences.

Finally, it's okay to admire Shakespeare without forsaking a multi-layered critique of the world order. As the poet Robert Graves once said, 'the remarkable thing about Shakespeare is that he really is very good, in spite of all the people who say he is very good.'

THE CONCEPT OF THE WEST

Jasper M. Trautsch

When did the concept of 'the West' emerge? How is it related to what (until recently) was referred to as the 'Orient'? And what has 'the West' come to connote in the twentieth century? It is important to have analytical clarity on these questions if we are to shed some light on the foundations of 'western' identity, understand the role Islam played in its formation, and appreciate how some of the present misperceptions between 'the West' and the 'Muslim world' can be avoided.

Reconstructing how the modern notion of the West came into being and what it has come to mean, it is necessary to distinguish between its two separate conceptual origins. Before the twentieth century, the notion of the Occident and Western Civilisation had developed distinct connotations. The 'Occident' – referring to a cultural community of Western and Central Europe – is a concept that developed at the advent of the early modern period at the turn of the sixteenth century and found its imaginary Other in the (Muslim) 'Orient'. 'Western Civilisation', by contrast, is a concept that emerged only in the nineteenth century in an intra-European context, mentally dividing the continent (and later the Euro-Atlantic world) into two political-ideological spheres: a liberal 'West' and an autocratic 'East'. It was only in the twentieth century that both notions merged and that 'Western Civilisation' consequently referred to a political community of liberal democracies and a cultural community based on a common history and religion. Recognising that 'the West' has come to connote both a political and cultural community might help to clear up some misunderstandings about what constitutes 'the West' and allow us to better understand the sometimes paradoxical attitudes of 'western' publics towards developments in the 'Muslim world'.

The Concept of the Occident

A mental East-West divide had already existed in antiquity and the Middle Ages but its foundation was fundamentally different to the Occident-Orient dichotomy that became prevalent in the early modern period. In antiquity, Islam, the most significant imagined Other for the modern 'Occident', had not yet formed. The most meaningful cultural division within the Mediterranean world was between a 'Latin West' (the coastlines from the Atlantic to the middle of what today is Libya in the south and the centre of the Western Balkans in the north) and a 'Greek East' (the eastern part of the Balkan Peninsula, modern-day Turkey, and eastern North Africa). After the split of the Roman Empire in 395 AD, this partition became institutionalised in the resultant Western and Eastern Empire.

The Muslim conquest of the Arab Peninsula, large parts of the Persian and Byzantine Empires, the Maghreb, and the Iberian Peninsula in the seventh and eighth centuries also did not immediately lead to modern concepts of Christian Occident and Islamic Orient. First, the emerging rift between western Catholic Christianity and eastern Orthodox Christianity – developing divergent rituals, religious doctrines, and attitudes towards state-church relations – became almost as significant as the rivalry between Western Christendom and Islam. In 1204, it was, in fact, Constantinople under the Byzantines that was the target of the Fourth Crusade and was stormed and sacked. Second, although northern Europe was Christianised and a synthetic Germanic-Latin culture emerged in the western part of the continent, the 'Occident' as a civilisational-geographical concept referring to Christian Western and Central Europe did not yet make sense in view of the Muslim possession of Sicily and Andalusia.

It was only at the turn of the sixteenth century that the modern concept of the Occident could emerge. First, the Reconquista – the expulsion of Muslims from the Iberian Peninsula – came to a close in 1492 with the fall of Granada, ending all Islamic rule in Western Europe. (Sicily had already been 'liberated' in the eleventh century.) As a result, the western part of Europe became religiously homogeneous. This then provided the concept of the Occident referring to Catholic Western/Central Europe with geographical-cultural plausibility.

Second, Orthodox Christianity lost importance as a significant Other for Western Christendom when, in 1453, Constantinople was conquered by Sultan Mehmed II, and the Byzantine Empire, the centre of the Eastern Orthodox Church, finally collapsed. As a result, the dichotomy of a Christian 'Occident' versus a Muslim 'Orient' replaced the mental division of the Euro-Mediterranean world into a Latin-Catholic West and a Greek-Orthodox East that had been prevalent since antiquity.

Third, Western Christendom felt directly threatened after the forces of the Ottoman Empire under Suleiman the Magnificent advanced into south-eastern Europe, taking Belgrade in 1521, decisively beating the Hungarians in 1526, and besieging, albeit unsuccessfully, Vienna in 1529 (and then again in 1683 when Mehmed IV was Sultan). Consequently, Western and Central Europeans became more strongly aware of their commonalities as they faced a mutual enemy.

Fourth, the Reformation and the political division of Europe into confessional states called the ecclesiastical unity of Western Christendom into question and created the need for a more neutral term than 'Christendom', 'Imperium Christianum', or 'res publica christiana' to describe the cultural unity of Europe. While the term 'Occident' still carried a strongly religious connotation, it was not dogmatic but rather referred to the larger cultural community of Western and Central Europe. Moreover, partly thanks to the Renaissance, Western/Central Europe was no longer exclusively justified by its Christian foundations but also increasingly through an appropriation of its pre-Christian Greco-Roman heritage. According to Renaissance humanists, a long historical continuity stretching back to the beginnings of antiquity characterised Western/Central European history and gave the area cultural coherence.

While the term 'Occident' continued to refer to the civilisational unity of Western/Central Europe and to be set apart from the 'Orient' in the southeast, its meaning changed during the Age of Enlightenment alongside the decline of the Ottoman Empire, which ceased to be a threat. As a concept, the 'Occident' was gradually secularised in the eighteenth and nineteenth centuries and increasingly connoted a politically, economically, culturally, and technologically superior civilisation rather than a religiously defined non-Orthodox Christian Europe. It now became imagined as progressive and rational and was thus demarcated from what appeared as a static and irrational 'Orient'. Importantly, the 'Orient' and the 'Occident' became essentialised as two fundamentally different civilisations, attributed with seemingly fixed and eternal characteristics. This mental juxtaposition of an advancing 'Occident' and a stagnant 'Orient' became even more entrenched when Western/Central Europe industrialised in the nineteenth century, widening the technological and economic gap between itself and the 'Muslim world'.

It is therefore unsurprising that, in the colonial context of the nineteenth and early twentieth centuries, Western Europeans used the concept of the advanced Occident to justify their colonisation of the 'Arab world'. It provided them with the rationale to spread their 'civilisation' allegedly based on reason, liberty, progress, and benevolence to what they imagined as the superstitious, despotic, backwards, and cruel 'Orient' – a discursive process that Edward Said would later term 'Orientalism'.

The use of the Occident to mean Latin-Germanic Western Christendom, however, was not simply given up. While the connotation of the 'Occident' as a religious community temporarily lost importance at the time of the Enlightenment, it re-emerged under new names in the context of the revolutionary developments in nineteenth century Europe. It was now more usually called 'civilisation chrétienne' in French, 'civiltà cristiana' in Italian, and 'Christian civilisation' in English while retaining its original name in German – 'Abendland', literally 'evening country'. Moreover, the concept of the Occident evolved into a fully-fledged ideology that opposed the principles of the French Revolution. It mainly became popular among those Western/Central European Catholics who deplored the mushrooming secularisation, the increasingly pervasive liberalism, the spread of nationalism, and the unchecked power of the modern state. They used it to conjure the medieval unity of Western Christendom, to lament the lost symbiosis of *regnum* (state) and *sacerdotium* (church), and to call for a re-Christianisation of Western/Central Europe to reverse what they saw as the 'Occident's' moral decay.

While the term 'Christian Occident' was thus complemented and gradually replaced by 'Christian civilisation', the spatial contours remained unchanged as the concept continued referring to the cultural unity of Western/Central Europe. A new development resulting from the concept's increasing politicisation, however, was the demarcation of

Europe from America. While opposition to the Orthodox Eastern Europe and the Muslim 'Orient' had defined the concept of the Occident from the beginning, it was now increasingly emphasised that the 'Christian Occident' also found a significant Other in the rising United States on the other side of the Atlantic. After all, the US was becoming not only a serious geopolitical actor to be reckoned with but also symbolised *par excellence* the liberalising and emancipatory thrust of the modern age that Western European conservatives so detested.

The First World War – by producing a pervasive sense of cultural crisis in Europe – further promoted this conservative and religious conception of the 'Occident'. The bloodshed between 1914 and 1918 was understood to be the result of the dissolution of the 'occidental' unity which had supposedly characterised Europe before the advent of secularisation, materialism, liberalism, and nationalism. The conflict also provoked fears that Europe's global dominance was about to end and that the new powers in the west and east were becoming hegemonic. It was in this context that Oswald Spengler published his hugely influential two-volume bestseller *Der Untergang des Abendlandes* (*The Decline of the Occident*), which, originally published in 1919 and 1922, was quickly translated into a dozen languages and contributed to the widespread popularity of the 'Occident' concept in interwar Europe. The German historian-philosopher insisted that the 'Occident' whose demise he predicted included neither the Slavic and Orthodox peoples of Eastern Europe nor Europe's offspring in North America.

By the first half of the twentieth century, the 'Occident' had thus developed two distinct connotations. In the context of imperialism in Africa and Asia, it referred to Western European powers such as Britain, France, and the Netherlands, which used their technological and military superiority to rule over non-European peoples. In the context of Europe's relations to the emerging world powers in the west and east, it was now called 'Christian civilisation' and referred to a cultural community that was spatially confined to Western/Central Europe (particularly Germany, the Alpine countries, Italy, the Benelux states, France, the Iberian Peninsula, and the United Kingdom) and historically shaped by Latin/Germanic culture and Catholic/Protestant Christianity. While still set apart from its original significant Other – the 'Islamic world' – it was now mainly imagined in opposition to the Orthodox 'East' and the 'New World' across the Atlantic Ocean.

Admittedly, the terms employed to describe these concepts were not always used consistently. At the turn of the twentieth century, the expression 'western civilisation', for example, could be increasingly found as a synonym for 'Occident' in discussions of colonial affairs. In Germany, the term 'Abendland' meant both 'Occident' in the imperial context and 'Christian civilisation' in the Euro-Atlantic context. Moreover, the connotations of the concept were not completely congruent in different languages. While the German 'Abendland' implied that Western Europe's culture was based on a synthesis of Latin and Germanic traditions and of Catholic and Protestant Christianity, the French 'civilisation chrétienne' usually referred more to the Catholic countries that had been shaped by Latin culture.

Nonetheless, two different concepts – referring to Western/Central Europe either as a technologically advanced 'Occident' in an imperial context or as a 'Christian civilisation' in a Euro-Atlantic context – did emerge and should be distinguished for analytical clarity. Also, while the concepts' specific meanings varied in different languages, a transnational understanding of the general contours of the 'Occident' as a 'superior' civilisation and 'Christian civilisation' as a religiously-defined cultural community was reached across Western/Central Europe.

The Concept of Western Civilisation

The concept of the Occident as a cultural community emerged in response to a threat from the Ottoman Empire at the turn of the sixteenth century and demarcated Western/Central Europe, as a civilisation, above all from the 'Muslim world' in its southeast. In the nineteenth century, it was complemented by the notion of a Christian civilisation set apart from both Russia in the east and America in the west. The concept of the West referring to a political community of liberal regimes, by contrast, was an invention of the nineteenth century and for several decades was applied only in an intra-European context.

It was in the 1830s that the concept of the West connoting a spatially congruent political community emerged, as Europe became mentally divided along a North-South axis. This was caused by an increasing ideological polarisation between liberalism – ascending in Western Europe

— and autocracy — dominant in Eastern Europe. In the so-called July Revolution of 1830, the French bourgeoisie ousted King Charles X, installed the more liberal Louis Philippe of Orléans, and considerably extended the powers of the parliament, gradually turning France from a constitutional to a parliamentary monarchy. In the same year, the predominantly Catholic southern provinces of the Netherlands, inspired by the events in France, successfully revolted against the dominance of the largely Protestant northern provinces and the rule of King William I whom they perceived as despotic. The Belgian National Congress drew up the most progressive constitution of the time, which contained an extensive list of fundamental individual rights, established a separation of powers, created a powerful bicameral parliament, and strictly limited the powers of the new king, Leopold I, turning newly independent Belgium into a parliamentary monarchy. Great Britain, which had already been a parliamentary monarchy since the Glorious Revolution, also liberalised during the 1830s. A major step in this process was the Great Reform Act of 1832, which increased the electorate and redrew the boundaries of the parliamentary boroughs in England and Wales to account for the ongoing urbanisation. This strengthened the power of the middle class at the expense of the landed gentry. The Act was followed by similar legislation relating to the election laws of Scotland and Ireland.

While the nations in the western part of Europe liberalised in the 1830s, developments in Eastern Europe took a contrary turn. The Polish national movement — encouraged by the events in France and Belgium and upset by Russia's frequent violations of the Polish Constitution — established a provisional national government and dethroned the Russian Tsar in his function as King of Poland in late 1830 and early 1831. In response, Nicholas I militarily crushed the Polish insurrection, suspended the Polish Constitution, annexed the previously semi-autonomous Kingdom of Poland to Russia, curtailed civil liberties, and dissolved the Polish army. Nicholas also refused to abolish serfdom, suppressed non-Russian peoples in his realm, and ruled in absolutist fashion without any constitutional restraints, further eroding Russia's image in the liberalising Western Europe.

As a result of these diverging political developments in the different parts of Europe, an east-west divide became dominant on Europeans' mental maps. The notion that Western European nations formed a political community characterised as liberal and progressive and defined in opposition to what was perceived to be an autocratic and reactionary 'East' emerged. Indeed, it was in the 1830s that the term 'western civilisation' was first used in the British press to characterise Western Europe as fundamentally different to Russia. The Crimean War of 1854 further promoted the emerging ideological East-West divide between liberal systems in the west and autocracy in the east. As Great Britain and France sought to prevent Russia's territorial expansion into south-eastern Europe at the expense of the Ottoman Empire, the Western European press elevated the conflict to a struggle between 'Western civilisation' and 'Eastern barbarism'.

Although the nineteenth century saw no further military confrontation between Western European nations and Russia, the mental division of Europe into a liberal 'West' and an autocratic 'East' became increasingly entrenched as the political developments in both parts of the continent continued following diverging trajectories. Great Britain proceeded with its progressing liberalisation in the second half of the nineteenth century through political reforms and the expansion of the franchise. France turned into a republic again after Napoléon III, who had usurped power and established the Second Empire in 1851, was dethroned in 1870; the Constitution of the Third Republic provided for universal male suffrage for the elections of the Chamber of Deputies. The suffrage was also extended in the Netherlands, and in 1893 universal male suffrage was introduced in Belgium.

Russia, meanwhile, remained an absolutist monarchy – the power of the Tsar was unlimited by constitutional restraints. While the Revolution of 1905 in the wake of Russia's defeat in the Russo-Japanese War began a reform process, the incipient Russian democratisation proved too feeble and short-lived to affect Western European contemporaries' mental maps. The Tsar did indeed abdicate in 1917, as the demoralising effects of the First World War triggered the so-called February Revolution. Yet the provisional government, seeking to initiate democratic change, was toppled at the end of the same year by the Bolsheviks who took power in the so-called October Revolution and founded the Russian Soviet Federative Socialist Republic.

Against the ideological polarisation of Europe over the course of the nineteenth century, Western Europeans interpreted the events in Russia in

1917 as a confirmation of their view that Eastern and Western Europe were fundamentally different. The victory of Bolshevism in Russia was placed into a continuum of Russia's past as the despotic 'East' that threatened the liberal systems characterising Western Europe. The political-ideological East-West conflict — existent since the 1830s — was therefore not an 'invention' of the twentieth century. In the wake of the October Revolution, the interpretation of the conflict was simply transformed from a struggle between a liberal 'West' and an autocratic 'East' to a battle between a democratic 'West' and a totalitarian 'East'.

It was at about the same time that the recently united Germany joined Russia as a major antinomy of 'the West'. The position of the German states — located between Western and Eastern in Central Europe — in the emerging East-West conflict had been ambivalent during the nineteenth century. However, the German Empire, founded as a constitutional monarchy in 1871 and occupying an ideological middle ground between the Western European parliamentary monarchies or republics and the Russian autocracy in Eastern Europe, was increasingly imagined as non-'western'. In World War I — which was elevated in Great Britain and France as a conflict between 'western civilisation' and 'German barbarism' — Germany was even perceived to be a defining Other for 'the West'. The Second World War, too, was not interpreted as a war within 'western civilisation' but as one between 'the West' and German fascism.

Another new element in the discourse on 'the West' that emerged at the time of the world wars was the mental inclusion of America. Despite the fact that the US had been a pioneer in the development of liberal democracy, it had initially not been thought of as a 'member' of 'western civilisation' when the concept emerged in the nineteenth century. One explanation for the concept's exclusive focus on Western Europe might be the fact that the US played no direct role in European affairs such as the Revolutions of 1830, the Revolutions of 1848/49, and the Crimean War. Another reason for the exclusion of America from 'the West' might have been that, on both sides of the Atlantic, many believed that the conditions in the 'New World' were just too different to those in the 'Old World' and that the political and social developments in both hemispheres therefore had to follow different paths.

This perception of the Atlantic Ocean as a civilisational dividing line gradually began to change at the turn of the twentieth century. It was partly because large democracies – comparable to the US – had emerged and proven sustainable in Europe, too, for example in France. New communication and transportation technologies also led to a perceived contraction of space making the Atlantic Ocean increasingly less of a barrier and more of a bridge between Western Europe and North America. However, it was only during World War I that the notion of Western Civilisation became widespread in American public discourse, since it legitimised America's entry into the European conflict. In 1918, the federal government, moreover, established the so-called Students Army Training Corps (SATC) to prepare army recruits at universities for their upcoming military duty. Part of the program were the 'War Issues courses', taught at more than 500 institutions, which justified America's participation in the conflict by highlighting the political differences between the western allies and the central powers. When the war was over, they were transformed into the mandatory 'Western Civilisation' courses that came to be offered at universities throughout the US in the 1920s. New generations of Americans would hereby become acquainted with the idea that North America and Western Europe were both part of the same civilisation based on shared political values and common forms of government.

By the beginning of the twentieth century, the concept of Western Civilisation had thus come to refer to the political community of democratic states on both sides of the Atlantic. It was defined by a commitment to liberal values and found its defining Others first in what were perceived to be autocratic Germany and Russia and later in the fascist Third Reich and the Bolshevik Soviet Union.

The Merger of the 'Occident' and 'Western Civilisation' Concepts

While the concepts of the Occident and Western Civilisation had different origins and developed distinct meanings, they merged in the twentieth century to form the notion of the West as a political and cultural community as we understand it today. More specifically, both forms of the 'Occident' concept became integrated into 'the West'.

First, at the turn of the twentieth century, the term 'Western Civilisation' – referring to the democratically organised nations bordering the Atlantic – began to be used interchangeably with the term 'Occident'. The concept of 'Western Civilisation' therefore inherited connotations of being the most modern and advanced civilisation initially developed in the Enlightenment and subsequently used to justify European imperialism. The gradual merging of the two concepts became strikingly visible when Spengler's bestseller *Der Untergang des Abendlandes* was imprecisely translated into English as *The Decline of the West* rather than correctly as *The Decline of the Occident*. In French, the conceptual merger was even clearer, since there was only one term – 'Occident' – to describe the group of nations that were both committed to democratic principles at home and imperialism outside Europe. It was also – besides the US – the nations of *Western* Europe that played the imperial game most successfully. Austria-Hungary had no colonies, Italy's colonial ventures were confined to North Africa, and Germany lost its comparatively small colonial possessions at the end of the First World War. It is thus unsurprising that the terms 'Occident' (referring to the colonising powers) and 'Western Civilisation' (referring to the association of liberal regimes) were increasingly used to refer to the same group of nations and became synonymous.

The fusion of both concepts can be most clearly observed in textbooks on 'Western Civilisation'. These followed an overarching narrative in which the history of Western Europe and later North America was characterised by rationality, progress, and the continuous expansion of freedom from the classical world through the Middle Ages up to the present day. This account thus set Western Europe and North America apart *both* from the technologically less advanced societies in Latin America, Africa, and Asia *and* from the less democratic states in Eastern Europe.

Second, after World War II, the concept of the Christian Occident or Christian civilisation merged with that of Western Civilisation – a development made possible, if not caused, by the beginning of the Cold War. As the Euro-Atlantic world became politically divided into a 'western' and an 'eastern' military bloc leaving no room for a separate and neutral 'centre' in-between, it became paramount to mentally integrate (West) Germany into 'the West', even though it could not boast a democratic success story after the dismal failure of the Weimar Republic and the

National-Socialist dictatorship. It also needed to be justified why the former fascist enemy state of Italy and the authoritarian regimes of Spain and Portugal ended up in the 'western' sphere of influence. While these countries had not historically belonged to 'the West' as a political community of liberal democracies, they could, however, lay claim to being part of the historically grown cultural community of 'Christian civilisation'.

This merger of the concepts of Western Civilisation and Christian civilisation – exemplified by the increasing use of the term 'Western Christian civilisation' in the press at mid-century – involved two simultaneous processes. On the one hand, 'the West' was no longer exclusively thought of as a political community of liberal democracies but also as a cultural community of non-Orthodox Christian nations. Hereby, non-democratic or newly emerging democracies in Central and Southern Europe could be easily included in 'the West' on people's mental maps. On the other hand, the 'Christian Occident' no longer referred to a Latin-Germanic Europe that was set apart from both the Orthodox 'East' and what was dismissed as the materialistic US; it now began to include fellow Christian North America and found its only significant Other in the atheistic communist 'East'. In this manner, 'the West' and 'Christian civilisation' began to refer to the same community consisting of Western Europe (now including Germany, Italy, and the Iberian countries) and North America.

This is not to say that 'the West' ceased to be defined by democratic forms of government and liberal values. To the contrary, West Germany and Italy did indeed democratise, and West European and North American nations put constant pressure on the Franco and Salazar regimes in Spain and Portugal to liberalise and thus make 'the West' politically homogeneous. However, 'the West' was transformed into more than simply a group of liberal democracies, which also explains why democracies emerging outside Europe and North America would not necessarily be considered 'western'.

This merger of the two previously distinct concepts thus justified and made sense of the post-war division of Europe. It was facilitated by the fact that both 'Western Civilisation' and 'Christian civilisation' found their most significant Other in the atheist totalitarianism of the Soviet Union. To reiterate, the concept of Western Civilisation had emerged in direct opposition to illiberal Russia in the nineteenth century and Bolshevik Russia in the twentieth century and the concept of the Christian Occident had always excluded not only the Muslim Orient but also Orthodox Russia. Moreover, Russia (after the October Revolution) and all of Eastern Europe (after the Second World War) were 'Orientalised' in 'western' discourse – traits traditionally ascribed to the 'Arab world' were projected onto the countries east of the 'Iron Curtain'. Most significantly, in the late 1940s and the 1950s communism was represented as an Asiatic ideology that threatened Europe's unique culture. In this way, communist-ruled Eastern Europe was excluded from 'Europe', whereas the nations west of the 'Iron Curtain' were equated with 'Europe' as such.

The fusion of the 'liberal West' and the 'Christian Occident' was an 'invention' of the Cold War that not only justified the reconceptualisation of Germany, Italy, Spain, and Portugal as 'western'. It also allowed for the rapid mental relocation of East-Central European nations such as Poland, the Czech Republic, Slovakia, Hungary, and Slovenia into 'the West' after the end of the Cold War. After all, as historically Catholic and Protestant countries, they were part of the cultural community of the 'Occident' – once the communist regimes were replaced by democratically elected governments they also fitted into 'the West' as a political community.

'The West' and the 'Muslim World' today

'The West' was able to expand to include countries that had previously had no successful democratic traditions such as Germany, Italy, Spain, and Portugal through a merger of the concepts of Western Civilisation and Christian civilisation in the mid-twentieth century. At the same time, the incorporation of a Christian element would also establish stricter limits to the further enlargement of 'the West'. As a cultural community, 'the West' would be necessarily circumscribed – despite the secularisation of 'western' nations since the 1960s, 'the West' would still be set apart from regions shaped by non-Christian religions. In other words, not every liberal democracy would automatically be mentally integrated into 'the West', as the examples of India, Japan, and South Korea – stable and exemplary democracies but hardly imagined as 'western' – demonstrate. It also explains why there was and is so much principled opposition to a

Turkish membership in the European Union (EU). Turkey's bid for inclusion into the EU, while not rejected outright, has provoked much more hostility and proven more difficult compared to widespread support for the relatively easier entry of countries like Poland and the Czech Republic into NATO and the EU in the 1990s. Importantly, Turkey's accession to NATO in 1952 also followed a different rationale to that of other member states: it was justified by Turkey's strategic importance rather than its cultural commonalities with other members of the alliance. Put differently, Turkey was perceived to be a valuable partner for 'the West' rather than a part of 'the West' itself.

One valuable insight from the analysis of the conceptual history of 'the West' is that it is not merely a 'club' of liberal democracies that found its defining Others in autocratic Russia, fascist Italy, Nazi Germany, and the communist Warsaw Pact. 'The West' is also a cultural community that for the past 500 years has been defined in opposition to the 'Orient' or what today is better called the 'Muslim world'. The continuing importance of this dichotomy became strikingly visible in the reception of Samuel Huntington's bestseller *The Clash of Civilisations*, published in 1996. Even those who criticised Huntington for alleging a superiority of 'western' culture, for positing Islam's incompatibility with democracy, and for considering a conflict between 'Western Civilisation' and the 'Muslim world' as unavoidable usually did not call his civilisational categories into question. Most accepted the assumption that there was a clearly distinguishable 'western civilisation' and an 'Islamic civilisation' (the actual linguistic, ethnic, and cultural heterogeneity of Muslim nations between Morocco and Indonesia notwithstanding). In sum, since 'the West' is a cultural community for which the 'Muslim world' has always served as the most significant Other, its connotation would have to change dramatically for it to be able to incorporate non-European Muslim societies.

It is, however, not inconceivable that the notion of the West as a largely homogeneous cultural community will lose importance in the next decades, as the large-scale immigration of Maghrebians and Middle Easterners will further diversify European societies. The fate of the 'Western Civilisation' courses in the US might serve as an illustration for the challenges the concept of the West will face in the future. As the student body of American universities became more diverse in the 1960s, these courses became subject to severe criticism. African Americans, Latin Americans, and Asian Americans could not be expected to sympathise with the 'Western Civilisation' narrative, which was based on the experience of white Europeans and which ignored or downplayed the 'dark sides' of 'western' history such as slavery and colonial exploitation. As the ideology of multiculturalism spread through US academia and as an increasing number of non-white students enrolled at universities, many of the 'Western Civilisation' courses – not adequately reflecting the cultural diversity of American society – would be terminated. Possibly, the notion of the West as an historically grown cultural community rooted in the heritage of ancient Greece, the Roman Empire, and medieval Christendom will equally be called into question and dismissed as outdated as Europe's populations become increasingly multicultural.

Another conclusion that can be drawn from the conceptual analysis of 'the West' is that, while merging with the concept of the Christian Occident, it has retained its character as a political community of like-minded liberal democracies. While accepting autocratic regimes such as Spain and Portugal into its fold because of their membership in the cultural community of 'the West', there was constant pressure on them to liberalise to make the political and cultural 'West' congruous. There has certainly been more pressure on rogue 'Western' regimes to democratise than was exerted on dictatorial regimes in the Middle East. Interpreting 'the West' as both a circumscribed cultural community and a political community based on universal values also explains why 'western' nations can be sincerely interested in the spread of democracy to other parts of the world while they simultaneously retain apprehensions and prejudices, if not animosity, towards non-'western' cultures. It was striking how quickly the enthusiasm about the 'Arab spring' and predictions about the global triumph of democracy in 2011 turned into indifference and defeatism about the compatibility of democracy and Islam when, about a year later, the 'Arab winter' set in.

Finally, understanding 'the West' as both a political and cultural community allows us to analytically distinguish between both aspects of 'western' identity and avoid mistaking this demarcated community for a set of universal values. On the one hand, simply equating 'the West' with liberal-democratic principles at least implicitly denies the applicability of these values in other cultures (or casts doubt that they can be practised in non-'western' societies and successfully be maintained there). A case in point is the dichotomy of an 'enlightened West' versus 'fundamentalist Islam' that has structured many 'Westerners'' perceptions of international relations in the wake of the terrorist attacks of 11 September 2001. The universal values of the Enlightenment were claimed for one's own community, which was set apart from a 'Muslim world' allegedly incapable of separating church and state and using reason rather than relying on faith. This argument was also conveniently used by secular autocrats and dictators in the 'Arab world' such as Hosni Mubarak or Bashar al-Assad to legitimise their 'enlightened' regimes by representing themselves as the only bulwark against their nations' 'Islamisation'.

On the other hand, identifying 'the West' with liberal democracy also bears the risk of discrediting liberal values and democratic forms of government. It allows illiberal critics of an open society from political extremes to interpret any blunder 'western' nations make (such as America's illegal invasion of Iraq in 2003) as the result of allegedly flawed 'western' values.

Accepting that 'the West' is not just an association of states with similar forms of government but also a cultural community based on a common past, by contrast, makes it possible to distinguish between 'the West' as a civilisation and as, in the words of historian Heinrich-August Winkler, 'a normative project'. It allows us to imagine that 'the West' can exist without claiming the principles of liberal democracy exclusively for itself. Finally, it would enable non-'western' societies to fully embrace liberal-democratic values, as they would not have to fear a loss of their cultural peculiarities if they followed the political model of 'the West'.

THE STRUGGLE FOR WORLD POWER

Roger van Zwanenberg

To understand how the West has acquired so much wealth and power, and the route it has taken towards world domination, it is useful to look at history in broad, global terms. Around 1600, some of the richest parts of the world were in the East – China, India, Indonesia and Japan. The pre-modern world's trade routes remain a good indication of the flow of material wealth from the East through to the Eastern Mediterranean, trickling to Europe via Venice and other Italian city states. The notion of a world or global power is a more recent concept even though colonial and imperial power formed part of the ancient world – from Egypt's pharaohs to the Persians and the Romans.

After 1600 however, with the creation of monopolistic European trading companies, the ancient patterns of wealth and power altered. By 1800 India had already been impoverished through European intervention and by 1850 so had China. Instead of the West buying Eastern products, trade had been reversed and the East began buying Western products. Power and wealth had swung from the Eastern side of the world to the Western side. So how did power and wealth first move from the East to the West? How was it fought over in the two World Wars? And, is it now moving back again to the East?

I first became interested in these question as a young man. I left home at nineteen, with no historical knowledge of the world and having failed most exams at school. The two previous years had been spent trying to find my way in the city of London as a representative of Unilever, selling margarine. Nothing seemed to work, so with my sister's advice I left Europe. My mother gravely said to me on leaving, 'Always remember darling, you are British – we are an honourable people. Never forget this.' With these words ringing in my ears I set off to Israel and then India, where I came across gross poverty on a scale I had never imagined. If my people were so honourable, as my mother had intoned, why had we left India in 1947, at its Independence, in such poverty? Everyone I asked had no answers.

On my return from India, I managed to find my way to university. I happened more by luck than judgement to find myself studying economic history. My professor excited my imagination when he described the role of steam engines in boats that allowed them to progress across the seas, against the prevailing winds. Soon after at Southampton University, in a special course given by the republican Irish historian Miriam Daly – who was assassinated during the civil war upon her return to Belfast – I learnt why Britain conquered Ireland, how she held it as a colony, and what happened to those who resisted. My mother's advice began to ring thin.

From there onwards, the rest of my university career was spent exploring these great issues of history. I was lucky enough, after my doctorate, to be allowed to teach in East Africa where I attempted to show my students why Britain had colonised their lands. I was surprised and a bit shocked to discover that those who had been offered an education during the colonial era had not been taught their own history but rather the history of England. They had been told they had no history and many had forcibly been given English first names. This was my experience in deracination, or the humiliation of the 'Other'. But I still needed to learn more about how the British had created sufficient wealth to dominate the world.

The German-American economic historian Andre Gunder Frank began turning the big story of British economic history and the Industrial Revolution on its head through works such as *Development and Underdevelopment*, published in the 1960s. In the 1990s Frank wrote widely about the Silk Route and its development in the Orient. In essence Frank had begun upending the story of British Economic History and the Industrial Revolution – a trend developed by other academics such as the political scientists Janet Abu-Lughod and Sandra Halperin. According to this retelling of history, before the Industrial Revolution in Britain, China, India and the Near East had civilisations and wealth far beyond the imaginations of scholars and students in the West. These powers had developed industries largely made of smallholder production and financial services long before the invention of the steam engine in the West. Capitalism, in the form of trade, banking and small scale commodity production, was widespread for millennia across huge areas of what we now term the East. Halperin argued that the Asiatic traders wanted freedom of movement, sanctity of contracts, property rights, stable currency and reliable banking. Abu-Lughod contended that trade actually flourished during the Mongol period as the Mongols were able and willing to protect trade routes.

Meanwhile, Europe was witnessing bitter political and religious struggles from the fifteenth to the seventeenth centuries. In England, the struggles of the Tudors against the Vatican resulting in the creation of the Protestant religion are part of the same story. Because the Church had always been one of the major owners of farm land, much of this land was then confiscated by the King and parcelled out to his favourites, some of whom began to farm on a commercial basis. Thus began the process of commercialisation of land which was absent under the pre-Reformation system. The growth of the natural sciences during this period then increased agricultural productivity through the creation of improved farming techniques. Scientific discoveries also improved the quality of sea-going ships, so essential for the island kingdom of Britain. These sciences were institutionalised through a variety of Royal Societies in many fields, such as medicine and physics, which in turn spearheaded the translation of classical works of knowledge from Arabic into English.

This commodification and commercialisation of land ownership and the growth of secular sciences catalysed the conditions for Western Europe to catch up with the Orient. However, the transformation leading to the creation of a world power required more fundamental changes. In the fifteenth, sixteenth and seventeenth centuries, monarchies in Europe believed that one person's gain had to be another person's loss so far as trade was concerned – a logic that came to be called mercantilism. The English supported their wool trade and so up and down the country, wool products were bought and sold at local markets. Spinning and weaving wool were specialist activities in villages across the land. The state encouraged the export of woollen products and discouraged their import by imposing heavy taxes.

At the beginning of the 1600s, Britain, France, Spain and the Netherlands created their own monopoly companies to trade across most parts of the world. I will concentrate on the British East India Company whose remit was to trade in the East – India, China, Japan and their surrounding regions. Britain's East India Company was in direct competition with the French and the Dutch who created similar government-supported monopoly companies, each competing against the other in the East. In the early years, they had little to export as the Indians did not want anything Europe had to offer. As a consequence, the Europeans traded with gold and silver, much of which came from their invasions of the Americas and the destruction of the Inca Empire.

Wealthy Europeans, however, wanted Indian cotton goods which were the best in the world. The British East India Company, with the government's support, went from solely being a trading company focusing on towns off the Indian coasts to becoming a military company able to wrest its own territory. Company officials settled and intermarried with Indian elites and started taking part in the internal conflicts of the Indian subcontinent. The British East India Company eventually defeated the French East India Company and reached a separate agreement with the Dutch, who would claim monopoly over the Indonesian archipelago and Japan, while the British would have monopoly of the Indian subcontinent. Additionally, over the Company's life, it repeatedly called on the British government to bail it out when it went bankrupt, used money improperly and was implicated in stock market bubbles and eye-watering corruption. The Company thus began by buying spices and textiles and selling them all over Europe and then innovated on its ownership model, pioneered shareholding corporate ownership and provided the basis for modern business administration. It achieved market dominance, executive malpractice and immense human oppression by colonising India.

Nineteenth century European colonialism was bolstered by the idea that Western man had a superior civilisation and was part of a superior race – non-European peoples of 'colour' were considered inferior. (Being conscious of my Jewish origins, I have always been fascinated by the existence of race and racism.) The nineteenth and early twentieth century colonisers never considered that the people they were colonising had a pre-existing culture and civilisation made up of laws, religion, language, music and other ways of living. There was of course widespread violent resistance to colonisation but wherever people rose to fight colonial oppression, leaders and large numbers of their followers were slaughtered. For instance, armed uprisings in German East Africa (present-day Burundi, Rwanda and mainland Tanzania) and in present-day Namibia were totally suppressed.

Even lands that were not directly colonised suffered from the machinations of European powers. Western traders in Canton, for example, were horrified that the Chinese authorities should attempt to forbid the opium trade – they felt entitled to sell whatever the Chinese would buy. The Chinese authorities' responses to their attitudes are captured in a letter sent by Commissioner Lin Zexu, personal representative of the Chinese central court, to Queen Victoria in 1839. An exasperated Lin wrote:

> The Way of Heaven is fairness to all: it does not suffer us to harm others in order to benefit ourselves…your instincts are not different from ours; for nowhere are there men so blind as not to distinguish what brings life and what brings death, between what brings profit and what does harm…. So long as you do not take it upon yourselves to forbid the opium but continue to make it and tempt the people of China to buy it, you will be showing yourselves careful of your own lives, but careless of the lives of other people, indifferent in your greed for gain to the harm you do to others….

The British responded by sending a gunboat and so began a hundred years of humiliation of the Chinese alongside the colonisation of India.

The Steam Engine, Slavery and War

Although the British East India Company turned the world upside down, this fundamental change in global geopolitics was not enough to make Britain a world power. Britain also had to be the unconditional master of Europe. Spain and Portugal were previously Europe's pre-eminent powers, annexing much of the Americas for gold and silver. Spain was weakened in the sixteenth century, however, because of its conflicts with the Muslim world. Britain, on the other hand, was gradually defeating major European powers at various battles, culminating in the defeat of France's Napoleon in 1815 which paved the way for British dominance in Europe.

Britain's military dominance was made possible by the invention of the steam engine. Steam power was initially utilised to lift water out of holes in the ground to allow coal miners to dig deeper. Once invented, the steam engine had applications across every form of production and transport. When applied to the spinning and weaving industries it sprouted industrial factories and rapid urbanisation. The steam engine also revolutionised transport – the railway was invented while steam power helped ships to drive against the wind. Yet the growth of the steam engine had one unforeseen consequence – the constant annual growth of the economy which pushed Britain and then the rest of Europe to advance faster than the East.

Alongside the wonders of the steam engine also came the trans-Atlantic slave trade. Slavery was nothing new – people were sold as slaves from ancient times. What was new was the scale of the slave trade from Africa into the Americas and the Caribbean. Without slavery there would have been no raw cotton and no finished cottons to export to India. And although Britain abolished slavery in the first half of the nineteenth century, her cotton mills were not shy of buying raw material from the southern states of the US where slavery lasted until the civil war in 1864. Britain hugely benefited from slavery – in Liverpool and Bristol, boats were built to transport slavers and British settlers in the Caribbean made their fortunes from sugar using slave labour. Slaves and slavery were as fundamental to the Industrial Revolution as the steam engine.

The short thirty-one years from 1914 to 1945 were then hugely destructive on an unprecedented scale, not least because of the dramatic social and political changes that accompanied the Industrial Revolution. The major powers fought each other with degrees of savagery as never before in the First and Second World Wars. New technology kept producing weapons of war that increased the ability of humans to kill each other exponentially. One of Britain's main purposes for entering both wars was to maintain her world dominance. She failed.

Since the 1870s, a unified Germany had wanted a place in the colonial firmament. Britain, however, did not wish to give any more than had been agreed in 1884 when Africa was divided between European powers. There was a minor alteration when the Congo was removed from the direct control of Belgium's King Leopold II in 1908 and became annexed as the Belgian Congo but the balance of colonial power essentially remained unchanged. Germany was thus competing with Britain for a share of global influence but there were no international mechanisms to control two such great powers sparring for dominance, except war.

Up to 1914, many of the pre-capitalist empires around the world were still in place. China had been on the wane since the Opium Wars and the great Southern and Central American empires had already been destroyed by the Spanish and Portuguese, but the Austro-Hungarian, Ottoman and Russian Empires were still very much in existence. The First World War saw the collapse of Austria-Hungary while France and Britain wrestled for colonial influence over the defeated Ottoman Empire's oil-rich Arab territories. By 1922, the British and French under the Sykes-Picot agreement divided up the Arab world into a new collection of nation-states. The British and French ran these as colonies up to 1939 and after 1945 they were handed to various authoritarian rulers. The creation of the state of Israel in 1948 altered the balance of the region, with the arrival of Jewish settlers from the West and emerging diplomatic ties between Israel and the West.

Meanwhile, the decades after the Russian Revolution in 1917 consumed the imaginations of most American and European socialists against a backdrop of global socialist movements that had formed around the Communist, Trotskyist and Maoist ideologies. Instead of forming national parties struggling together for a just society against a common enemy, socialists largely fought each other over what was 'correct' socialist analysis.

At the end of the First World War, however, the British and the French were ill-equipped to foresee these changes – for more than a century, they had been convinced of their superiority in world affairs. So in 1919, they imposed humiliating terms on Germany in the Versailles Treaty, which the economist John Maynard Keynes argued had prepared the way for the Second World War. Under the Treaty, Germany could not grow her economy and recover and so the way was set for the rise of Adolf Hitler's Nazi party which eventually took power in 1933. I would argue that the German attitude towards Jews and other minorities, as well as Eastern European Slavs, was an extension of the racism that could be found in the British and French Empires. In the end, neither Germany nor Britain achieved their major war goals and Britain lost everything she had been working towards over the previous 250 years.

The Rise of the USA

Between 1914 and 1945 the control of world power therefore altered significantly. Up to 1914, Britain was accepted as the dominant global power, with the pound sterling as the world's preeminent trading currency. From the mid-nineteenth century, the British central bank offered international traders security by their willingness to exchange sterling pounds into a given weight of gold, hence the 'gold standard'. This limited the volume of sterling available at any time and currency security was assured for all European and American export traders. In the opening decades of the twentieth century, the British government had placed the maintenance of the gold standard above all other priorities as the national interest. However, the two World Wars and recurring recessions destroyed the ability of the British exchequer to maintain this for long.

The interwar years also saw intense turmoil in many other parts of the world. Japan had tried to expand and create an Empire of its own and had invaded China and parts of Southeast Asia. Horrendous war crimes were committed. When I visited China I saw the permanent memorial to the Japanese atrocities which made me think of the joint British and US bombing of Dresden in 1944.

The British economy and military were so seriously weakened by 1944 that when the British and US governments met at Bretton Woods, New Hampshire, to discuss post-war arrangements, British views were effectively side-lined, marking the beginning of a new era. Henceforth, the US was in charge of world affairs. The British had been victorious in both World Wars but eventually lost their Empire, with the Americans insisting that Britain's former colonies were opened up to international trade. Among these were some of Britain's most prized possessions, especially India.

Yet the Americans had not arrived on the scene unprepared. The US economy had already surpassed the wealth of Britain well before 1914. Like other 'developing' capitalist states the US had encouraged exports and taxed imports throughout the nineteenth century. But by 1945, Britain was deeply in debt and the end of Empire was a fact of life that simply had to be accepted.

The US's first act of power was to drop two atomic bombs on Nagasaki and Hiroshima to end its war with Japan, effectively also telling the rest of the world to 'watch out'. Many scholars have since shown that Japan was not the US's prime aim because the Pacific War was effectively over by then; rather it was a message to the Soviet Union that they were potentially next in line.

By 1945, world power had swung out of Europe for the first time in 250 years. Europe was devastated, much its infrastructure had been destroyed and it was deeply in debt. It was the US that decided on the terms for peace after the Second World War. The US economy was three times the size of their nearest rival the USSR, five times the size of the British economy and the US produced half the world's industrial output and owned three quarters of the world's gold reserves. Yet for the US, the post-war 'threat' of Communism loomed large. During the War, local communist parties had been the backbone of the resistance against the Nazis and were ready to take power in many parts of Europe after the defeat of Germany. And so the US army remained in Europe after the war to fight the local communist parties, culminating in the creation of the North Atlantic Treaty Organisation (NATO) purportedly to defend the region against a Soviet invasion.

The rise of communism was not confined to Europe. The rise of leftist movements in ex-colonies and the success of Mao Zedong's guerrilla war in China in 1949 meant that large parts of the world were out of the control of major European powers. Within Europe, the British Labour Party took power through democratic means and for the following two decades or so, the British people enjoyed a pretty good deal in terms of education and other opportunities on offer. Many had access to higher education for the first time – but this situation was short lived. Similarly in the rest of Europe, left-leaning Social Democratic political parties took power over the next couple of decades and people's living standards generally improved.

Outside Europe and the US, there were mixed attempts – some of them violent – to create socialist states in Korea, Cambodia and Vietnam, with only the latter succeeding. In the Philippines, Central and South America, South Africa, Mozambique, Angola, and the Congo, Communist parties of varying hues struggled to take power. Socialist leaders like Gamal Abdel Nasser in the Arab world, Kwame Nkrumah and Julius Nyerere in West and East Africa and Sukarno in Indonesia worked to advance their ideals through the ballot box.

Many of the new anti-colonial and postcolonial leaders were, however, assassinated or 'disappeared' – among them India's Mahatma Gandhi in 1948, Congo's Patrice Lumumba in 1961, Morocco's Mehdi Ben Barka in 1965, Nigeria's Ahmadu Bello in 1966, Mozambique's Eduardo Mondlane in 1969, Guinea-Bissau and Cape Verde's Amílcar Cabral in 1973 and Guyana's Walter Rodney in 1980. Many of these leaders were succeeded by anti-Communist dictators. In fact, in South and Central America, the US trained local anti-Communist terror squads amid a political context in which numerous people were disappeared, tortured or killed.

Democracy outside the US and Western Europe was tolerated as long as it did not get in the way of global power. One of the lessons from this period is that democracy cannot easily alter a society except towards some form of US-friendly capitalism. We should all recall Salvador Allende, the democratically elected Marxist president of Chile who was ousted in a bloody coup soon after coming to power. He was replaced by the US-backed dictator Augusto Pinochet who presided over a reign of terror and bloodily purged Allende's support base.

After the end of the Second World War, Britain and the rest of Western Europe became allied to US interests in an embrace that has endured for over 70 years. In Britain, this is known as the 'Special Relationship' which is probably more important to the Brits than to the US. This relationship ensures that Britain shares intelligence and surveillance with the US and that the US maintains a number of military bases on British soil. It can be argued that while the relationship has ensured that Britain did not become a third rate political power after the breakup of its Empire, it nevertheless denies Britain full military independence. And so despite the upheavals of the first half of the twentieth century, Britain was one of the few countries after 1945 that had not been invaded by foreign troops. The structure of the old society has remained intact especially its monarchy, Parliament (including the House of Lords) and landed ruling classes. Like Britain, the European Union has also cultivated a strong alliance with the US and certain political and ideological trends have flourished on both sides of the Atlantic, namely neo-liberalism, anti-Communism and so-called counter-terrorism policies after the attacks of 11 September 2001.

Emerging Transformations

Reminiscent of post-1871 Germany and the Soviet Union post-1945, China is now a contender for global power, but the challenges facing it are significantly different. There is the legacy of the Opium Wars before which Chinese civilisation had flourished for thousands of years. Yet China's export-led GDP growth over the past 30 years has also been remarkable – millions upon millions of people have been released from absolute poverty. China has further built up the largest reserves of US dollars in the world and it has now exported some of this surplus in concrete infrastructure investment projects globally. Growth has been led by the Chinese Communist Party which is ironic because it can be said that China is indeed a capitalist success story. These facets of China's rise are significantly different to the earlier emergence of Germany and the Soviet Union. In fact, it appears that China has no wish to challenge the US militarily but prefers to supply financial aid to various smaller nations. China is in the process of developing an international bank – the Asian Infrastructure Investment Bank – that is poised to challenge existing financial institutions such as the World Bank, the Asian Development Bank and the International Monetary Fund.

If China has ambitions of expanding its influence in other parts of the world such as the Middle East, however, it will have to deal with pre-existing, complicated geo-political landscapes. For example, in the Middle East, the US is still in a special alliance with Israel which in turn appears to resist any workable solution that would accord Palestinians any semblance of autonomy and self-determination. At the same time, Israel and other Arab states such as Saudi Arabia have become deeply dependent on US financial and diplomatic support. Along with the ongoing turmoil in Syria, Iraq, Yemen and other surrounding states, the situation in the Middle East remains grim.

On a more general level, China or any other potential contenders for global power must deal with the 'c' word – capitalism. Despite a brief period of left-leaning social democratic euphoria in the West after the Second World War, from the 1970s onwards capitalism was back – this time with the US leading the charge. The US pursues the idea of 'free trade' with the same zeal that the British East India Company did, if not greater. What some people now term 'neoliberalism' is simply a more sophisticated version of the British Empire's mantra of free trade. Into this mix, however, we now have new digital technologies, which first emerged in the 1960s and then continued to grow at an exponential rate, and have eventually altered human relationships so fundamentally.

New technologies have allowed people to organise differently and more organically on one hand, but they have also enabled transnational capital to grow exponentially.

I followed this growth in book publishing from my experience in founding and heading progressive publishing houses. The major companies of twenty or thirty years ago have all either been bought out or have themselves become the giants of the twenty first century within a broader field of media. Worldwide, the big companies have invested in new technologies since reading books, listening to music and watching film and television have all become or are becoming intertwined. All these companies see themselves as global rather than national and their interactions with each other include buying up a bit here and selling another bit there.

Leaders of liberal democratic Western states facilitate the growth of monopolistic firms by initiating an ever growing labyrinth of trade deals such as the Transatlantic Trade and Investment Partnership between EU and the North America (TTIP), the Trans-Pacific Partnership between America and the Pacific Rim (TPP) and the negotiations between the EU and Eastern and Southern African states. These are in addition to pre-existing blocs such as the North American Free Trade Agreement (NAFTA). Negotiations are presided by representatives of big companies and governments and hardly ever include grassroots communities or activists.

Common to these new arrangements is the method of settling disputes between states and investors, or the Investor State Dispute Settlement (ISDS), which allows companies to claim damages against specific governments for obstructing investment. This legal instrument bypasses a sovereign state's domestic legislation arguably even in cases where the state's laws are meant to protect local populations. Conflicts of interest arise because some judges in these courts are corporate lawyers appointed on an ad hoc basis. There is also a lack of transparency when the tribunals decide the size of the fine to be paid by a state. And once a decision has been made, it is final.

Of course, we need to pay attention to emerging trends that are likely to complicate or challenge this grim picture. What needs to be remembered is that in the seventeenth and eighteenth centuries monopoly companies from Europe had a relatively free hand to do what they wanted because it took so long for information to be gathered and transmitted to their European headquarters. It might seem that there is now hope for a more vibrant and transparent information exchange, but new monopoly companies are increasingly able to bypass national governments through instruments such as the ISDS. Then and now, monopoly power posed and continues to pose a major threat to people's aspirations for a truly representative and participatory democracy.

History has shown us that monopoly powers can change and have changed the world. We should take note.

POSTWEST ANXIETIES

Gordon Blaine Steffey

Phlebas the Phoenician, a fortnight dead ... Consider Phlebas, who was once
handsome and tall as you.

The Wasteland, T.S. Eliot

French sociologist Michel de Certeau argued that 'narrations about what's-going-on constitute our orthodoxy'. We can say the same about narrations about what's-next. From journalism to political representation, from legacy to new media, the torrent of narrations engulfing our waking hours and encroaching on our sleep 'organise in advance our work, our celebrations, and even our dreams.' These narrations – which de Certeau also terms masks, simulations, and the 'results of manipulations' – fabricate the realities to which they seemingly refer and are thus 'circular' and 'objectless.' The unrelenting sound and fury of de Certeau's 'recited society', or in the absence of any 'believable object' of abyssal reference to the belief of others, or the 'citation' of experts and public opinion polls, certifies the validity of the mask. If our credences are emphatically entangled with and conceivably produced by the multiplying mechanisms of discipline, by a global control culture and normalised systems of surveillance, if selves too are 'recited,' then we must seek without delay the formulae for transmuting credence into 'denunciation' and dissent and thus 'manipulate the mechanisms of discipline and conform to them only in order to evade them.'

Such quarry led de Certeau to an exposition of the customary network of antidisciplinary tactics whereby the 'dominée' already ensnared in disciplinary nets also engages in 'free' and 'creative' work. If our futures are the 'development projects' of predatory totality or have long since been occupied by the plutocrats who own our world, if Thatcher's 'there is no alternative' (TINA) named an incipience not yet in fullest flower and therefore yet to come, the question stands: is idiosyncratic work disguised as work for the proprietors (what de Certeau termed *la perruque* or 'the wig') a tactic available to knowledge workers on the trail of a viable PostWest from within the embrace of the West and its institutions and beneath its superintendence? More, if we retain some regard for a West or fathom both the intensity and extensity of its dissemination, then we should ask with Boaventura de Sousa Santos, 'is there a non-Occidentalist West?' Is there an 'other West' open to 'counterhegemonic globalisation' and to participation in ecologies of knowledges and productions with differential, context-dependent, real-world interventions and outcomes? Is such a West, which would constitute a veritable PostWest, not only thinkable but even more urgently actionable?

An obituary of the West is untimely and as deliriously naïve as prophecy. I prefer then to engage in critical play the conditions that organise our dreams and dreads of a PostWest. Suffice it to say that an overprovision of prefixes signals a civilisation sunk knee-deep in overcoming or the desire to overcome. It is difficult to plumb the surging glamour and circulation of trans-, inter-, and the veteran post- without detecting therein a gestation and portent of categories and forms of life beyond those which stammer and miscarry without the relief of prefixing. To be sure, our prefixation is no overture to the 'great noon' envisioned by an imagined Zarathustra, no preamble to the reappearance of 'wild dogs' in the cellar, but it suggests that the categories in terms of which (at least) the denizens of English-speaking societies have articulated and lived their lives are fatigued and ever more uninhabitable. To dress out racial, normal, and now West with the prefix post- befits an interim of transit between plateaus (neither named Eden or *Gehenna*) and leans forward and backward in anxiety.

About what are we anxious? Prevarication of labour markets from São Paulo to Seoul and the emergence of a new global class structure and Precariat; ballooning populations of conflict-related refugees and internally displaced persons; accelerating deadening of the biosphere beyond the reach of (even the myth of) technological remediation and national and transnational environmental policy; patent laws that secure for pharmaceutical companies monopoly control over the manufacture and sales of life-saving and life-enhancing drugs. These brutalities and indignities provoke us to anger, advocacy, and political action. They irrigate and aggravate our anxiety, but neither severally nor collectively comprise it. Western canons of knowledge follow the lead of European existentialists in reckoning anxiety to be 'indeterminate' or generalised, which is a country mile from holding it to be 'about nothing' (technically, anxiety is about more than any particular thing or set of things). Existentialists argue that the signature feature of anxiety is its insistent, inalienable, and enigmatic unclarity about its aboutness. In a formulation fathered by the tarnished Heidegger, anxiety is the extraordinary experience of rupture from the world wherein I am ordinarily, practically, and complacently absorbed. If such rupture or detachment is squired by 'nausea,' by a vulnerability whose sire is facing up to groundlessness, it is also attended by a fleeting (often missed or misspent) occasion for spontaneity and creativity.

For those alive to the idea that the writing is on the wall, that they are living at the extremity of their world, anxiety seems a fitting response. What lies on the far side of the limit, the fine textures of lives and futures on the other side, is stubbornly resistant to human intelligence despite titanic efforts in foresight. In this chaotic environment wrought of accelerating change, informational ambience and superabundance, and the 'sense of an ending' ('real' or 'recited,' but who can tell?), there is considerable pressure to explain what's happening in conventional terms and thus to carve out safe harbour for this storm-tossed vessel. 'Round up the usual suspects,' indeed. In the immediate wake of the Great War, Valéry wondered, 'Will Europe become what it is in reality, that is to say: a tiny cape on the Asian continent? Or will it abide as what it seems, that is to say: the precious share of the terrestrial universe, the pearl of the sphere, the brain of a vast body?' In that so-called 'age of anxiety,' a somewhat recent interval along the arc of the tradition of writing about the health of the West, Paul Valéry and others configured the PostWest as a 'crisis' of disarticulation and dislocation from the centre to the periphery or from a localised universality (Europe or West as 'brain') to a 'tiny cape,' what Valéry (in delightful wordplay) terms a 'deminutio capitis' or, literally, a 'decrease of the head.' The Latin he borrowed from Roman legal discourse wherein it referred generally to a winnowing of aggregated legal attributes and most often to a reduction in status. Flight to a sanitised, idealised past from a fallen present remains a popular form of explanation (and self-collection), but time travel cannot expel the suspicion that much (perhaps far more than ever before) remains perilously unsaid, that the world is no more 'mine oyster,' and that this strange sense of insecurity, however individuals and communities metabolise it, might never resolve into another dominion, another 'oyster,' nor permit a relapse into the drowsy optimism of youth.

In spring 2007 erstwhile educator turned neoconservative pundit Victor Davis Hanson startled up from a slumber disturbed by dreams and apparitions. As he chewed over his reveries, he attained insight into what he terms the 'new religion' and 'new creed' of a 'surreal present,' in a word, capitulation (he prefers the clumsier locution 'gospel of the Path of Least Resistance,' which ostensibly differs from that *other* gospel in substituting 'gratification' for 'sacrifice'). Hanson published his reveries in the *National Review Online*, the digital face of the semi-monthly magazine founded in 1955 by the godfather of American conservatism, William F. Buckley, Jr. Carrying the fertile title, 'The Postwest,' and headily developed by the tagline, 'A civilisation that has become just a dream' (not so 'merrily, merrily, merrily,' it will turn out), Hanson's editorial posits as a sequence of dream tableaux what is in fact a feeble litany of supercilious, starboard-listing flummeries. Among the latter, I include the following, 'I also dreamed that ... Europeans would advise their own Muslim immigrants, from London to Berlin, that the West, founded on principles of the Hellenic and European Enlightenments, and enriched by the Sermon on the Mount, had nothing to apologise for, now or in the future. Newcomers would either accept this revered culture of tolerance, assimilation, and equality of religions and the sexes — or return home to live under its antithesis of seventh-century Sharia law.' Beneath the diaphanous surface crouches the 'love it or leave it' jingo, a longtime darling of flag-waving tub-thumpers and more suited to automobile bumpers than to public policy deliberation on immigration or war. 'Equality of religions and the sexes,' the recipe for the West, and other follies I set aside with the observation that Hanson's memory of the West looks like 'screen memory,' Freud's term for a vivid 'mnemic image' that memorialises (displaces) the 'relevant experience itself' and is thus a shield against repressed trauma and/or desire and a retroactive formulation of a subject's wishing.

On Hanson's account, the passing or ongoing transit of the West into strictly oneiric realms (or, to my eyes, nostalgia for a West that never was) is visible in the North Atlantic refusal to chide an insolent Iran with an iron fist, in American hand-wringing over its 'valid' invasion of Iraq, and in the general flaccidity of 'defenders of the liberal tradition of the West' on violent extremism. It is a desperate errand to account for the role of the Sermon on the Mount in Hanson's make-believe or in any dispassionate analytic of Western origins. Suffice it to say that Hanson's West shares far more with the parade of empires that extracted resources from the Galilee than with the displaced Galilean who practised the *basileia* of God among the poor and at risk. The terrain mapped in Hanson's dreams is a range patrolled by the 'picturesque' American cowboy so ably disenchanted by Philip Ashton Rollins, a place where men (emphatically men) 'wild up' in order to secure preemptively the dominion to which their 'revered culture' entitles them: 'When I'm hungry I bites off the noses of living grizzly bears.' When swagger falls flat, 'white man's metal' is the last line of defence. In the absence of grizzlies, Hanson develops a taste for the Democrat bosses and liberal media who make of his waking hours a nightmare. In sweet sleep, by contrast, there is no 'retreat' and 'no more concessions [by North Atlantic powers] to the pre-rational primeval mind, no more backpeddling [sic] and equivocating on rioting and threats over cartoons or operas or papal statements. There would be no more apologies about how the West need make amends for a hallowed tradition that started 2,500 years ago with classical Athens, led to the Italian Republics of the Renaissance, and inspired the liberal democracies that defeated fascism, Japanese militarism, Nazism, and Communist totalitarianism, and now are likewise poised to end radical Islamic fascism.'

This holy and puissant West has naught to answer for save its brilliance of light and liberty to an ungrateful world lately unwilling to make the sacrifices required for its maintenance. In Hanson's frothing, the titular 'Postwest' appears as the strictly implicit, reverse side of an obverse text soaked with 'castration anxiety' and 'masculine protest.' The summons to rally to a sacred empire besieged by 'primeval minds' is a simple case of 'nothing new under the sun'; new is the robust undertow of resignation, new is the pervading disbelief in Gibbon's sanguine assurance that fluctuations in power and prosperity 'cannot essentially injure our general state of happiness, the system of arts, and laws, and manners, which so advantageously distinguish, above the rest of mankind, the Europeans and their colonies.' The 'Postwest' is the incidental (and nocuous) domain wherein the gloomy Hanson and his wakeful votaries exchange bogus dreams and 'screened' tales of the loss of Atlantis beneath the sea. Indeed the 'rise of the rest' is a mere derivative of a primary theft of the phallus (which Hanson takes to have been an inside job) or the onset of its dysfunction.

If the prospect of a PostWest excites (and it ought to arouse a quantum of passion), enthusiasm must surely be dulled and perhaps deferred by the chilling family resemblance of 'the rest' to Phlebas the Phoenician. What I mean is just that the PostWest is a discourse of the West and thus recycles many if not most of the very categories that define it here, replicate it there, and everywhere police its integrity with 'recitation' and black sites. You will have guessed some of the categories I mean: development, race, sustainability, labour, religion, democracy, STEM (not as a set of disciplines, but as a set of expulsions and exclusions), and freedom (among others). The grammatical and lexical bases of nation-state, prosperity, market, and even knowledge itself have been formulated according to the European and North American experiences of these phenomena (and/or to their advantage). Thus while boundaries and borders are instantly overflown by digital communication and information technologies and driven by information economies, presumptively broadening our aperture of understanding on the world, the networks and systems that discipline and move knowledge have coarsened knowledge and narrowed that aperture at the expense of indigenous, local, marginal, and expelled knowledges. This is what Boaventura de Sousa Santos terms 'epistemicide,' the superordinate's murder of the knowledge of a subordinated culture. In this 'information phase' of capital there is grave need for inclusive and unyielding critique of the cultural forces gelding human knowledge and for insurgency against the increasingly sadistic attenuation of 'useless' forms of knowledge or of sense-making not readily commoditisable.

Who lacks ears to hear how the PostWest will be? It is recited. How many have yet to learn the words to speak of a 'shift' in the 'balance of power' or of the 'new geography of power'? Who cannot yet enumerate three to five variables that precipitated the 'decline' or 'final decay' of the United States (habitually and problematically seen as the terminus of the West)? Who cannot learnedly announce the 'loss' of American power and influence to 'emerging powers' like mighty China, India, Brazil, a resurgent Russia, and a shortlist of not-yet-mighty 'others'? It is recited. The standardisation and wide dissemination of this script are far from fatal to its claim to truth, however crude and dubious seems the linear analytic of 'rise' and 'fall.' While that analytic invites and warrants suspicion, far more vexing are the categories and instruments used to frame and measure phenomena like 'rise' and 'fall,' which in the main exhibit negligible variation from West to PostWest. The resuscitation of classical growth and development strategies in progressive, new left, and socialist governments of the global South despite the welcome and well-publicised demise of classical Western development theory is a case in point. The global struggle for perpetual economic growth inspired Eduardo Gudynas to term development a 'zombie category' or a simultaneously 'defunct' and uniquely feasible model (precisely because the ontology of Western modernity remains largely uncontested). It must be contested because the fetish of profusion or perpetual growth violates a basic law of ecology and invites the attentions of Nemesis. The second iteration of Ecuador's 'The National Plan for Good Living' defines *buen vivir* (literally, 'good living') precisely in opposition to the 'quest for opulence or infinite economic growth'.

A Spanish translation of Quechua and Aymara expressions *sumak kawsay* and *suma qamaña*, *buen vivir* is a viable, working contestation. It names a family of Latin American epistemic systems and lifeways incongruent with the legitimating discourses and institutional frameworks of neoliberal capitalist and statist hegemonies. With roots in the ancestral values and practices of indigenous communities in the Americas, these diverse lifeways suffered five centuries of Hanson's 'hallowed tradition' before re-emerging to source scepticism about and opposition to a developmentalist and (neo-) extractivist productivism responsible for cultural, ecological, and social destruction across Latin America. Invoked in Article 8 of the 2009 constitution of the Plurinational State of Bolivia, *suma qamaña* posits 'good living' in terms of the cultural and ecological landscapes of the Andes, specifically in terms of the relations of complementarity and reciprocity that characterise the *ayllu*, the local community of animals, ancestors, persons, plants, and Pachamama (lit. 'Mother Earth') wherein material and spiritual well-being are collectively sought. Gustavo Soto Santiesteban explains that nature here is a 'complex system of relations ... conceived of as a living being and not as a thing of which to make other things,' a subject then and not a factor of production or natural capital. The sticker price attached to maintaining a state while financing and executing a transition to a new economy and sociality means that the worldview implied in *buen vivir* has yet to decompose the worldview undergirding the old economic organisation (whether in Ecuador or Bolivia). This means that contradictions are possible, likely, and even temporarily inevitable. It means that increased oil production, aggressive mining, and mega infrastructure projects measured more to global than local interests (e.g., the proposed Corredor Ferroviario Bioceánico Central or transoceanic railway from Santos, Brazil to Illo, Peru by way of Bolivia) sit cheek by jowl with constitutional and popular affirmations of *buen vivir*. *Buen vivir* nevertheless remains an available ethical, political, and communitarian logic for life and the practice of dissent in the Amazon and Andes, but not beyond these territories to which they belong and by/to which they have reference. Indeed, Gudynas argues that 'there is no sense' in appropriating the Aymara *suma qamaña* and Guaraní *ñande reko* outside of their local ecologies and encourages other cultures to 'explore and build their own Buen Vivir' that are engaged with and responsive to their unique local ecologies.

There is something beautifully distinctive and disturbingly unfamiliar about the Latin American lifeways collected plurally and non-hierarchically under the expression *buen vivir* (this may be a function of perspective). In a 2009 conference presentation entitled 'The Meaning of the Commons,' Louis E. Wolcher offered an analysis of 'commoning' that may raise a window on the unsettling unfamiliarity of indigenous or mixed lifeways like *suma qamaña*. Wolcher argued that commoning or the unscripted social practice of autonomy and subsistence was 'bred into the bones of [medieval] people'. When the development of private property rights (the enclosure acts) threatened commoning, dissent and resistance were capacitated by this experiential polestar, by the memory of a 'different form of living'. He continues: 'global capitalism has eclipsed the common imagination to such a degree that we have lost contact with this earlier memory if we ever had it. There is nothing for us to fall back on, or, to put it differently, for most people, ordinary people, the only solution they can think of to the failures of the market that are roiling us right now in so many different ways is the market, more market, different market. And so, unlike the medieval peasant or the medieval commoner, we do not have this cultural memory of a different way of being or at least the average person does not in the United States.' The truth of Thatcher's TINA lies in late capitalism's unremitting obliteration of different ways of being not only in the global South but also from the memories and imaginations of people who were once more than merely Western. In Hanson's 'The Postwest,' the titular subject matter appears as an unplayed B-side – his mind is free of alternatives.

With no alternative in the offing, no memory of an alternative, and that unshakeable 'sense of an ending,' the way of life in the West is anxious. Our prefixation chafes against the constriction of the world to the terms of ontologies that are idle or defunct in some ways and inhumane in others. Like the West wherein it first draws breath, the PostWest is differentially configured and configurable precisely because there is no object to which it must or could correspond. How it is configured depends principally on the West written as lost, transformed, overcome, dispensable, usable, or redeemable in its projection. I follow Boaventura de Sousa Santos in thinking of the modern West as a sociopolitical paradigm founded on the 'tension between social regulation and social emancipation,' a paradigm that has lately generated vast global inequities and calcified into the intensely toxic formation described by Michel Foucault as neoliberal govermentality. Santos poses the problem of epistemicide (and thus the production and perpetuation of TINA) in terms of the 'abyssal thinking' that characterises the modern West. Abyssal thinking is a system of distinctions grounded in the imposition of radical lines that hierarchically divide metropole from colony, regulation/emancipation from appropriation/violence, and existent from nonexistent. By way of example Santos cites the epistemological hegemony enjoyed by modern science over the universal distinction between true and false 'to the detriment of two alternative bodies of knowledge: philosophy and theology.' The visibility of tensions between science and philosophy/religion lies on *this* side of the abyssal line and is thus predicated on the invisibility of the 'popular, lay, plebeian, peasant, or indigenous knowledges on the other side of the line'. The latter are unthinkable both in terms of scientific truth/falsity and in terms of the scientifically undiscoverable 'truths' of philosophy and theology. They belong rather to the other side of the line where dwell 'beliefs, opinions, intuitions, and subjective understanding, which, at the most, may become objects or raw materials for scientific inquiry,' but cannot rise to the level of real or acceptable knowledge. Not only does abyssal thinking reduce 'existential problems' to what may be said scientifically about them, but also deterritorialises and disappears the agents and agencies of these discarded cognitive experiences. This 'radical denial of co-presence' or sacrifice of (sub-)humans in order to affirm the universal humanity on this side of the line means that the struggle for global social justice is indivisible from global cognitive justice ('post-abyssal thinking'). Alternatively put, general epistemology must consent to its impossibility and to the possibility of an ecology of knowledges, a non-hierarchical plurality of heterogeneous knowledge and ignorances. Such post-abyssal thinking may be found in the Bolivian constitution's non-hierarchical and pluralistic articulation of linguistically and culturally heterogeneous values: 'The State adopts and promotes the following as ethical, moral principles of the plural society: *ama qhilla, ama llula, ama suwa* (do not be lazy, do not be a liar, or a thief), *suma qamaña* (live well), *ñandereko* (live harmoniously), *teko kavi* (good life), *ivi maraei* (land without evil) and *qhapaj ñan* (noble path or life).'

Just as the communitarian ecologies of the Americas inspired the first European utopians so too the political activists and rearguard intellectuals of Latin America tutor the West in alternatives which the West could not efface, recall, imagine, *or* disavow. By disavow I mean that *buen vivir*, say, is as indebted to the critiques of capitalism that originate inside modern Western thought as it is to the organic antagonism of the lifeways of a pre-Columbian antiquity. Let me be clear that the ascendancy of China is not an alternative, which is not to deny (substantive) difference between the dominion of the United States and China or India. The rules of the game do not change because the gamers do. There are more PostWests *in potentia* than can be tallied, but how many are credible (the scariest are the most credible), and of those how many desirable because they reflect the internal plurality of local needs and knowledges and respond to and enhance the social well-being of that distinctive ecology? It is only some kind of *buen vivir* that can change the rules of the game enforced by the logic of capital, but not a *buen vivir* that parrots the idiolects of other ecologies.

Many cultures use dreams to extend the scope and nature of their insights into the world. In the mid-nineteenth century a young Crow boy named

Alaxchiiaahush (lit., Many Achievements) or 'Plenty Coups' had a medicine dream while questing in the wilderness. Jonathan Lear argues that the Crow used Plenty Coups' dream to 'struggle with the intelligibility of events that lay at the horizon of their ability to understand' (namely, the devastation of their world by the modern West). In his medicine dream, Plenty Coups encounters a 'Man-person' who shows him the departure of the buffalo from the plains and the arrival of 'spotted-buffalo' (cattle), a vision later interpreted as the displacement of the Crow from their lands by white men. He also dreams that the Four Winds flatten a forest save for a lone tree in which sits the 'lodge of the Chickadee'. The Man-person explains that while weakest in body, the Chickadee is strongest in mind: 'He is willing to work for wisdom. The Chickadee-person is a good listener. Nothing escapes his ears, which he has sharpened by constant use. Whenever others are talking together of their successes and failures, there you will find the Chickadee-person listening to their words … He never intrudes, never speaks in strange company, and yet never misses a chance to learn from others.' Undoubtedly the object of collective revision, the dream was given its normative interpretation by the Crow elder Yellow Bear. In exposition of the Chickadee-person, Yellow Bear concluded that 'He [Plenty Coups, who would lead the Crow into their future] was told to think for himself, to listen, to learn to avoid disaster by the experiences of others.' In consequence of this interpreted dream and under the leadership of Plenty Coups, the Crow made common cause with the whites and were able to retain (some, but increasingly fewer acres of) their ancestral lands. Lear makes the case that Plenty Coups offered the Crow a 'traditional way of going forward,' using the traditional force of Crow spirituality, the Chickadee, to open up the Crow to seeing as wisdom what they needed to learn from others (including non-Crow) by listening. Thus an indigenous folk of North America models the courage required by post-abyssal thinking even as their culture confronts and suffers the abyss. As the West faces up to transformations far, far milder than the brutal devastation faced by the Crow, it can do no better amid the insecurity and anxiety of transition than to observe the rite of the Chickadee: to listen to and learn from those who sheltered their lifeways and wisdoms from the violence of its abyss.

WHERE IS THE EAST?

Amrita Ghosh

What do we do when we talk about, or think of, the West? Consciously or unconsciously, we envisage the West in terms of its binary opposite: the East. But what is the East; and where exactly is the East located?

The term 'East' has always been in vogue in the Eurocentric visions, usually conjuring ideas of mysticism and certain cultural and ideological differences between the East and the West. Lately it has also been loosely synonymous with a new age interest and invention of 'eastern yoga' and discovering the spiritual self through what is constructed as the East. But locating the spatial denomination of the term raises some curious problems. Which part of the world shall we unanimously agree is the East? East of what? The word 'East' undoubtedly invokes a certain spatial imaginary, a topographical production which is both a real and imagined concept, but it also ushers in crucial questions about its frame of reference – is it the Far East, Middle East or the Near East that is being conjured in the term; or is it a strange amalgamation of all three that curiously becomes the 'East?' Thus, what has become of this term is a problematic monolith in the western eye.

Furthermore, the question of spatiality also needs to be merged with 'what' the idea or construction of East means historically and in contemporary culture. Certainly, the discursive multiplicity of the term has changed or been reshaped over a vast span of time and space. Benjamin Disraeli's famous uttering, 'The East is a career', that Edward Said famously used as an epigraph in his seminal work, *Orientalism*, perhaps still becomes the best possible answer to analyse the practices of the term. More specifically, there is a growing trend that frames the East as a way of consumable exotic, selling Bollywoodian sensibility in the global market. In what we understand as the post 9/11 world, the word invokes a vision of radical alterity of the Middle East, as the threatening Other against Western modernity, which itself is extremely problematic as it diffuses various historicities and specificities over a vast space.

The earliest usage and production of the term has its foundation in the East India Company and the British Empire. The East was initially prevalently used in the imperial framing of British colonies in India and parts of South Asia. Later, with the British imperial expansion and oceanic travel explorations, the term became analogous with China, Japan and some other countries in the far eastern topography. Thus, one notices that from the early discursive emergence of the word East, there begins a problematic homogenous construction, which was by no means a natural cohesive existence. Along with this awkward homogenising of geographical space, the Far East had already been tagged with the 'wondrous' discourse that peaked during the Renaissance and the Enlightenment. The cultural historian Surekha Davies explains that:

> from classical antiquity to the Enlightenment, the distant East was associated with wondrous beings in the European imagination.... From the fifteenth century, European oceanic exploration began to reveal hitherto unknown regions of the globe...The distant East—often termed India—was sometimes conflated with a region called Ethiopia which was variously placed in Africa or Asia.

Davies' work tracks this idea of 'wonder, disbelief, surprise' about the East and its peoples and culture by charting a chronology of travel writers and mapmakers from the medieval times to the seventeenth century. Clearly, there was confusion in delineating precise geographical regions to the Eastern spaces and as Davies notes, cartographers and travel writers dealt with ambiguity and tension in the aspect of verisimilitude and not everyone attempted to sensationalise the East. She argues that ultimately the mapmakers and writers allowed the readers to ascertain what they would believe about the narrative on the East based on the multiple doubts and lack of realism in many accounts. However, one thing is still certain in the various narratives that emerged during this time: even in a discourse on the East fraught with contradictions, its codification as exotic and wondrous was a palpably common practice that seeped into the popular imagination which could not be erased from any discourse of the 'problematic' East.

Gradually, the Far East became slowly synonymous with China, Japan and some countries in the far eastern rim, and the term Near East and Middle

East came to be dubiously interchanged. The geographer Karen Culcasi suggests that 'Great Britain's possessions in South Asia made the Middle East not only a geo-strategically important region but also the middle of the journey east to India; hence the term "Middle East".' However, despite the imperialist genesis of the term, the space denoted by the imperial framework was still vague, implying anything between the 'Far East' and the 'Near East,' between the Mediterranean and Indian oceans. In 1948, the United Nations defined the Middle East to be spread across three continents including Afghanistan, Iran, Iraq, Syria, Lebanon, Turkey, Saudi Arabia, Yemen, Egypt, Ethiopia, and Greece. The administration of George W. Bush adopted the label as recently as 2004 for a region extending from Morocco to Pakistan. Whatever be the larger and problematic categorisation of countries for understanding the term, it is crucial to note that the term comes with an ideological production in hegemonic narratives that reflects a violent, backward region with Islamic fundamentalism, oppression, and lack of freedom or democracy. Such a spatial denomination has clouded our minds especially in the post 9/11 world, with East having a synonymous undercurrent of religious Islamic fundamentalism, crisis, bloodshed and lack of peace. Thus, a certain current imaginary about the East has become merged with this idea of the Middle East, whose spatiality is still not clear. Most significantly, as Culcasi rightly points out, this kind of lumping areas with an Islamic culture 'not only ignores non-Arab/Muslims living in the region but also potentially merges these two distinct cultural traits into one uniform characteristic'. It also fails to realise that 'the Arabs from Morocco to Egypt to Iraq differ immensely in their history, local practices, and dialects'. A larger problem of such a construction of Middle East is the creation of a homogenous, monolithic vision of Islam as a religion, ignoring the nuances and diversities amidst the Muslim people, who are then lumped together into a dangerous representation that gains currency in popular, normative culture.

The East is thus a non-space, difficult to locate cartographically, a term which is more socially and politically constructed and shifted in different temporalities and power discourses. The best understanding of the problematic monolithic representations of the East comes from Edward Said's *Orientalism*, which remains, I would argue, as important now as when it was first published in 1978. In the introduction, Said explains orientalism as:

a distribution of geopolitical awareness into aesthetic, scholarly, economic, sociological, historical and philological texts; it is an elaboration of not only a basic geographical distinction (the world is made up of two unequal halves, the Orient and the Occident) but also of a whole series of 'interests', which, by such means as scholarly discovery, philological reconstruction, psychological analysis, landscape and sociological description, it not only creates but also maintains; it is, rather than expresses, a certain will or intention to understand, in some cases to control, manipulate, even to incorporate, what is a manifestly different (or alternative and novel) world.

Said sees the ideological and discursive emergence of the Orient as a constructed antithesis to the Western imagination. And this imagination exists on an uneven exchange of power, where the Occident has the capability of constructing, discovering and imagining the east in ways that invoke wonder, monstrosity, barbarism, violence, backwardness and lack of reasoning. Evidently, the representation of the Middle East is not much different from Said's explanation of the genesis of the Eastern Orient held in the Western imagination. Lately, the construct of East in contemporary culture has emerged with an orientalism redux where locating the spatiality becomes insignificant to a large extent. Apart from far east cultures of China and Japan, where the discourse is one of more benevolent wondrous exoticism, the terminology presently holds on to what Said long ago labelled as the idea of East in the Western yardstick.

If one extreme of knowing what the East means is through the prism of the post 9/11 world, another extreme can be stated to be the post-*Slumdog Millionaire* interest in the East in a very specific fetishised way. Bollywood's large diasporic audience and wide popularity across cultures has been distinct since the post-liberalised economy of India opened its markets and borders. At about the same time as Danny Boyle's 2008 movie, a plethora of films and media programmes gave rise to a resurgence of interest in the East (*The Darjeeling Limited* [2007], *Eat, Pray, Love* [2010], *The Best Exotic Marigold Hotel* [2012]). This construction of East in the entertainment industry, designed for the consumption of West, is intrinsically sprinkled with a benign orientalism.

Under the project of globalisation, the once accepted binaries of the North-South and West-East have supposedly broken down, generic borders have vanished or at least they have been problematised and questioned. Also gone, as Gayatri Spivak reminds us, are 'such nice polarities as modernity/ tradition, colonial/postcolonial'. Globalisation has not only connected the world but is also transforming a range of social relations be they culture, economic or political. While globalisation may have dissolved all kinds of boundaries, it takes place, as Spivak reminds us, essentially in terms of 'capital and data' – that is, the flow of capital via the transnational companies who have the power to decide which 'data' and information would construct a certain 'worlding of a world.' Here, the age old essentialised binaries of Occident and Orient are not only maintained but pose a grave problem in a world where intermixing of communities, cultures and religions are increasingly common. They project a more damaging aspect of stereotyping and essentialist elements of culture, religions and regions that broaden the North-South gulf even more. Not surprisingly, globalisation and orientalism go hand in hand, because a western hegemony is still maintained in this flow of capital and certain kind of data. The 'universalisation of capital' through a corporate-funded thrust for the global then becomes responsible for the production of a redux orientalism, which caters to an evolution of a universal 'eastern subject.'

A good illustration of the emergence of redux orientalism in the post globalised world is provided by Oprah Winfrey's two-episode film, *India, The Next Chapter* (2012). Our heroine travels to India, visits various Indian cities, and 'educates' Western viewers about the elites and subalterns of the Indian socio-cultural fabric. Oprah's goal, as stated by her, is to 'spread little pieces of light in this world'. To depict a more 'authentic' representation of India, Oprah visits Mumbai's slum dwelling population, as well as a wealthy upper middle class family in her journey. The camera first pans through the urban city, and stops to focus on a gathering crowd that has collected on the roads to see the shooting. Oprah turns to the camera and notes, 'even though there's lots of people and there's lots going on, there is sense of karma'. Elsewhere, during an interview with Indian journalist Barkha Dutt about her Indian experience, Oprah stresses that:

> whether it is Jaipur, or Agra, whether you are in Mumbai, or the countryside with the widows, or with glitterati, you feel like you are in the centre of some-thing bigger and greater than yourself. *And although everybody kinda looks the same* [italics mine], there is a lot of diversity in India, you feel like you are in a

part of humanity, where your humanity is being expanded; I feel opened and expanded by this experience.

There are two narratives that are critically worthy of our attention here. First, the epistemological production of a spiritual essence of India and its people, where the chaos of people and 'lot going on' still has the undercurrent of a karmic solution. The problem with that kind of ethnography is that it not only misrepresents a culture and the people, but it exhibits a sense of spirituality as a spectacle, a new-age spirituality pill that provides instant solace and therapy to the western subject and helps in its consolidation of self-hood against the native other. How, one wonders, one can look at a crowd on the street and experience a karmic essence? More problematically, Oprah's interview with Barkha Dutt echoes Joseph Conrad's journey into the 'heart of darkness' where all native subjects are devoid of individualised identity: 'they look the same' and yet their 'othering' affirms the opening and expansion of the Western subjectivity. It is distinctly reminiscent of Edward Said's claim that the discourse of orientalism is not about the orient; rather, it is instrumental in defining the western, European self. Oprah's assertion that her humanity is being expanded and opened, no matter how benevolent and seemingly innocuous it sounds, serves as a token to this kind of manifest orientalism where the Western self is reaffirmed in its difference – yes, the eastern subject is human, but is a different human subject, and in this difference lies the 'opening' and construction of the western self-hood. People from the East still remain quasi-caricatured figures of exotic wonder and spirituality.

Ultimately, this has become the other extreme of tokenising the East in postnormal times. Oprah's television programme is just one glimpse of the many representations of the East in popular culture, media, films, which highlight that the nature of neo-colonial imaginings of orientalism are still relevant and thriving in the present context. Disturbingly enough, in the renewed codes of a globalised world, this representation of an othered space and its people commodifies a new passage to the East as the consumable exotic whose projection is good for consumption in global markets. It reaffirms the new age orientalist discourse of finding oneself in an exotic escape to the 'East.'

The East is thus an imaginary construction to be found somewhere between spatial and ideological stations. Yet, it would still be valid to ask, where does one nonetheless find and locate the East between the two extremes in the post 9/11 and post-*Slumdog Millionaire* world? It would be fair to say that the dilemma of the question precisely indicates where the answer lies. That is, locating the 'East' is not possible. No matter how certain social and political discourses attempt in defining or framing the East, it is not a homogenous space, nor is it an essential realm. Such discourses only reflect the hegemonic power that ideologically produces an idea of East that is not a naturalised state, only adding to harmful projections of an ever-increasing North-South faction. And yet, one may argue that the 'real' East lies somewhere, where the hegemonic flattening of history and spatiality ends.

In *Provincializing Europe*, the Indian historian Dipesh Chakravorty provides a glimpse of a potential answer. He calls for a rewriting of history from within the 'East'; a history that would become an alternative to the established ideas of framing, locating and defining the East. Perhaps, only then we can move towards finding the East, in reconstructing our imaginations towards, what Chakravorty calls, the 'anti-modern' consciousness. In the end, one needs to go beyond the East-West binary in order to truly break the impasse. This is where the overarching question of locating and understanding the East becomes a critical one. Only by breaking and shifting the age-old existing status quo will we be able to rethink afresh and move towards more viable and humane dimensions of representations of identities and cultures.

INDIA'S RISE TO SECONDARINESS

Shiv Visvanathan

You ask me: whatever happened to our desperate aspiration to be a superpower? It is a good question; particularly now that Narendra Modi has been voted out of power. You may find the reply of a retired mandarin, a member of a club of bureaucrats, a bit whimsical, nostalgic, even contentious. As you know, I was an administrator who was an authority on Nehru, who was sidelined by Mrs Gandhi, who closely watched the power play of the Modi regime. So I speak with some experience. And it is my hope that young thinkers like you may gain some valuable insights from my account of our recent history and use them to shape a better future.

I was sympathetic to the new regime which felt India was both third world and third rate and being treated as such. Our elite were desperate for a seat at the UN Security council, for the machismo of a superpower status. I remember one of them telling me: 'have you seen those American tourists in hoarding-size Hawaiian shirts, photographing the world they don't understand; illiterate but confident that American currency is stable, the American economy is secure, that American guns will rescue them if trouble begins, convinced that the world wants to be American. That is being a superpower and I want to feel like that'. Emphatically put. Citizens of a superpower no matter how individually insignificant behave like extensions of the superpower. There is a touch of jingoism in each visitor as if he or she comes wrapped in the US flag.

The word superpower is like an advertisement for an energy drink, promising a boost of masculinity and decisiveness. Superpower envy has always haunted us. At the end of seventy years of nationalist effort the West labelled India as a BRICS nation, the B team of the world. Colonialism was bad but not being taken seriously by the post-Cold War world; where the West itself had begun to decline, this was demoralising. China hiccupped and the world read meaning into it. India protested and the world ignored it. Something, somehow had to be done to wipe our sense of B plusness. We had the third largest army in the world, a huge economy, the third largest pool of scientific talent; most of our population was under twenty-five and yet all these demographic dividends did not add up to superpower scores. Our inability to convert advantages into achievements was devastating us. The Modi government tried to do just that: convert India into a superpower. So let me reply to your question as a post-mortem of that exercise.

Constructing Mediocrity

What broke India down was the deep sense of the social, not the implicit social as lived and breathed in as a life world but as constructed, built and injected into the policy documents, social as in social science and social policy. A good humanities education could have saved us from the philistinism of social science. We treated the social like engineers treat pipes, as acts of plumbing. There was no mystery, no play as in a jigsaw puzzle. We were living fragmented lives based on fragmented theories. A mediocre social science built on inane words like development, nation state, smart city. To erase or side line the idea of civilisation, to enact the script of the nation state was like destroying forest and expecting a tribal people to survive. A nation state is like a prefabricated house with a limited sense of hospitality and a narrower sense of diversity. Without a sense of civilisation, the tacit worlds of meaning, the layers of nuance and understanding, the weave of paradox and contradiction, the ecologies of ambiguity disappeared.

The BJP (Bharatiya Janata Party) realised that the sooner the sense of civilisation gave way to the nation state, the sooner could the world of panopticons, security and surveillance be constructed. They knew in their bones that while a civilisation was a commons, a nation state was a contract and contracts do not work with memory and meaning. You have to lobotomise a civilisation to create a nation state. India became the third largest producer of social science of the most mediocre quality. No nation state can survive without mediocre social science. The logic of the discipline is insidious. With science, the nation watches in awe, too much in fear of it. Becoming scientific is more demanding than being patriotic. Yet social science became a mix of experts' lingo and folklore. It was managerial and could be taught as technique, blending claims to science with a whiff of the spiritual. The use of management as a folk discipline by media, journals like *India Today* conducting celebrations of each bestseller long forgotten in the West, the tutorial colleges which downloaded Western knowledge, all created a world of Kitsch which our elite gorged on. Kitsch does not have the rituals for the civilisational sense of memory or aesthetic. Our elite survived on a gruelly mush of best sellers. When Indian authors like Chetan Bhagat and Sekhar Gupta can simplify the world, why read the classics. Intellectuals such as Ashis Nandy became irrelevant. Nandy, in fact, admitted that his work was not relevant for the new era. He claimed the upward mobility of backward minds was destroying us. What compounded the error was our sense of the double, our mirror the Non-Resident Indian (NRI).

The NRI lived in an American world but often attributed his success to his innate qualities – like hard work, solidarity and prudence without giving enough recognition to the American melting pot. His patriotism, prudence, and professionalism made him appear like a full-time worker for the RSS (the extreme rightwing organisation, Rashtriya Swayamsevak Sangh, the parent organisation of the BJP), with an openness to consumption. The NRI by becoming the Indian double destroyed the sense of citizenship in India. The NRI was the new Puritan, the *Pracharak* (worker) of the second modernity. Between Silicon Valley and the RSS headquarters at Nagpur, one derived a new definition of the world called India.

It was a tragedy of the parts being lesser than the whole. The individual narratives of the NRI were rich, the social science morals extracted from it were poor or rather impoverishing because they captured little of life in its everydayness. Ironically, alongside the rise of the NRI, the new developments of social science added to the mediocratisation of India. To have a few mimic men, sounding like an echo of the West, was affordable. To become a mimic nation in the global age was disastrous.

We also misread our science confusing it with technology. Let us call it the crime of Bangalore. Bangalore and Delhi created the new consortiums of the mind between the corporate right of entrepreneurs such as Kiran Mazumdar Shaw and Nandan Nilekani, and the new bowdlerisation of myth to facilitate governance and management theory of Dev Dutt Pathaik, combining nation and corporation in lethal ways. Whether it was a management festival or a literary festival, India thrived on a mulch of superficiality, an intellectual cuisine served out as the latest dish. We imitated Oxford, Harvard, Singapore because our children were at home there. There were certain consequences of this that people did not notice at first.

People misread the creativity of Bangalore misunderstanding both the role of the early Dewans like Visvesveraya and the later imagination of scientists like Dhawan and Ramaseshan. Bangalore was a science city built around paradigmatic institutions like the Raman Research Institute (RRI) and Indian Institute of Science (IISC). Science as a mode of enquiry created a playfulness, a professionalism and a culture of its own embodied in such exemplars like C V Raman (1888-1970), RS Krishnan (1911-199), GN Ramachandran 1992–2001), Sivaraj Ramaseshan (1923-2003). The city became a paradigm for a university. Even today, IISC ranks as the highest Indian Institution in World Rankings. But Bangalore as a city turned at right angles when the city became a centre for the IT industry. When technology as an instrumental imagination dominated, the city became managerial. Instead of a playful community, what emerged was a technocratic elite including the likes of Nabdan Nilekani and Narayan Murthy at Infosys, Azim Premji at Western India Products Limited, or Wipro. All of them read knowledge in a different way and felt that their experiences should impact the city and the nation. Interestingly the philosophical imaginations were secondary or anecdotal in the Bangalore group. The philosophy that emerged was that of a right wing corporation, which wanted science to pay returns and wanted to use it to create a managerial revolution. Nilekanis' *Aadhar* (identity) card was an example. Narayan Murthy's speech at IISC showed his sense of science and technology was illiterate. He thought Ford and Tesla were products of the university interactions. The Infosys role in creating a classics selection equivalent to the Harvard Loeb series showed the limits of the imagination. Murthy did not know that myths and classics exist in numerous versions, that the Ramayan is told in 300 variants. To create a canonical variant of this as the only version displayed a classic sense of elite philistinism masquerading as philanthropy.

The official emphasis on science and technology narrowed the visions of a knowledge society. To think one could create a knowledge economy without the ecological framework of a knowledge society marked the elites' misreading of the dynamics of cognition. The university as a community was the worst victim of this three pronged attack. Firstly, the elite was already exporting its children to universities abroad. Secondly, the right was determined to create a university on the lines of party syllabus where history, parts of science, economics followed the party's idea of the subject. Thirdly, the university dominated corporate managerialism which was more concerned with evaluation and rankings but had no sense of the intellectual process. As the university shrank under this triple assault, populist politics was happy with the nominal dole of an IIT (Indian Institute of Technology) to each state. Think tanks and policy institutes, literally clones of institutions abroad, began to determine the contours of research and scholarship. Instead of the legacy of institutions like the Delhi-based Centre for the Study of Developing Societies (CSDS) or Centre for Policy Research (CPR), we now relied on Brookings, Hastings or Vivekananda. India's rise to secondariness was self-inflicted and eventually arose in the domain of ideas. John Maynard Keynes once pointed out that even the worst dictators only lived out the text book ideas of some forgotten philosopher. But even Keynes could not comprehend the nature of scholarship and its contribution to the idea of India being content with its secondariness. Only our secondariness was greeted as a victory. B team status was something we welcomed and were content with.

The Challenge of the Civilisational

India could have been a superpower in two ways. It could have played out its imaginaries as a plural civilisation, as a country where Hinduism was syncretic, as a nation which had more Muslims than any country except Indonesia, as a society where Christianity was older than in the West, as a source of the origin of Buddhism and Ambedkariti neo-Buddhism, or it could play out as a hegemonic nation state with a will to dominance over the smaller societies around it. As a civilisation India had possibilities of outthinking and out-imagining the West. The nationalist movement had that imagination not only in its openness to the dissenting West but its attempt to create futuristic possibilities and alternative ways of thinking. Our nationalist movement dreamt of alternative science, multiple time, syncretic encounters, thought of cities beyond the Western idea of the industrial city but India as a nation state only sought to domesticate the dominant West. In 1947, the choice was not just about liberation from the British but whether India and hopefully China would retain their sense of civilisation. China chose to be a nation state and so did India. In fact, it is only as a nation that one can be a superpower because a superpower internalises the categories, the puritan categories of a nation state to invent its superpower status. This involves a commitment a certain kind of science, economics and a certain theory of development. Partly because of the devastation of partition, India decided not to follow the civilisational path. Being civilisational allowed you the plurality of time, to live with both your masculine and famine sides in balance in a society where Copernicus and Gandhi were contemporary. Being civilisational meant that the oral, the textual, the digital, the tribal, the peasant and the post-industrial would not be assimilated into the factory called development. By choosing to become a nation state without civilisational moorings, India decided to live in historical unilineal time where pluralistic options became secondary to the official imagination of the West. Somehow the ravages of partition and the Bengal Famine made it almost an act of necessity, to adopt planning, modernity and the planned march towards history.

Sometimes other countries shape the way we think of ourselves. China did not have much of an impact in the first years of independence. In fact, till the 1962 military defeat China was another competitor. Mao Zedong (1893–1976) and Zhou Enlai (1898-1976) acquired a charisma as American media created a magic around them. Between the US build-up and the Indian military defeat, the Indian elite realised the US preferred China. India and the US were democratic twins but when it came to policy, pragmatic USA preferred China. The Mao jacket displaced the Nehruvian one. But it was not in a literal military sense that China threatened India. What China threatened was our confidence in our democracy. Our democracy seemed a poor delivery system for health or nutrition. Totalitarianism seemed better at governance and at delivering welfare. Our democracy suffered from China envy. When Chinese fans and electronics invaded our markets, took over our crafts, the China in us was revived by the likes of Narendra Modi and others. It was clear that China was the dominant superpower. It could threaten the US financial system. US trade with India was insignificant next to China. China's Jack Ma made Tata look like a midget. China possessed a brutal masculinity our elites coveted. Because the elite were not confident of challenging China as nationalist imagination, we began playing second fiddle to the US and Japan in their actions against China. But it was not security that broke the elite psyche, it was the fact we could not be true to our way of life, our sense of heritage. China emasculated us not by making us more Chinese but by making us less Indian. China more than any other society made our elites feel that there was no Indian way. Suddenly our think tanks felt we could neither out-think the West or China. It was a psychological secondariness that would haunt us for decades. There was no Gandhi in our midst who could remark 'yes, Chinese civilisation would be a good idea'. The Dalai Lama reminded us gently of it calling India 'his elder brother' but by now Tibet was just another defeated country. Spiritualism was fine but national security was the true soul of a country. India as a country seemed to inspire ambivalence unlike China which inspired fear or Islam which triggered hate. At this level, India was second division history. Sadly the social movements that could have challenged interpretation were suppressed by the Modi regime. The irony was we saw civil society as activists without realising they were interpreters, epistemologists who could offer an alternative world. As nation states became national security states, globalisation triumphed over internationalism. India could have claims to becoming a superpower in the international world where the UN as an idea was more relevant, but with globalisation the world changed drastically.

The Indian elite had no sense of classical time, of the need to wait and consolidate; it had no sense that vintages take time to brew, that the yeast of ideas take time to work. The elite had been spectators for too long to be genuine players. They were a bit like their cricket matches, no rather more like their cricket commentaries. Commentaries as narratives provided the template, the discourse for the way the elite looked at the world. There was a touch of hysteria to every sentence, as if every move was pregnant with impact. It was like expecting the speed and frenzy of Chinese checkers from a long drawn-out game of chess (may be one day some scholar could write about hysteric elites and their impact on a nation). But when hysteria is accompanied by historical expectations, media and elite misread every event. It sounds adolescent but elites do become adolescent when they do not go back into history or thrive on bowdlerised or Ersatz history. Take Modi's quick visit to see Pakistan's Nawaz Sharif in December 2015, a mere stopover, or his much touted meeting with Shinzo Abe of Japan. It was like a skit and his parade of dresses portrayed like a costume ball. As a wag put it 'the British Empire was a costume ball. The Victorians understood symbols and enacted out the costume ball of an empire, Modi, sadly is what kids call a fancy dress'. The Chinese, Abe, Obama assumed they had power. It was casually implicit in their body language. Modi's body language said more about his tailor than his politics. Indira Gandhi could semiotically out-think a Kissinger, outwit a Nixon. Modi was purely aspirational, hoping wish could become reality. His world of make believe does not become a self-fulfilling prophecy without good propaganda. Indian efforts at image building were too naïve and lacked self-confidence.

There were several reasons for the failure of strategy. Firstly, our new elites were not like the old ones, who enjoyed power and enjoyed discussing power. When one reads a Sardar Pannikar (1894-1963) or a K.P.S. Menon (1898-1982), or a B.N. Rau (1887-1953), one senses a reflexivity about power. These men understood power, had a vision; our new Modi elite had only a wish list. They were shopping at a mall at the whim of every salesman, they were not philosophers of desire. Secondly, the elites which operated through clubs which socialised decision makers in a systematic way, provided them with all the tacit dialects of power. The club might be condemned for its exclusiveness but it did perform a creative function providing continuity in framework and value. Third, there was a continuity of families, where the Bajpais, the Pandeys, the Menons, the Mukherjees provided a mnemonic continuity with the past. As power moved to think tanks, the old style with its values and its wisdom disappeared. Think tanks like Vivekananda, Aspen, and the new CPR were data based. As the political scientist Rajni Kothari once said about psephologists, 'they could tell you all about elections but little about democracy'. The think tanks were data points but had no strategy, no philosophy, they were more like marketing agendas who moved with the clients' whims. They had no anchor points of responsibility and perspective, no vision of a nation which went beyond interest politics. Also in the gap between Nehruvian strategies and Modisque nationhood, there was little transmission of the folklore of foreign policy. The new think tanks wanted to create a science, a methodology. They had all the trappings of scholarship but lacked style, the tacit webs that made a tactic comprehensible at several layers. You could sense it in the memoirs that emerged. The older lot wrote about who thought what; they were better storytellers and one must confess a bit snobbish. The new lot were behaviourists, creating an overt history of who fought who. It was the difference between reading a record of a journey and being faced with a memo pad and a timetable.

Deeply and fundamentally there was a failure of semiotics in comprehending the relationship between symbolism and power of the lived world, of behaving like a great power, of understanding the symbolic short hand for a certain relationship between politics, technology, economics and law. Just think of it in a performative sense. When one says 'China is a great power', the statement is performatively convincing. It has the concreteness of 'this is a table'. When India says it is a superpower, it sounds like a wish, a collective Rorschach of an elite, a hypothesis, like a sketch which needs to be filled up. Linguistically, performatively our foreign policy statements sounded hollow. The symbolism was missing or weak. Our civilisation had a symbolic power but as a nation-state, we sounded weak, even unconvincing.

What puzzled observers was the way we responded to Islam. Oddly, India read Pakistan through the lenses of fundamentalism compounding the tragedy of partition. Partition was one of the great genocides in history but at the end India still had more Muslims than Pakistan. Earlier we had the confidence to watch Pakistan as if it were a failed state, an extension of American power but the rise of Islamic fundamentalism has confused us. India saw it opportunistically through knee jerk crises as a moment to label Pakistan as another terrorist nation. Every time there was an attack on New York or Paris, our elite felt closer to the G-13 or the 7/11 club. Our policy makers wanted the violence to work for us, not work against the violence. Indian foreign policy which once had a deep affirmation of Muslims countries now saw Israel as its true double. The presence of Islam in India made the government treat most India's Muslims in India as suspect citizens. It was an irony that escaped our elite. Strangely India which produced some of the world's most creative Islam, where Islam was an intrinsic part of everything from Bollywood to medicine, played down its Islamic self to play its superpower role. It was almost as if the word superpower meant a lessening of India as a place, as a mindset. It was like denying a part of you to create a new sense of history. India which could have battled idiot ideas like the Bush scenario of the axis of evil, demonised Pakistan; and in demonising Pakistan, we distorted Islam and erased or blunted a whole layer of the Indian self. Hindutva and the Hindutva roots of foreign policy impoverished the Hinduism of our imagination, of our tradition.

But there was something equally fundamentally wrong in the way we understood violence. Power can only be power if it understands violence, learns to moderate it or control it. One can use either the language of security or the dialects of peace. Security, the favourite word of our elite, is a Linus Blanket, a control term. It seeks dominance or parity in a technological or managerial sense but its sense of order derives from uniformity. Difference is perceived as noise. The idea of security is intrinsic to the logic of the nation state. However, the word peace is more community oriented, it seeks to read difference creatively and constructively. Peace requires an ease with plurality and its accompanying differences while security seeks to police order. Our reactions to violence are shaped by these perspectives. Violence becomes a law and order problem for regimes obsessed with security. Peace unravels the logic of difference but in an organic way. Peace prefers a commons, while security yearns for the Panopticon. Superpowers oddly are national security states. They want their boundaries intact, their citizens filed, and their monopoly of sovereign power clear and transparent. The enemy is a Manichean construct whether communist or Islamic, and needs to be suppressed or subjugated. As a result, these societies often create as the demonic other what is a genuine part of their self. For India to be a superpower, it was necessary to suppress its minoritarian and dissenting selves.

Enter South Asia

India had many chances to play a different kind of role. Yet the idea of the nation state blinded us to civilisational possibilities. There was first the whole issue of Nepalese democracy. The very word Nepalese democracy creates a sense of envy in India as India wanted to be unique in South Asia, a democratic plurality in a dictatorial or strife torn area. The idea of a Nepalese democracy threatened India's brand status. We puffed up like finches when people called us the world's largest democracy. We liked suffixes like first or biggest to emphasise our presence. Tiny Nepal moving to constitutionalism threatened us. We preferred Nepal as the last Hindu Kingdom. It made Nepal seem atavistic, a fragment of India's past or a

feudal fragment. But a Nepal emerging out of the morass of Marxism and
Kingship, to be a democracy made us feel secondary. When the question of
Madhesi representation came up, we decided to destabilise Nepal by
imposing a blockade. The Madhesis have suffered untold discrimination and
deprivation; but we did not hesitate to use bully boy tactics. India expected
Nepalese to knuckle in, even whine but they did neither. Worse the
Nepalese intellectuals pulled out a trump card for the future. Kanak Dixit
and other futurists around the journal *Himal* presented a futurist scenario
which went beyond the blockade to propose a new dream of the mind.
Himal produced a special issue on the new ontology of South Asia.

Dixit was a strange even quirky thinker who realised that Nepal as a
nation state was condemned to perpetual secondariness, either playing
second fiddle to India or being harassed to mediocrity by World Bank
consultants. Rather than being a creative republic, Nepal would remain as
a remittance economy of its NRIs. As Dixit sarcastically said at a conference
'the world does not gives us many options beyond being Gorkha or Sherpa'.
He said it in a wry hard unsentimental way which conveyed his realism, his
scepticism of the politics of the South Asian Association for Regional
Corporation (SAARC). Impishly he produced a new slogan, 'SAARC is
dead. Long live South Asia'. Dixit unravelled it as a plan for a beleaguered
Nepal arguing that to rescue Nepal, he had to rescue India, Bhutan and Sri
Lanka from the procrustean mindsets of the SAARC. Dixit was following
the old ideas of social scientists like Patrick Geddes (1854-1932) and
Radhakamal Mukherjee (1889-1968), who sought to replace the fixity of
the nation with the fluidity of the idea of region. The region, Dixit claimed,
reset the problem of SAARC. One needs to shuffle the pack before
changing the rules of the game. When your sense of reality, of the very
being of SAARC changes, your logic of politics changes. In rescuing Nepal,
you rescue India from the power of stereotypes it has been stuck in. Dixit
and Indian civil society created a pro forma for a different South Asia, which
is worth summarising.

They agreed that a nation state on its own is not a self-sufficient entity.
Firstly, it is not an ecological fact. It carves out regions into artificialities.
Even as a theory of culture, it is inadequate because a nation lacks a sense of
a cosmos, an inkling of the grand ending of time. A nation without a set of
accompanying concepts is impoverished, denuded of a possibility of being

a whole. A system is a formalised even closed idea of order. A whole is open and the relation between parts has a sense of the unfinished. The idea of the whole is something we perpetually negotiate between past and future. There is no sense of scale, only boundaries and partitions. When Gandhi gave India the concepts of *Swadesi* and *Swaraj*, he provided an ethical gradient that went beyond geography. Swadesi provided a sense of locality, neighbourhood, nativeness, of dialect and vernacular, of indigeneity. Swaraj was a sense of the planetary where a neighbourhood could echo a cosmos. Swaraj gave a sense of planetary responsibility. As concepts Swadesi and Swaraj were not dichotomies but captured the idea of micro and macrocosm as in the relationship of dew drops to ocean. Swadesi and Swaraj were linked together to an idea of oceanic circles. There was a sense of music, an accordion effect as you pushed and pulled, an architectonic of scale.

An India without the idea of South Asia seems hegemonic while an India as an inventive part of Bhutan, Sri Lanka, and Nepal brings a sense of playfulness back to the culture and the geography of South Asia. Instead of the closure of boundary, we have the openness of hospitality. Let me suggest what appears as a farfetched example. Tibet in literal sense is a thought experiment. Here is a country without being a nation, a set of refugees, exiles who have repaid Indian hospitality by providing a sheer pollination of ideas. Tibet plays the civilisational conscience while waiting to return to nationhood. Meanwhile, as Tibet (as a metaphor) and as a Buddhist experiment and through the charisma of the Dalai Lama, Tibet creates an availability of new imaginations. Tibet is an ethical challenge to China as an idea. Its Buddhism creates new conversations with the West on physics, on economics, rethinking ethics, giving a new meaning to Satyagraha. Tibet reinvented a sense of intimacy of place even if it has lost its original space, its territory. Tibet redeemed the idea of India. One understands this when we look at the plight of Syrian citizens and contrast it with what India did for Bangla and Tibetan refugees. The idea of India changed from a constipated nation state to a hospitable ecology thanks to this. Similarly, each country has to invent a new or a renewed idea of South Asia.

Each country has to reinvent the idea of South Asia but we have to move from the South Asia of the imagination to a South as a set of imaginaries. South Asia cannot only be a literal map. It has to be a set of topological spaces rewriting relationships. Sri Lanka, Bhutan, Nepal have to be experiments that India needs to join. It might need a new notion of a no war pact or attempts to rework a new idea of a regional social contract beyond the stereotypical frame of small to big nation. One senses that the idea of South Asia has to go beyond SAARC for new models of dreaming and alternatives to enter this domain. What if Tibet were to be given SAARC membership or honorary status? Could we create more active engagements without alternating between passive spectatorship (as in Sri Lanka) or active hostility as in the Nepal Blockade? Could the idea of South Asia as a trans-region give other little regionalisms a different future? What we often call secession might be an alternative way of constructing an imagination. Beyond the aridity of the Commonwealth as a colonial hangover, could there have been a commons, a common wealth called South Asia? Why was it secondary in articulation to the common wealth? Could an ecological imagination centring around rivers, mountain systems or the idea of the sea help rethink South Asia? Could giving tribes, nomads and pastoral groups the right to travel across boundaries help change the nation state? Think of Tagore's *Kabuliwalah*, we read as children, which nation did he belong to? Think of a Green Cross project, a type of Red Cross for the environment, a common responsibility for South Asia where no work of heritage is destroyed by war or violence. Could the Bamiyan temples have been saved as a common heritage site or do we shrug off its destruction as a local event? Could we invent sustainability as a regional style for subsistence cultures? What new connectivities could we add to create a South Asia which sounds like a warm human organism rather than a creation of clerks? How do we rethink the politics, culture, ecology of the idea of a region in response to Atlantic theatres and the European Commission idea? Is trade the only defining feature of treaties or can we centre the battle around violence, climate change, a new notion of a regional university? How do we rescue SAARC from secondariness and yet not give the bureaucratic idea of SAARC a primariness? Is there a South Asian way of thinking that can help redeem the nation state impasse? What does a new idea of a playful South Asia mean to identities and everydayness? Imagine a Shadow cabinet of South Asians acting as a floating critique of regimes in this area. How does one create a therapeutic idea of South Asia? One is looking at the idea of region at three levels. Firstly a transnational idea of region, secondly a concept of regions within the nation state and thirdly how the idea of region is at right angles to the nation state. Does a folklore notion of South Asia help in terms of cultural memory of old song lines?

The idea of South Asia cannot be equated to the banality of SAARC. South Asia, even just to recognise its possibilities, had to be presented as an outrageous hypothesis. The concept was first coined by the American sociologist Robert Lynd (1892-1970). One can interpret it to mean a novel idea whose very presence ambushes the normal mind, an idea which becomes acceptable after a mental struggle. South Asia has always been seen as inferior and second rate. As Kanak Dixit once observed, the idea coerces and given the current politics, Nepal, Bhutan, Sri Lanka are condemned to being secondary and second rate. We need a different set of ideas to emancipate us. Think of a new Legislative system. India removes the Rajya Sabha and replaces it with the South Asian Parliament. Imagine a South Asia, a Parliament which allows for dual citizenship, where the Bhutanese idea of Gross National Happiness and Sikkim's plea for Organic Farming get extended. Think of a Parliament with the custodianship of the Himalayas, to preserve and protect it as the domain of the sacred. Think of a Parliament which creates a Green Cross, not just to defend cultural monuments like buildings during war but which also legislates on sustainability and diversity, which confronts violence with a new notion of peace. A parliament which believes that to be ecologically sound the idea of the region needs a new idea of economics, a sense of the knowledge commons which creates a limited secession from the world's idea of intellectual property. A parliament which adopts prisoners of conscience which it seeks to protect in order to enhance the idea of rights and ethics, which offers citizenship and refuge to the likes of Julian Assange and Edward Snowden. Imagine a parliament which introduces an idea of coercive holism, insisting trams serve tea in traditional terracotta pots and not in plastic. Think of a Parliament whose secretariat is a set of futures research centres. Think of a Parliament which has as an annexe the new idea of a South Asian University debating and clarifying every idea in progress.

Narendra Modi ignored the debates. In fact, official agencies panned the idea seeing its roots in anti-national and sentimental sources. But somewhere civil society and our sense of the civilisational made India feel it had lost an opportunity for a different future.

The Climate Change Fiasco

There was a feeling that somehow India under Modi was happier playing a sibling to Israel than in thinking through what Nepal or Bhutan or Sri Lanka meant to us. Global power in an abstract sense rather than the diverse creativity of the neighbourhood meant more to Modi's menagerie.

However, the biggest disappointment came during India's role during the climate change conference. Sustainability was a word that troubled third world countries. They read it as a blend of care, concern and conscience with that touch of hypocrisy the first world always displayed. It exemplified the schizophrenic piety all critiques of development displayed. Conscience could soften the paradigm of development but not replace it. It violated a sense of history. All this was valid but the centre-periphery model of industrialisation had no real sense of the planetary world and its future.

Whether it was the suave Jairam Ramesh, the economist and politician of the Congress party or Modi's minister for environment, one sensed they both used the same formula, an Old Testament version of nationalism. Here history becomes the measure of justice. Time becomes compensatory and if the first world began industrialisation first, the third world feels it needs equal time to pollute. There was little debate about alternative energy, the nature of waste, and the rights of future generations. In fact, history seems to exhaust both ethics and the imagination. The third world claims history justified its delayed response to the ethical issues of the planet.

Few countries did a hermeneutical reading of the idea of sustainability. A few dissenting intellectuals showed that sustainability is not a holistic term but a fragment confronting two other fragments called security and safety. All these were managerial exercises which lacked the holism of place. One sensed that while the West was declining, and we were edging towards a post West era, the categories of thought it had introduced had found new converts.

I remember it was a poet, a Kannada poet, who told me sustainability is not poetic enough because it is not playful enough. It is still a part of the Western puritan conscience, a distant cousin of Malthusian science. Critics felt that India was not being civilisational. A Bhakti movement would have been more apt. Asceticism can be built in as an option, an ethical or aesthetic or religious response to a world rather than treating it technically and economically. It is a pity India insisted on a secular framework when alternatives were possible. India as a civilisation had to see sustainability as a secular orphan which needed to be reviewed civilisationally, across the great religious imaginations, providing dialects of the sacred. Unfortunately, Hindutva was too rigid to allow for the play of Hinduism.

The centre-periphery model within which the Indian nation state read modern history proved too unforgiving. It turned the third world into Shylocks demanding their pound of flesh. It forgot India as a civilisation was always more hospitable to the other. When the sustainability debate occurred, we lack the civilisational literacy and confidence to present a different argument.

I remember the author U R Ananthamurthy (1932-2014) telling me centre-periphery frameworks are recent fictions. India he claimed dealt with the other in terms of other models. One was the myth, the heuristic of frontyard and backyard. The response was modelled on the traditional house. The frontyard was masculine, official. It was where my father dealt with government officials, foreign visitors, and village elders. The backyard was feminine, the source of intimacy of the kitchen and storytelling. The frontyard was official, English, scientific while the backyard was informal, a world of translation, of dialects. Nehru was a frontyard intellectual, Gandhi and Tagore belonged to the backyard. Between frontyard and backyard we domesticated most alien systems. Gandhi added an even more interesting dimension to it.

He provided the concepts of Swadesi and Swaraj. Swadesi encompassed the local, the vernacular, the neighbourhood; and Swaraj, the sense of the planetary. For Gandhi, India had to create new Ashrams of the mind to think planetary. Ashrams were domains of prayer and experiment. A Gandhian idea would have led to new experiments in energy, new metaphors of the body, and new ideas of a sacrament with nature. Instead of leading the debate on climate change, India remained obtusely a third world country. Somehow the question of new imaginaries left Modi cold. His was a Prussian idea of development married to an RSS idea of everydayness. Somehow the regime lost its roots in creativity. Our great ideas are cosmic or marginal. Dissent becomes a creative blend of both to scale. Little happened in the Modi era. He kept shrinking. By 2020, one realised that BJP as an alternative idea of India was over. What was pathetic was that there was no sense of ending, except that sense of deflation. The country is at a lull now. The ideas of civil society are stirring but have lived in suspended animation for a decade. Our mediocrity seduced us. Now life is tentative but I feel the new generation might dream differently. Democracy will hopefully invent new possibilities for India.

Pass my reply to others. Tell them, it is essential to remember. It is not the excesses of the Right that destroyed BJP or thwarted India's dream of global prominence and greatness. It was sheer mediocrity.

RUSSIA'S IDENTITY CRISIS

Julia Sveshnikova

Coming back to Russia in the spring of 2016, I am all ears, eyes and soul. I want to see the changes on the ground after Russia was battered by sanctions and other diplomatic consequences as a result of its policies – particularly its claims on Crimea and military intervention in Syria. Russia's attempts to accelerate the coming of the post-Western order – specifically, a multi-polar world with powerful anti-American allies trumpeting victorious slogans – have cost Russians dearly. True, the same morose aura I encounter on the underground train is merely a sign of the continuing depression of recent years. And there are the same people on the streets – they marry, give birth and go to work – so things seem to be at the level of the 'usual normal'. Yet there are so many layers of reality – taking shape in the media, on the Internet and in public discussions among intellectuals; in 'kitchen talks' about politics that we inherited from the Soviet era as a quiet way of expressing our disenchantment; in witch-hunts against NGOs that are suspected of conducting political activities with foreign funding; in the unheeded warnings by the watchdog Transparency International; the list goes on. These aspects of reality also exist, even if not everybody sees or gives them any importance. All the while, people talk about needing values, identity, religion and ideology almost surreally alongside the need for investment into various industries, infrastructure and improved living standards.

Located at the plexus of Europe and Asia, Russian identity continually fluctuates between both Slavophile and pro-Western tendencies, a phenomenon that is at times painful and disturbing. Our disputes still divide us, reminding us of the centuries-old standoff between 'West' and 'East'. The term *'vatnik'* – derived from the name of an iconic Soviet uniform jacket issued during the Second World War – is now applied to the so-called patriot, 'an outspoken follower of Putin, who aims to compensate his meaningless life by glorifying the motherland' (as defined by the online translator Multitran. ru). The term was coined as a response to the government's crackdown on Russia's liberal opposition and the so-called 'creative class' and was meant to be insulting. However, now it is getting more common for supporters of Putin or the Russian government to adopt the term proudly, especially in response to Russia's policies in Ukraine and Syria.

Proud *vatniks* bash liberals supposedly for their pro-US imperialism and for falling for 'American cookies' (as the Western funding of non-commercial activities is derogatorily referred to); 'liberals' blame the government for its imperialist post-Soviet aspirations, most recently in the Middle East. Both are not exactly right in their mutual antagonisms, but as a result of this impasse most Russians end up paying the price domestically and internationally. Domestically we fail to work on more important problems while still suffering from sanctions. Internationally we look like a vulgar, clumsy bear that everybody wants to avoid. But we should not judge the majority of Russians for not being meticulous in analysing the conflicts that some of their leaders have instigated on their behalf. They are unable to see the bigger picture either due to the state of the media or because they have more pressing personal issues to struggle with.

Meanwhile, the intellectual and political rhetoric carries on. In an emerging post-Western world there are still pro-West Russians who believe that Western sociopolitical systems, society and culture should be emulated. However, it is the Slavophiles who have the ideological upper hand at the moment. Russia's 'special mission', according to Slavophiles, began with its adoption of Eastern Christianity but is now expressed in terms of the country's geopolitical aspirations. That is, Russia's 'special mission' now is to unite the post-Soviet space or 'the Russian world', to promote Eurasianism, to support other poles of power and to stand for Russian interests in different parts of the world, even if there are not enough internal resources to achieve this.

'*Sobornost*' – the organic unity of Eastern Orthodoxy and the local parish, or a kind of a unity through communalism – is now rather perceived as unity through traditionalism and conservatism. Here we can observe the minister of defence Sergei Shoigu crossing himself before opening the Victory Day parade on 9 May 2016, as he did in 2015. Presidents of the new Russia ostentatiously attend religious services in the Cathedral of Christ the

Saviour, whose crystal-white walls are still blushing after the female punk group Pussy Riot's scandalous 'punk protest' there in 2012. But if these devoted servants of the nation are worshipping as mere mortals, why are they always filmed by so many cameras, their bowed heads occupying so much broadcasting time during Christmas or Easter?

These contests about 'Russian' identity often serve certain political purposes – a matter of interest as well as a source of frustration for millions. The majority who are fighting for their daily bread do not usually bother to contemplate this. But there are thinkers and truth seekers concentrated in Moscow and St Petersburg, and scattered in other cities, tackling painful questions about self-identity.

As far back as the 1990s, in a desperate attempt to bring Russians' mind-set to order, the late president Boris Yeltsin assigned a special commission to devise 'a national idea' but the project nearly failed. The best it could come up with was 'do not pee on a staircase', according to Georgy Satarov, who was on the commission and is now head of the NGO Information Science for Democracy (INDEM). Of course, what the commissioners meant was that Russians need to be self-conscious about our actions which could damage our surrounding environments – from rubbish in the streets, corruption in the country's management and polluted thoughts in our minds. So we spent the beginning of the twenty-first century fighting off dirt but it feels like we've piled up more garbage. So many of us now hope that this dirt is in fact a kind of mud with healing properties. Or as the popular comedian Michail Zhvanetsky puts it: 'I see the light at the end of the tunnel...but the damned tunnel doesn't end.' Neither does the pollution.

Given Russia's interventions in the Middle East, it is important firstly to understand the complicated role that Islam has played in the development of Russian national identity throughout the centuries. And although they share the same religion as Muslims in the Middle East, Russia's Muslims do not have a united response to the events in Syria, Crimea, or elsewhere. The tight confluence of Islam with ethnicity, or political preferences, or pre-Muslim backgrounds (for converts) makes distinct lines of division and results in very diverse responses towards governmental policies among Russia's Muslim population. Besides, after the media fuss about Russia's interventions abroad subsides, some common issues remain for the country's Muslims and non-Muslims – namely the economic pie that keeps shrinking. Russians — Muslims and non-Muslims — are still searching for their 'true' selves behind the media façade. How do we define ourselves in relation to the 'West', the 'Muslim world' and our own heritage?

Scattered *ummah*

The face of Russia is European, Slavic and Orthodox Christian but it is also Asian, Turkic, Muslim and Buddhist, among other things. Russian identity is so multi-layered — ethnically, religiously and historically — that it appears impossible to dissect it. The Muslim face of Russia is no less complex than 'Russian identity' on the whole. A religion that was 'tolerated' during the time of Russia's historical territorial expansion, Islam came to shape the perplexed notion of Russian citizenship. At the turn of the first millennium A.D., Vladimir Sviatoslavovich the Great, ruler of Kievan Rus', allegedly needed to choose a religion to unite the peoples in his lands. Rumour has it that he had some sympathy for Islam but only if the religion allowed the consumption of alcohol. Fast forward to 2003 when President Vladimir Putin declared Russia 'an Islamic country' and 'part of the Muslim world', and then to 2005 when Russia joined the Organisation of Islamic Cooperation (OIC), albeit with observer status. In fact, Islam became an officially recognised religion in 1788 through the edict of Empress Catherine the Great which established the institutional coordination of mullahs and Islamic religious leaders, launched in 1789 in the city of Ufa (in modern Bashkortostan). Catherine also signed an edict establishing the 'Mahometan Religious Administration' chaired by the Mufti in Tavricheskaya Oblast (roughly corresponding with modern-day Crimea) in 1794.

The Soviet era, 1917-1991, somewhat fragmented Russian Muslim identity. Religion was officially not welcome in the militant secularist state and as with other places of worship, mosques went underground and ritual practices were limited and persisted in secret. This period created the conditions that would characterise the religious landscape in post-Soviet Russia — a lack of professionals in the religious field due to the absence of specialised religious education. From the 1980s onward, the Soviet Union observed a rise in religious and nationalistic attitudes in its southern republics. This foreshadowed the penetration of more radical elements in the 1990s, filling in the post-Communist ideological vacuum. By this time, there was no strong intelligent governmental narrative to counter rising Islamic radicalisation and separatism. Against this backdrop, the 1993 constitution proclaimed a secular state with equal respect to all religions, and Islam again received recognition and support. Madrasas were reopened and new mosques erected, but the absence of a long established tradition of Islamic education drove eager students abroad – to Saudi Arabia and Egypt in particular – who brought back new visions of Islam.

At present, there are at least one million ethnic Muslims in Moscow who are especially visible during major religious celebrations such as Eid-al-Fitr. According to official estimates, out of a population of 143 million, there are 16 million Muslims with Russian citizenship and five million comprising migrants – the numbers are very rough. Muslims in Russia are inadvertently affected in the country's two recent foreign policy undertakings. Russian military intervention in the Middle East involved its responses to multiple Muslim actors – radicals from the so-called Islamic State (IS), Sunni Arabs, Kurds and Turks as well as Alawites and Jafari Shias. The seizure of Crimea affected Crimean Tatars who are Muslim. Muslims within Russia reacted differently to these political trends as part of their diverging quests for self-actualisation. On one hand, in response to the growing involvement of the Orthodox Church in politics, many Muslims feel impelled to fortify their own ideological and cultural particularities. On the other hand, with regards to Crimea and Syria, Russian Muslims exhibited varying political preferences as with other citizens who were observing these developments.

Take Tatarstan. It is home to Sunni Muslims of the Hanafi *madhab* who are generally perceived as 'gentle' and 'secularised'. But recent years have witnessed the strengthening of ethnic, cultural and religious sentiments in Tatarstan. In the 1990s it was a matter of embarrassment to speak Tatar on the street as the speaker risked being considered rural and uneducated. Now speaking Tatar publicly is a matter of pride. Expressing religiosity has become fashionable. More hijabs can be seen in the streets. Largely secular graduates of Turkish and other colleges are giving up cigarettes and alcohol in pursuit of the 'straight path' even if they did not feel shy about these indulgences previously. Religious leaders who returned after studying in the Arab world only reinforce this trend. Similar trends of rising religiosity, especially among younger generations, can be observed in the Caucasus, where the population mostly follows the Shafii *madhab* of Sunni Islam. But landlocked Tatarstan – which once dropped its claims for independence and submitted to Moscow – reacts calmly to the reported discrimination against its Tatar brethren in Crimea. Perhaps this is because the Russian media do not focus on what is actually happening in Crimea. But it is also because of the prevailing perception, even in Tatarstan, that Crimea was rightfully 'returned' to Russia, a country it has always belonged to, especially among Tatars who grew up during the Soviet era.

The resurgence of Islam includes those who, in search of their identity, reclaim and reinterpret the religion into which they were born, for example Geydar Dzhemal, the eccentric leftist Muslim writer-activist of Azeri origin and head of the Islamic Committee of Russia. There are others who make a conscious choice to convert. According to very rough estimates, there might be some 10,000 Muslim converts but this figure is unreliable. The new converts – active, bold, sometimes militantly religious – consist of another notorious group in the Russian social landscape. They might not be numerous, but they try very actively to make their voice heard especially on political issues. Converts are free to choose which schools of Islam they want to follow, and this allows many to get creative. While Hanafi and Shafii *madhahib* were traditionally practiced in Russia, converts have enriched the landscape through their engagement with the Maliki *madhab* in Sunni Islam, Shiism, and Salafism.

On the whole, non-traditional Muslim groups are more successful in attracting their followings from converts rather than from Muslims born in established Sunni traditions. This is understandable, since those who embrace the faith anew are doing it through active choice – in search of 'the Truth', or a solution, or a safe haven for mind and soul. Many converts engage with their newfound religious convictions with no more or less intensity than other religious believers. However, the more committed converts are also more vocal in asserting their new identity publicly, something which affects both the wider public discourse and the landscape of Russian Islam. Although Islam can be seen as a universal religion, it is also often perceived as having particular ethnic or traditional trappings. For new Muslims, the easiest way to understand and express Islam and to internalise it is to become immersed within a cultural context of so-called 'indigenous' Muslims – usually Arab, but sometimes Iranian, Turkish or even Pakistani. As converts look for the source of their newly discovered truth, they may travel to Egypt, Iran, Syria, Turkey, or elsewhere. Depending on their experiences, they might get disillusioned with the discovery that 'indigenous' Muslims are rarely 'ideal' Muslims or they might deepen and strengthen their knowledge and fascination with Islam. For the disenchanted, the trajectory can take another twist – this is where they return and invent a special Russian Islam ('Russian' in the sense of ethnicity, so it could also be referred to as Slavic Islam). They distinguish their version of Russian Islam from Russian ethnicity as well as from other Russian Muslims, creating their own *ummah*.

It is difficult but still possible to preserve faith in a cultural vacuum, although it requires Herculean conviction and motivation. But conventional Islam stresses on the collective idea of the larger *ummah* to which believers need to be bound. Within this context, there used to be a group called the National Organisation for Russian Muslims (NORM) founded by Vadim (Harun) Sidorov in 2004. It was joined by another outstanding Russian Muslim figure, the former priest Vyacheslav (Ali) Polosin. Initially NORM had a Salafi orientation. After the Shia faction headed by Taras (Abdulkarim) Chernienko left, NORM decided to focus on promoting the Maliki *madhab*. As its founders explain, their purpose was to produce the merger of Muslim and Russian ethnicity. In order for this group of 'Russian Muslims' to distinguish itself from other 'born Muslims', it chose the Maliki *madhab* to set itself apart from the historically established Hanafi and Shafii schools. Sidorov himself began his journey in leftist groups and carried his past into his newfound religious identity. However, despite internal conflicts, some founders like Polosin decided to embrace Crimean Muslims with open arms and welcomed the erection of the mosque in Simferopol in 2015.

There is another non-traditional element in the Russian Muslim landscape consisting of converts to Shia Islam. The presence of Shia Muslim converts can be attributed to the introduction of Iranian culture to Russia as the two countries maintain friendly ties and arrange cultural exchanges to a significant extent. Some Shia converts thus explore opportunities to study in religious seminaries in the Iranian city of Qom. Prominent Shia converts include the already mentioned Taras Chernienko (Abdulkarim Mashhadi), Anastasia (Fatima) Ezhova, long standing author and editor of the journal *Musulmanka*, and the imam Anton Vesnin (al-Rusi) who currently resides in the Iraqi city of Najaf. Alongside the Shia converts are historically Shia

Azeris, many of whom have also attended seminaries in Qom and engage in *dawah* (missionary activity) with the wider Russian public despite not always being entirely fluent in the Russian language. The Shia sector is distinguished by a very specialised type of discourse to the extent that at times it appears irrelevant to the current problems of Russia and even its Muslim population. For instance, there are strong intra-Shia debates about being *'zedde wilayat'*, that is, against the concept of governance based on the authority of religious jurists as practiced in Iran. These debates might sound like a parallel reality for the daily concerns of the majority of Russians, yet they exist.

And so within Russia's Muslim population there are those who support intervention in Syria because they support Putin's strong hand and/or Bashar al-Assad's Alawi regime, which they consider Shia. Then there are those who oppose Russia's intervention precisely because it is tantamount to supporting an Iranian-backed Shia regime that is killing Sunnis. Some support the annexation of Crimea because of the presence of Muslims there and because 'it has always been ours'. Others resent the reported discrimination against Crimean Tatars. Some, like other Russians, are indifferent. Others are disappointed that money is being channelled to Crimea, and that instead of heading to their usual comfortable Turkish and Egyptian resorts, they have to travel to 'our' peninsula at triple the price for lower quality services. Group and individual priorities and political boundaries can go unnoticed, however. Opinions are not necessarily spoken out loud.

The numbers game

Despite existing international tensions, it is fair to say that within Russia the dust has already settled about Crimea and Syria – but there are other issues now to consume people's interest. The newly acquired Crimean region will not promise a swift payback and will rather require large-scale investment. Shabby infrastructure, the necessity to build a bridge over the Kerch Strait and social payments will not be compensated by the strategic acquisition of the permanent naval outpost in Sevastopol. Shortly after the jingoism of the annexation of Crimea had evaporated, average Russians started resenting the amount of spending – taken out of mainland Russia's budget – that was supposed to be injected there.

As the findings of Levada Center opinion poll conducted in August 2014 showed, the number of people happy with the acquisition of Crimea dropped from 23 per cent to 16 per cent within four months after April. Overall approval fell from 47 per cent to 40 per cent, and the number of respondents feeling shame or explicitly disapproving of the government's actions remains at nine per cent. The controversy here is that while 73 per cent (compared to 64 per cent in March 2014) stated that Crimea should be a part of Russia, which can most likely be attributed to the skilful work of the Russian media and its effect on public sentiment, 28 per cent (compared to 19 per cent in March 2014) were not ready to pay for the government's actions from their own pocket. Also, despite the mainstream media not making much noise about the deaths of Russian soldiers in East Ukraine, many respondents still had concerns about military action.

Polling data provided by the official Russian Public Opinion Research Center (VCIOM) in the spring of 2016 demonstrated that the media effect was crucial. Over 90 per cent of those polled were sure that Russia's assertive policies proved its ability to defend national interests. Fifty-three per cent were sure that these policies strengthened Russia's image internationally; 73 per cent concluded that Crimea and Sevastopol play a crucial role in the country's defence shield. The detention of Crimean Tatars who constitute 12.6 per cent of the peninsula's population of 2.3 million – under the pretext of fighting extremism – was also not covered widely by the media and thus did not provoke much outcry. Sometime after Crimea was proclaimed a new region of Russia, the authorities welcomed the Tavrichesky Muftiyat into the structure of Muslim coordinating bodies in the country. Ambiguities in the Russian collective consciousness are also indicated by the answer to another question. From 2014 to 2016 there was an increase in the number of those who think that the overall standard of living overweighs concerns about whether Russia is a democratic state. However, democracy can have different meanings to Russians compared to how Western Europeans understand it but this is not very easily explained. Perhaps the following examples can help clarify the context.

The mass media played a huge role during Russia's intervention into the Syrian conflict in October 2015. It created the impression that Syria was just another region of Russia, albeit a troublesome one. In February 2016, according to the Levada Center, the war in Syria was better remembered than other major events in the immediately preceding months, ranking higher than the country's deadly influenza epidemic and the drop in the ruble's value. At the same time, public knowledge about the particularities and goals of military intervention was mostly superficial. The minister of defence stated that the US$2.5 million spent on the operation every single day was within the annual military budget. Yet attempts to continue portraying intervention as part of Russia's strategic interests were viewed sceptically by a significant number of Russians. In October 2015, 41 per cent of those surveyed by Levada felt that expenditures taken up by the Syrian operation could have been more usefully channelled to satisfy domestic social needs. The ambivalence in public attitudes over Syria was also reflected in the fact that over 50 per cent supported both arms supplies and humanitarian aid – not solely military invasion. Around 50 per cent agreed that Russia needed to support Assad in his fight against IS and other opposition to his government, and 34 per cent supported direct Russian attacks against IS and other opposition to Assad. Among the reasons given were that this would break the chain of 'colour revolutions' (non-violent resistance movements to overthrow authoritarian governments) around the world. The Russian authorities view 'colour revolutions' as part of a wider US-led plot to secure its military interests around the globe.

This narrative coincided with how Russia is more generally portrayed by its leaders as a beacon of resistance to Western dominance. And while things might seem more complicated at the level of political analysis, in lay terms they are more straightforward than one might think. Overall public approval of the campaign can be explained by the success of the simple message that Putin has carried since the early 2000s – Russia needs to fight terrorism through all available means. Currently the message is that if we do not fight terror outside the country, it will be threatening our own borders soon enough. So even without a clear understanding of the particularities of the conflict and their reluctance to pay for it out of their own pockets, the majority of Russians supported continued intervention in Syria. However, they were also against Russian boots on the ground and were not ready to receive Syrian refugees for economic reasons.

Russians want a role model who can help make the country great again, but the larger stakes are played out based on the geopolitical orientation of the ruling elite and its vision of the world. Take the issue of Crimea again.

As Daniel Treisman recently wrote in *Foreign Affairs* magazine, 'Putin has become willing in recent years to take major strategic risks to counter seemingly limited and manageable threats to Russian interests.' By 'Russian interests', he does not only mean the ethnically Russian population of Crimea or historical memory about Russian possession of the region, but Russia's naval stronghold in Sevastopol with its contract constantly on the verge of termination. So Putin gambled with both his own people and the West. And while the West was outraged, Putin's main audience – the population of Russia – gave him greater approval and even praise for 'returning' Crimea to Russia.

The ideological and emotional grounds for these policies in Crimea and Syria were prepared for quite some time before. In his famous Munich speech in 2007, Putin stated that Russia would not condone the unipolar world model. In his Valdai speech in 2013 he was even more critical of the West, insisting that Russia stands for traditionalism and considers globalisation, multiculturalism and the erosion of Christian values as threats to its identity. This speech stressed the importance of the idea of Eurasia and Eurasianism, as well as a turn to the East as a counterweight to Euro-Atlantic society which was framed as being in a state of spiritual, ideological and civilisational decline.

The ramifications of this positioning have become apparent, for instance, in the shift in the regime's and the public's attitude towards Joseph Stalin. After the intervention in Syria and the accession of Crimea, support for Stalin's legacy was higher than ever in post-Soviet Russia. The Syrian war and the standoff with the West after the annexation of Crimea harkened back to the glory days of the 1940s and 1950s for some. Public discussions juxtaposed Putin with Stalin as two Russian rulers on par with European leaders and capable of redrawing the map of the world. Opinion polls in 2015 showed that 45 per cent considered the sacrifices made during Stalin's regime as justified given his ensuing achievements. Significantly, twenty per cent expressed that Stalin was a wise leader who brought the country might and prosperity – these figures are likely to rise in the near future.

The strength of Putin's personality, his position and his track record of 'strong hand' governance, has even led some to speculate that there were personal motives behind the intervention in Syria; namely, Putin's sense that Assad needed help as part of a larger anti-Western resistance. The politics of personality thus mixes with the other historical and ideological layers in Russian history to create what appears to be an irrational and emotional national outburst. Russian public opinion seems to be able to compartmentalise anti-government sentiment about corruption, the status of minorities (especially Muslims) and admiration for Putin's 'strong hand'. The indifference among some is also a form of self-preservation. Public resentment is more likely to emerge, and could lead to a rebellion, when the national identity crisis begins to hurt people's pockets, rather than due to abstract calls for justice or freedom. Until that time comes, 'justice' and 'freedom' will continue to be empty slogans. In these conditions, there is a rising wave of anti-Western traditionalism and regime-sponsored calls for Russian society to return to its so-called Orthodox Christian and Eurasian 'origins'.

Paradoxically, any attempt to construct a so-called 'authentic' Russian identity in opposition to the 'West' seems to make people more apathetic about what real 'Russianness' consists of. Especially when demolished roads are not repaired, industrial enterprises are closed down, businesses underperform and the social ladder has broken rungs. A post-Western or 'turn-to-the-East' ideology is thus only a partially effective opiate for the Russian masses.

CHINA'S BALANCING ACT

Jalal Afhim

For much of the twentieth century, the Pacific Ocean was an American lake. After emerging triumphant from its struggle for dominance with the Soviet Union, the US went on to shape the geopolitics of the Far East with its alliances and enmities, through its projection of economic and military power. From China's perspective, the country was hung out to dry in the aftermath of the Second World War; South Korea and Japan were propped up with US support instead. Although a US ally during the war, and having paid an awful human price for resisting Japanese imperial expansion, China was excluded from many of the agreements which forged the post-war order. However, the status quo is being challenged by a newly assertive China. Having kept control of its currency, banks, and national industries, China now has the world's second largest economy. This is in spite, or possibly because, of stubbornly resisting pressure to conform to the neo-liberal economic consensus. The former East Asian powerhouses of Japan and South Korea find themselves once more in the shadow of a giant. China's momentum has also been matched by a recent surge in ambition. President Xi Jinping's 'China Dream' strapline seems to suggest an alternative to the American Dream, which speaks volumes on how the architects of China's rise see its trajectory.

The dream is already on the cusp of challenging US hegemony. It may not usher in a new PostWest world, but it will certainly be a different world. Xi's pitch to developing countries provides a good example: China will assist with infrastructure and trade, but without the ideological agenda which often comes bundled with US aid. For Muslim-majority countries in particular, partnership with China may prove to be more palatable in the long run. Where the US remains a strong ally of Israel, in defiance of almost the entire UN General Assembly, China supports an independent Palestinian state. With its 'no enemies' policy, there is neither partisan alignment nor rhetoric claiming knowledge of how other states should best organise themselves. But there is a new belligerence as well. China is showing its muscle by claiming disputed maritime territory, worrying US-aligned countries like Japan and the Philippines. However, at the same time it is reaching out to neighbours like Kazakhstan, offering expertise and foreign investment where these were previously sought from the West. The toxicity of the US brand for Muslim countries can only help China's cause, and with an estimated 23 million Muslim citizens, China surely has an asset in building fraternal ties with its Middle-Eastern partners. Indeed, in all the punditry about the rise of China, not enough attention has been paid to China's management of its Muslim minorities and whether this has any bearing on its international outlook.

Throughout most of the Cold War China was a bystander. But the fall of the Berlin Wall happened in the same year that Beijing sent tanks into Tiananmen Square, and troops from the People's Liberation Army (PLA) mowed down students gathered there to protest for political reform. The world changed. Tiananmen gave the Chinese people a clear message to stay out of politics. To keep them out, Communist Party supremo Deng Xiaoping had to offer something else – prosperity. He renounced the ideological commitment of his predecessor, famously saying of capitalism and socialism, 'Whether it is a black cat, or a white cat, what really matters is whether it can catch mice.' The goal was to move towards *xiaokang shehui* (a prosperous society). The cat was China's economy, and to catch mice it needed oil.

In 1993 China's oil needs were still met by domestic production. But by 2008, it was importing two million barrels a day, by 2013 this rose to 5.7 million barrels a day – it currently imports upward of seven million barrels a day. China's geopolitical strategy is significantly driven by its economy's reliance on fossil fuels from the Middle East. It has been Iran's primary trade partner for the last six years, receiving around sixty percent of Iran's exported oil. Qatar is China's largest supplier of natural gas, meeting around twenty percent of its energy needs, while Saudi Arabia is its biggest overall supplier of crude oil. China's approach to securing its energy needs could not be more different from that of the United State. The US has positioned itself in a role of leadership, building regional alliances and influence to ensure the globalised market economy has access to Middle

Eastern oil. Coercion, sanctions, and military intervention have all been deployed to achieve its goals. China on the other hand uses bilateral relationships and economic cooperation alongside political neutrality. This can sometimes be a delicate balancing act, but China has played its hand adroitly. For example, despite recognising Palestine as a state, China enjoys cordial relations with both Israel and Saudi Arabia. Both players have a vested interest in ensuring the Middle Eastern 'choke points' for oil supply are kept open – the Straits of Hormuz, the Gulf of Aden, the Red Sea and the Straits of Malacca. But the aftermath of the invasion of Iraq in 2003, the 2008 financial crisis and rise of the so-called 'Islamic State' or Daesh are taking a toll on the cachet of the US.

We may, therefore, see a major rebalancing of how the Middle Eastern states prioritise their relationships with China and the US. In 2016, Saudi Aramco and the Chinese state-owned oil giant – Sinopec – signed a deal worth $1.5 billion while President Xi Jinping visited the desert kingdom. This trip was followed by visits to Iran and Egypt, indicative of the ramping up of economic bridge-building in Central Asia and the Middle East that Xi Jinping's 'One Belt One Road' (OBOR) strategy aims to achieve. And the relationships are cosy in both directions. None of the 22 Arab countries officially recognise Taiwan, which China considers a wayward province. More significantly, neither do they voice support for the cause of independence pursued by some of their Uyghur co-religionists in China's far west.

The Middle Eastern states are looking East and West to make use of what both China and the US have to offer. China's rise increasingly works in their favour, providing a counterbalance to the historic primacy of the US – they now have an alternative.

But the way ahead for China is not free of obstacles. A major concern will be the fallout from China's crackdown on its restive Uyghur population. With its restrictions on worship, Islamic teaching, and the wearing of headscarves, China risks being seen as anti-Islam. With three-fifths of the world's Muslims living in the Indo-Pacific region, such a portrayal can only be detrimental to China's international relations and reputation. Relations with Indonesia and Malaysia have already been chilled by disputed claims to parts of the South China Sea. The Uyghur situation is already showing signs of shifting from a domestic problem to an international one. Hundreds of Chinese Uyghurs are reported to be fighting with Daesh in Syria and Iraq, and statements have been made by the Daesh leadership that China has been identified as an enemy. Should adversaries arise who are capable of portraying China as an enemy to Muslims, this could represent a significant headwind to OBOR and its current trajectory. A perspicacious approach to managing its Muslim population at home has never been more important.

Muslims in China

Media-driven stereotypes about China evoke images of vast quantities of cheaply manufactured goods and a massively populous and homogenous society. But when I moved there in 2005 to stay in a tai chi school in a small village in Henan Province, central China, I discovered a different world. China is a patchwork quilt of languages, cultures and identities. The State recognises 56 ethnic groups or *minzu* which belong within the Peoples Republic of China (PRC). Ten of these are Muslim peoples, and China's Muslim population, estimated at 23 million or around 1.8 per cent of the population, ranks twelfth on the list of countries with the largest number of Muslims after Uzbekistan and Saudi Arabia.

The nearest city from my school, Jiaozuo, was small by Chinese standards, with around a million inhabitants. It had a long history of coal extraction and poor air quality, with agriculture and coal mining the main industries. The university in Jiaozuo's suburbs where I went to teach was started by the British Syndicate Company in 1909 as China's first mining school. After a stretch as a contender for China's most polluted city at the tail end of the twentieth century, the local government closed many of the coal mines and invested heavily in tourism. The city's fleet of battered Volkswagen taxis now operate with hybrid petrol/gas engines to help keep the air cleaner. The street market in the centre of Jiaozuo is a rollercoaster smell-scape. The pungent whiff of *chou doufu* - 'stinky tofu' - is striking. Think about the transformation of milk into a pungent blue cheese, then apply the principle to soya milk instead of dairy. I would often hold my breath for the few dozen yards where it was most intense, while punters queued happily to buy lumps of it, deep-fried and served with a spicy sauce. Then there was a pleasant nutty fragrance, lifted into the air by the sizzle of superheated woks frying noodles. But what really caught my attention was the unmistakable smell of lamb cooking over charcoal. And I was puzzled by the appearance of the man fanning the charcoal with a scrap of cardboard. To me he looked more Middle-Eastern than Chinese. The sign above the mobile barbecue, which could be pushed like a pram, displayed the word *halal* in Arabic script. The man was a Uyghur, one of China's ten official Muslim minorities and a group I found to be present in small numbers in almost every Chinese town and city I visited.

A central Asian people, Uyghurs are just one of the 56 *minzu* to be found in China. They are most numerous in Xinjiang Province, an arid and semi-arid expanse in the west of the country about eight times the size of Great Britain. The Uyghur speak a Turkic language and, while ubiquitous around China, I found that they are regarded with fear and suspicion by the dominant Han communities into which they migrate. Han friends told me that the Uyghur carry knives, apparently a privilege granted by the government in deference to the role of knives in Uyghur culture. I was also told that if arrested, they are simply transported back to Xinjiang to avoid onerous paperwork on the part of the local police. While the credibility of these claims may be questionable, I nonetheless encountered them often enough to be convinced of their widespread existence in the public consciousness. During my four years in Shanghai, my friends and I had run-ins with Uyghur pick-pockets and this highly visible minority certainly arouses the most controversy among the Chinese Muslim *minzu*.

The case of the Uyghurs is simply one of the ongoing narratives, albeit the most controversial, of minority groups within China trying to define themselves in a rapidly changing society. China's breathtaking transition from a Maoist enclave into the world's second largest economy has been plagued by claims of inequitable sharing out of the cake. According to the World Bank, an estimated 600 million mostly rural people have been lifted out of poverty between 1981 and 2004 but over the last twenty years the distribution of China's growing wealth has become increasingly uneven.

But who are the Muslims in China? Where did they come from? How have they fared in China's transition from the 'sick man of Asia' to the world's second largest economy? How have they responded to contemporary developments in the rest of the Muslim world? There is a striking lack of material exploring these themes either in the press or in academia. Yet, the internal stability of an economically and politically resurgent China will be greatly affected by how the PRC treats its Muslim citizens.

The ten Muslim *minzu* in China include the Hui — by far the largest group — Sino-Muslims whose features are indistinguishable from Han Chinese thanks to centuries of intermarriage. Their ancestors were traders who, from the eighth century, came to China from the Middle East and settled there. The Arabic and Persian spoken by the first settlers have been replaced by local dialects, although some will learn Arabic as part of their Islamic education. Then there are the central Asian peoples: Uyghurs, Kazakhs, Kyrgyz, Uzbeks and Salars. They are visually distinguishable from the Han, usually lacking the epicanthic fold of the eyelid.

China's frontiers have for centuries been a melting pot of languages, cultures, religions and identities. There are Tibetan-speaking Muslims, Chinese-speaking Tibetans, Mongolic-speaking Muslims, Tibetan Hui and Hui Tibetans. Historically there has been fluidity between identities — an individual raised as a Tibetan Buddhist might convert to Islam, for example, for socio-economic reasons. The current official taxonomy of *minzu* is a relatively recent construct of the post-1949 PRC, designed to meet the administrative needs of the state. *Minzu* is a convenient classificatory tool that obscures the complex and often interwoven nature of Chinese identities; the concept probably has its origins in Western European efforts to connect a 'racial' identity to the new political entity known as the nation-state.

Slightly more clear-cut are different strands of Islamic doctrine to be found in China. Mainstream Chinese Islam is orthodox Sunni, following Hanafi jurisprudence. This is referred to as *gedimu*, a transliteration of the Arabic 'al qadim' (the old / ancient). While *gedimu* is considered orthodox Chinese Islam, Sufi orders are particularly prevalent in the North-West, where they had entered from South and Central Asia during the Qing Dynasty (1644-1912). There are a small number of Shia, mostly Tajiks. Conflict between Chinese Muslim communities has historically been less about matters of doctrine and more about political orientation, with *gedimu* Muslims often cooperating with the State to exercise influence or control. Sufi orders like the Jahriya adapted to local conditions, becoming patrilineal organisations with a great deal of political and economic influence, known as *menhuan*. Allegiances and enmities have depended not on doctrine, but on competition for resources, and ascendancy in the local contexts.

The government funds the Islamic Association of China, which is supportive of the *gedimu* orthodoxy, and aims to provide an overarching structure and governance of Chinese Islam and is responsible to the national congress. There is evidence that the Arabic language training opportunities offered by the Association tend to be accessible to Hui Muslims, with their recent history of co-operation with the State, but not to Uyghurs with their history of separatist agitation.

Muslims began settling in China as early as the eighth century, with merchants following the caravans along the Silk Road as well as the maritime route into flourishing trading ports like Canton (now Guangzhou). The merchants were not only Muslims and included people of other Abrahamic faiths including Nestorian Christians and Jews. The Song Dynasty capital of Kaifeng still boasts a community of Chinese Jews today. The next wave of Muslim immigration came with the all-conquering Mongols. When they established the Yuan Dynasty (1271-1368), large numbers of craftsmen, armourers and slaves were transported to China from the subjugated Muslim lands to the west. Central Asians were considered more trustworthy than Han Chinese by the Mongol rulers, and were employed as border guards and administrators. They and their descendants became known as *semu* which when written in Chinese script can also mean 'coloured eyes'. This period saw the establishment of substantial communities of Muslims in China.

In the seventeenth and eighteenth centuries, the expansion of the empire meant incorporation of predominantly Sufi Central Asian communities into the growing territories claimed by China, where they established the first China-based Sufi orders. These Sufi orders with Chinese characteristics would play an important role in the political organisation of Chinese Muslims in years to come, with the *menhuan* fusing features of mystical Islamic brotherhoods from the Middle-East with local customs of patronage and governance. The Sufism they practised, with its mystical doctrine and loyalty to the *shaykh* of the order, came to be known as '*xinjiao*' – 'new religion'. During the early twentieth century, there was a Wahabbi-inspired response to Sufism especially prevalent in the North-

West of the country and Yunnan Province in the South-West. This wave started during the Republican period (1911–1949) with Hui who had undertaken the pilgrimage to Mecca and returned to China influenced by Wahabbism. In the 1980s and 1990s, Saudi petro-dollars provided hundreds of scholarships for Chinese Muslims and build numerous mosques across China, thus entrenching the presence of Wahhabi ideology in China. The Chinese state has kept a wary eye on these activities, aware of Saudi connections with militant organisations.

The history of China's Muslim communities has been turbulent. In the mid-seventeenth century, a number of *menhuan* in the north-west took up arms in support of the failing and embattled Ming Dynasty while others aided the rebels. Conflict between rival *menhuan* in Gansu Province proved bloody and protracted, giving local bureaucracies of the succeeding Qing dynasty a governance problem they neither understood nor could manage. Inability of Qing officials to understand the Muslims they governed in Gansu was almost certainly a contributing factor in the outbreak of the Great Rebellion (1862-1873), which started as marketplace brawls and escalated into a series of bloody massacres. It is worth noting that there was no political rallying point for Chinese Muslims as a single entity. There were also a number of Muslim uprisings in Yunnan Province in the south-west; between 1856 and 1873 General Sulaiman Du Wenxiu presided over an independent sultanate in Yunnan Province, in defiance of the Qing emperor. Eventually, pockets of resistance such as this were crushed. The rebellions, including Du Wenxiu's *Pingnan* (Peace in the South) state, were never connected by a unifying ideology and the Muslim fighters who led them were rarely committed to political change. Their motivation was rather to obtain space for their own peace and prosperity. Uprisings were often retaliation against perceived injustice rather than the desire to subvert the existing order.

Just a few decades after Du Wenxiu was executed by the Qing, the last imperial dynasty crumbled. In its place Sun Yatsen's Republic of China attempted to consolidate a huge and diverse territory around a modern constitution. Held to ransom by General Yuan Shikai's threat of rebellion, he soon handed the presidency to Yuan. Yuan was a military strongman, and warlord politics moved into the space that had long been occupied by the imperial dynasties and which the institutions of the nascent republic were too insubstantial to fill. Hui warlords again fought both with and against other Hui, striving to create a space for themselves within China as Chinese, not motivated by political goals related to their religion or 'Hui-ness'.

Mao Zedong toppled the Nationalist regime of Chiang Kai Shek in 1949, riding a wave of rural discontent that he harnessed with an exciting new ideology of Marxist egalitarianism. While the communist state was officially atheist, the 1954 constitution granted freedom of religion to the Chinese people. However, intolerance and violence became hallmarks of the Mao era, especially during the Cultural Revolution (1966-1976). The protection granted by the constitution was not reflected in Mao's policies until the drive towards 'reform and opening up' under Deng Xiaoping in the 1980s.

Chinese Muslims see themselves, both now and historically, as part of the *ummah*, the global community of Muslims as well as Chinese (with some exceptions). The first recorded Chinese *Hajji* (the term given to Muslims who have taken the pilgrimage to Mecca) is the great Ming Dynasty admiral, Zheng He, who famously commanded a fleet of enormous ships which travelled to Arabia, India, and the Horn of Africa between 1405 and 1433. In Zheng He, as well as other historical figures, we have an indication that Chinese Muslims were not disbarred from achieving high office in the Ming period. That being said, there is also strong evidence that there was nonetheless a pejorative 'otherness' attached to their identity.

This is in sharp contrast to China in the modern era from which well-known public figures who are also Muslim are absent. In my eight years in China, I did not see a single film, television programme, or advertisement which featured a Chinese Muslim character. This absence is mirrored in the public sphere. Stereotypes romanticising minority *minzu* lifestyles, song and dance provide a fig leaf of inclusivity for Han institutions like the *Chunjie Wanhui*, the Chinese Spring Festival Gala – tuned into by possibly every Han household in the country during Chinese New Year celebrations – whilst denying those minorities any opportunity to craft and communicate their own stories. Han dancers will often perform folksy song and dance routines in the traditional garb of whichever *minzu* they are portraying. A small number of *minzu*, usually Mongolians or Tibetans, are more obviously treated to this occasional sentimental nod to superficial stereotypes. These are manufactured song and dance routines which usually invoke the clear-blue skies, or vast steppes, of 'home'. The Muslim *minzu* are almost invisible.

Acculturation and education

For centuries, the pressure for acculturation, that is, abandonment of identities other than Han, has been great. Confucian political philosophy held that even 'barbarians' could be civilised if converted to the Chinese way. The ethnocentric Han State has required non-Han Chinese to acculturate if they wanted to achieve recognition and status. Non-Han could become government officials as long as they passed the civil service examination, which comprised of the classics of Han literature. The Hui have adapted, creating a Chinese Islamic literature known as the *Han Kitab*. This is a syncretic body of work by a handful of Hui scholars who saw the essence of Islam as absolutely compatible with that of Confucian political philosophy. A perennial soothing factor in the Han-Hui relationship has been the ambivalence of Muslims in China towards proselytization. The spread of Islam in China was organic, not active, and conversion rates are very low.

Muslims also displayed great flexibility in accommodating the demands of both the dominant Han culture and their own religion. For example, during the dynastic period, each mosque was required to contain Imperial Tablets for mosque-goers to prostrate themselves in front of in homage to the Emperor. However, in doing so they would avoid contact between their foreheads and the floor, thus maintaining the requirement to worship none but Allah. This ability to adapt religious practice to local conditions did not detract from a firm resilience in guarding the core aspects of their faith as inviolate, and the kernel of their identity. Despite the tenacity of the Hui, who have maintained a separate identity and way of life based on Islamic principles for 1,300 years, acculturation has taken a toll. The numbers of Hui have shrunk by tens of millions.

In these conditions, education has a problematic duality for many of China's minorities. It is both a tool to serve state interests as well as a focal point for aspiration and access to opportunity. In Xinjiang Province's

Uyghur autonomous region, restrictions were placed on how many students an imam could teach at one time – just two in 2002, with the permission of the local bureaucracy. The same restrictions did not apply in other provinces. The phasing out of languages other than Mandarin in Higher Education has meant that rural minorities whose primary schooling is in their native dialect, such as Uyghur, are often excluded from higher education by their lack of Mandarin skills.

The other side of the coin is that non-Muslim Chinese are poorly informed about Islam. On a number of occasions, educated Han people told me that they knew why Muslims like myself don't eat pork. It usually went something like this: 'When the Prophet Muhammad was fleeing his enemies, he once hid amongst a herd of pigs. Now, pigs are regarded as a holy animal.' Such stories fill the void left by Islam's invisibility. In the service industries, awareness of the requirements of Muslim customers is very low and simply avoiding pork can be a challenge. When I explained to waiters that as a Muslim I didn't eat pork, which was why I had ordered fish, there would inevitably be an uncomprehending silence, after which the fish would be taken back to the kitchen, most of the pork mince which had been sprinkled on top of the fish removed, and the dish put back in front of me.

There is an upside, though. While levels of education about Muslims and their way of life is certainly low compared with the UK, there is also a refreshing lack of tension around the topic of Islam. As a Muslim and person of colour in the UK, the micro-aggressions encountered in many everyday contexts can be tiresome. In China, I remained free of the uncomfortable 'otherness' and unspoken negative associations that I encounter at home. This was certainly in part due to my status as an expat, but nonetheless, it is significant that Islam in China is not politicised for the most part.

Han-Uyghur relations are arguably the tensest in the mosaic of minority groups in the PRC today. While the Han state would argue that their policies seek to promote a sense of unity, Uyghurs often feel their religious and cultural identity is under attack. For example, public sector employees are not permitted to wear headscarves or prayer hats or participate in the fast during Ramadan. Communist Party members are also forbidden from attending prayers, creating a strong barrier to political access for Muslims.

On the other hand, the State provides funding for the Chinese Islamic Association as well as the construction and upkeep of mosques: according to official figures, there are currently around 34,000 mosques in China. The Uyghurs are beneficiaries of certain policies that give them advantage in entry to schools and in the realm of business, such as promotion, taxation and financing. There is really no question of whether the State is pro- or anti-Islam. It is simply that the potential rallying points for subversion of State control are closely intertwined with religious practice and markers of identity. That the Uyghur wish to maintain a strong sense of identity and community became evident to me when visited the local Uyghur community in Jiaozuo. I saw no Han amongst them; and struggled to communicate using my Mandarin. Years later, when living in Shanghai, an American friend who speaks fluent Kyrgyz told me he had his iPhone returned to him, with apologies, after speaking Kyrgyz to the Uyghur who had stolen it.

The Uyghurs still retain their language, while the Hui have lost their original languages, mostly Arabic and Persian, due to the pressure of acculturation. Hui musical traditions have also not survived. There is little historical record of the original music and song of the Hui, beyond accounts of Sufi devotional music which entered China through its north-western frontiers. But acculturation has brought benefits for the Hui: during my stay in China, I never once heard a Han refer to Hui in a negative light. In contrast, the Uyghur are often viewed as violent and criminal. While there have been numerous Hui uprisings in China's long history, there was little evidence of any sense of enmity. During the tumult of the late Qing Dynasty and early Republic it is true that Hui warlords sometimes fought Han. However, there are also numerous cases of Hui forming alliances with Han against other Hui. Hui were never a homogenous political entity, rather a patchwork of groups and interests, networked together by their Hui-ness. When turmoil erupted, their choice of ally was based on pragmatism, not ideology or identity.

Han-Hui encounters today are often commerce-based. The 'Lanzhou lamien' (Lanzhou pulled noodle) restaurants are abundant in every city and almost always run by Hui. In the tiny village where I pursued my tai chi studies, preserved beef was sold by a white-capped Hui man who cycled into town on a tricycle loaded with his product. But this is the extent of

Hui visibility. They are not on TV or in books read by Han. They live in separate neighbourhoods and their customs are poorly understood. The Hui are familiar but they are also strangers.

Maintaining the Balance

China's international charm offensive is undoubtedly productive. It has a clear, ambitious agenda: to supersede the US's dominance in the Asia-Pacific region, and to compete with the US and Europe for access to markets and resources in the developing world. It has been successful in initiating and attracting investors to a brand new Asian Infrastructure Investment Bank. Snubbed by the US, its 57 signatories include Australia, Brazil, Italy, Russia and the UK. President Xi has also made waves by prioritising Iran and the Arab nations in his 2016 diplomatic visits. Offering cooperation on energy and infrastructure, China's new OBOR strategy targets countries from China's borders all the way into Europe, seeking to pull them into a new system with China at the centre. The OBOR also seeks to rejuvenate commerce along the old Silk Road. Substantial investment has been promised for infrastructure and telecommunications from central China into the west and onward into Central Asia. Projects include the $46 billion ear-marked to build a warm-water port in Gwadar, Pakistan, on the doorstep of the Middle East as well as developing railway freight links between Ukraine – the breadbasket of Europe – and China.

These strategic seeds are being sown on fertile ground. China's appeal as a major economic partner is increasing; not least because of its consistently non-interventionist, non-judgmental stance on other nations' internal affairs. Its main business with other countries is focussed on developing infrastructure and trade, not wars and military bases.

Yet China struggles to offer a genuine alternative to Western modernity. The PRC has invested hugely to resist the soft power offensive from the West, which effectively equates globalisation with westernisation. While it has managed to fend off the post-Second World War neo-liberal consensus, the emerging generation is deeply entrenched in consumerist culture, brought up on *Friends* and drinking Coca Cola. Partaking in China's modernisation means getting an education, moving to a city, and being upwardly mobile. Of course, urbanisation has brought problems too, with 'left behind children' in the countryside and urban populations of struggling migrants who are often denied the social benefits available to those born in the cities. Modernity also has environmental cost: think of pictures of Beijing shrouded in thick poisonous fumes.

Undoubtedly, the biggest internal challenge comes from how it handles its Muslim minorities. Even the acculturated Hui are feeling alienated. A young urban and educated Hui woman that I spoke to was very much aware that while in China Muslims all reside in designated Hui areas, in other countries this is often not the case. She spoke of a conservative and traditionalist mentality in the older generation of Hui which rejects mainstream modernity with which she struggles to identify with. Young educated Hui may be adrift somewhere in between the anachronisms presented by the state and those espoused by previous generations of Hui, and feel ambivalent towards both. The disgruntled Uyghurs on the other hand, present a more urgent problem. Increasing numbers of them have been reported as joining groups like Jabhat al-Nusra in Syria. The security implications of large numbers of battle-hardened and brutalised Uyghurs returning to China are quite daunting. The 2013 suicide attack in Tiananmen Square, perpetrated by Uyghurs, made the headlines due to its high-profile location. But there have been dozens of incidents of unrest within Xinjiang since then which have gone largely unreported.

The challenge for China is in savvy management of stakeholders both inside and outside. The continuing rise of China, inspired by Xi's 'China Dream', depends very much on how it solves its Muslim puzzle as part of its larger political and economic balancing act.

SEESAWS AND CYCLES

Boyd Tonkin

'A great deal of demagoguery and downright ignorance is involved in presuming to speak for a whole religion or civilisation'.

Edward W Said, *The Clash of Ignorance*

'And now, what's going to happen to us without barbarians?
They were, those people, a kind of solution.'

CP Cavafy, *Waiting for the Barbarians* (translated by Edmund Keeley and

Philip Sherrard)

I

During the spring and summer of 2016, the Turner Contemporary gallery in Margate on England's North Sea coast hosted a new work by Yinka Shonibare MBE. Born in London but raised in Nigeria, the artist now uses the royal honour — which lends a ritual afterlife to a defunct imperial system — as part of his professional title. Pride, or parody? As with many of the attitudes struck by the Young (or at least younger) British Artists, it can be hard to tell. In any case, Shonibare's installation for the Turner gave visitors a firmer steer towards his core ideas. Commissioned as part of the 14-18 NOW programme of public art to mark the centenary of the First World War, 'End of Empire' takes the form of two figures who sit on either end of a seesaw. It swings slowly up and down as sea breezes waft into the gallery. Those rising and falling figures wear the European formal dress of the early 1900s; their clothes, however, are woven from the kaleidoscopic batik fabrics of West Africa in which Shonibare often drapes his work. Instead of a head, each rival bigwig sports a globe.

As one 'statesman' with a head stuffed with world-devouring ambition ascends, so the other sinks. Both, meanwhile, betray through their flamboyant threads the distant origin of their comfort and luxuries. As a mobile visual image for the European power-plays that culminated in the Great War, 'End of Empire' packs a lot of meat into an entrance-hall attraction for a gallery in a faded Kentish resort engaged in its own battle for renewal. The swollen-headed imperial centres vie for supremacy in a zero-sum game of advantage and setback. However, each depends for its grandeur on the exploited hinterland made visible in Shonibare's rainbow batiks.

Such, you might say, was the world that consumed itself in the fires of 1914–1918. In 1913, on the eve of the deluge, eleven Western powers occupied more than half the world's land mass, and ruled 57 per cent of its people. Their domains, according to the historian Niall Ferguson, 'accounted for close to four-fifths of global economic output'. But the Great War ended with the once-stable seesaw of Great Power rivalry shattered beyond repair. Four imperial monoliths fell from it into utter oblivion: the German, Russia, Austro-Hungarian and Ottoman empires. Two more, the victorious British and French, received a life-extending shot of territory and influence in the peace settlement of 1919, only to expire from their wounds within half a century.

A hundred years later, other actors perch on that seesaw. As the 'American Century' fades into memory, and Russia seeks to punch its way back into the fearsome authority of the Soviet decades, a new – or, rather, revived – counterweight takes its place on the other end. The problem is that no one knows quite what to call this ascending force, or even whether it can fit into the seat vacated by the vanished hegemons of the twentieth century. A shelf of books with titles such as *When China Rules the World* (Martin Jacques) or, alternatively, *The China Boom: Why China Will Not Rule the World* (Ho-fung Hung) confidently identify the new boss and speculate on its prospects and performance. Other players in the ancient game of rise-and-fall maintain that the globalised economy will mean that any future seesaw looks more like a switchback or a roundabout. In 2006, Ferguson himself and Moritz Schularick identified the double-headed dragon of 'Chimerica': a hybrid monster that united 'parsimonious China and profligate America' in unstable economic co-dependency.

For some analysts, a generalised 'East' stands to profit from the retreat of an equally nebulous 'West'. To archaeologist-historian Ian Morris, 'The shift in power and wealth from West to East in the twenty-first century is probably as inevitable as the shift from East to West that happened in the nineteenth century.' A monolithic 'Asia' sometimes takes a bow as history's latest protagonist, unified beyond the wildest dreams of a Song emperor or Mongol warlord. Now powered by microchips or carried on container ships, this renewed model of pan-Asian supremacy updates for a hi-tech age the dream of past challengers to Western arrogance such as the Japanese nationalist writer Kakuzo Okakura. In 1903, he proclaimed that 'Asia is one', and that 'Arab chivalry, Persian poetry, Chinese ethics and Indian thought all speak of a single Asiatic peace... nowhere capable of a hard and fast dividing line'.

Other long-term trend-detectors exult in the crackle of economic growth that (despite spells of crisis and paralysis) sparks from the so-called BRIC states of Brazil, Russia, India and China. Some forecasters sprinkle their recipes for a rebalanced globe with a sprig of MINT (Mexico, Indonesia, Nigeria, Turkey). This alphabet soup revives, within a neoliberal economic order, the hopes (or fears) for a revolutionary 'Third World' that accompanied the binary face-offs of the Cold War era.

Pundits, economists, forecasters and historians differ in the names they give the new guys on the seesaw. Few seem to doubt the presiding metaphors of rise and fall, ascent and decline, that govern our explanations of far-reaching and deep-rooted historical change. Today, a re-emergent 'East' may hog the limelight: a belated recompense, its cheerleaders would say, for two or three centuries of plunder and humiliation. History's wheel has spun out its payback. In the words of the cultural historian Pankaj Mishra, in his study of the Asian intellectuals who plotted the comeback of their cultures, 'the dominance of the West already appears just another, surprisingly short-lived phase in the long history of empires and civilisations'. For Mishra, 'The rise of Asia, and the assertiveness of Asian peoples, consummates their revolt against the West... it is in many ways the revenge of the East.'

But whose 'West', and whose 'East'? Wholesale labels applied to peoples and cultures have caused so much mischief and mayhem that the wise observer might prefer to shun them altogether. Beneath the clumsy rubrics of East and West, Europe and Asia, Muslim and Christian, millions of individuals pursue and enjoy hybrid, plural and mingled lives, just as they always have. When Edward Said condemned Samuel Huntington's 'Clash of Civilizations' theorem after the attacks of 11 September 2001, it was this confinement of human complexity in a simplistic straitjacket that outraged him. Huntington, wrote Said in 'The Clash of Ignorance', is an ideologist 'who wants to make 'civilisations' and 'identities' into what they are not: shut-down, sealed-off entities that have been purged of the myriad currents and countercurrents that animate human history'. That history contains not only 'wars of religion and imperial conquest' but also 'exchange, cross-fertilisation and sharing'. For Said, 'unedifying labels like Islam and the West... mislead and confuse the mind, which is trying to make sense of a disorderly reality which won't be pigeonholed'.

The Bengali polymath Rabindranath Tagore, one of the most searching critics not only of Western imperialism but Asian responses that flattered it by mimicry, took care to distinguish between 'the spirit of the West' and 'the nation of the West'. His 'West' contained its own otherness, its internal forces of resistance and dissent. A binary politics that raised a monolithic and spectral 'Eastern' or 'Asian' nationalism against it would merely echo the faults of its enemy. Yet even a mind as fervently anti-chauvinistic as Tagore's was prepared to use such seemingly metaphysical categories in order to further dialogue and enable progress. He argued that 'the West is necessary to the East. We are complementary to each other because of our different outlooks upon life which have given us different aspects of truth.'

We can agree that all such overarching terms deserve to appear within mental, if not actual, scare-quotes. Still, for all their ghostly and even delusional qualities, they have served to quicken the pace of intellectual and political change. When Sayyid Qutb, the literary godfather of jihadi radicalism, railed against Western degeneration in his testament *Milestones*, his targets may have been composed of straw and wind. That did not prevent Qutb from succeeding in his task of inspiration or incitement.

Along with the giant shadow-puppets of continents, creeds or just compass-points that populate the rhetoric of cultural clash and rivalry comes the master-metaphor of growth and decay. Borrowed from the lifespan of human and other natural organisms, the patterns of rise and fall, youth and age, ripeness and rot, vigour and senility, have all tried to make historical sense of societies that lived alongside each other in harmony or (more often) tension. In those circumstances, the life of a culture or a dynasty might plausibly look like the grand amplification of the life of a man.

Around 750 BCE, Homer's Iliad – a Greek epic poem about a semi-mythical battle in Asia Minor – gave voice to this perception in a figure of speech that poets have re-animated ever since. In the early eighteenth century, Alexander Pope's translation – one of dozens – turned the archaic Greek of Homer into neo-classical English: 'Like Leaves on Trees the Race of Man is found, / Now green in Youth, now withering on the Ground. / Another Race the following Spring supplies, / They fall successive, and successive rise. / So generations in their course decay, / So flourish these, when those are past away.' Whether you think of your society as a healthy green shoot or dry, yellowing waste, organic metaphors may stimulate and energise, comfort and console. They may excite the 'risers' of any age, and solace the 'fallers'.

The perennial lure of these comparisons pays no heed to borders of nation, period or faith. In the late fourteenth century, the historian, sociologist and philosopher Ibn Khaldun gave this cluster of ideas its canonical expression in Islamic historiography. Writing in present-day Algeria, but the proud descendant of an Andalusian family which left Spain during the Christian re-conquest of the south, he scoffs at the idea that human action alone can halt the decline of a great house. 'If, then, senility is something natural to the life of a dynasty, it must come about in the same way natural things come about... Senility is a chronic disease which cannot be cured or made to disappear because it is something natural, and natural things do not change.'

With its sociological analysis of the transition from nomadic to civic life ('badawah' and 'hadarah'), and its cyclical model of growth and disintegration, Ibn Khaldun's Muqaddimah created a template that scores of later rise-and-fall narrators would adopt. After specifying the decadent delights that presage social downfall - apparently, they include cultivation of the red and white oleanders still grown across the Mediterranean lands – he insists that 'the goal of civilisation is sedentary culture and luxury'. However, 'When civilisation reaches that goal, it turns towards corruption and starts being senile, as happens in the natural life of living beings.'

Ibn Khaldun sees civilisation as perennially prone to collapse under the burden of its own achievements. Later wide-screen historians, from

Giambattista Vico and Edward Gibbon to Khaldun's disciple Arnold J
Toynbee, play endless variations on this theme. Toynbee, whose ten-volume
A Study of History updated the *Muqaddimah* for the bewildered readers of
the mid-20th century, called his forerunner's treatise 'the greatest work of
its kind that has ever been created by any mind in any time or place'. Later
panoramic narratives of the cycle of civilisation often read like footnotes
to Ibn Khaldun. 'Prosperity ripened the principle of decay,' wrote Gibbon
about the fall of Rome, until 'the stupendous fabric yielded to the pressure
of its own weight'. For Vico, surveying human history from his Neapolitan
backwater in the 1720s, 'Men first feel necessity, then look for utility, next
attend to comfort, thence grow dissolute in luxury, and finally go mad and
waste their substance.'

II

By the 1370s, Ibn Khaldun's arc of growth and decay was already a time-
honoured trope in historiography. His cross-cultural comparisons, his
curves of grandeur and decline, had emerged with the dawn of history-
writing itself. Our urge to contrast societies and civilisations, and to devise
rules for their life and death, may embarrass thinkers who refuse to treat
the past as a glorified soap-opera or game-show. Yet that drive lies as deep
as the need to make sense of human history.

In 2010, Ian Morris's book *Why the West Rules — for Now* staged another,
vaultingly ambitious, bid to 'look at the whole sweep of human history as
a single story', from the close of the last Ice Age to the third millennium.
Morris presents an overarching epic drama in which the Eastern and
Western 'cores' — roughly, China and its adjoining territories on one side,
Europe and the Near East on the other — match each other in social
development almost step-by-step for much of the last 10,000 years. After
the fall of Rome, the Chinese world strides confidently in front, between
550 and the 1770s (Morris knows how daft some of his exact dates sound).

Then the West and its North American offspring (literally) steam ahead,
thanks to the double lucky-strike of a revolution in fossil-fuel use and safe,
easy Atlantic commerce. Morris dismisses both discredited racial and still-
active cultural theories of Western supremacy over the past 300 years or
so. He rejects both 'long-term lock-in' and 'short-term accident'

explanations of the West's advantages. And he usefully widens his lens so that (say) classical Islamic cultures fall within, rather than outside, the fold that covers the Western end of the Eurasian landmass. The Arab conquerors 'came not to bury the West but to perfect it', and by 700, 'the Islamic world more or less was the Western core'. Still, Morris does maintain that the modern West lucked out in its resources and its location: 'The West rules because of geography'.

Would Morris's new determinism of coal, wind and water satisfy sceptics for whom every effort to portray history as a slugfest between heavyweights, in Huntington's 'clash of civilisations' mode, must be a disreputable exercise? At the time of publication, it prompted me to ask some historians about the validity of such a broad-brush narrative. Some historians answered that tales of West-against-the-Rest have outlived whatever usefulness they had. However, Paul Cartledge – the eminent classicist who is now emeritus professor of Greek culture at Cambridge University – gave a robust defence of such super-sized comparative story-telling. For Cartledge, the dialogue or dispute between systems helped to kick-start history itself. As he argued, 'The founding father of (critical, explanatory, objective) history... Herodotus, was also the founder of the West-East cultural dialectic.'

Writing in the Greek world of the mid-fifth century BCE, Herodotus (who came from what is now Bodrum in Turkey) not only studied and compared the various cultures that he knew across the Mediterranean and Middle East. He asked why the vast and sophisticated forces of imperial Persia had failed to prevail against the tiny city-states of Greece in the wars that ended with the victory of a Greek coalition against the armies of Xerxes I at the Battle of Plataea in 479 BCE. If he concluded that civic democracy and the rule of law did give Greeks the edge over Oriental despotism – a heroic fable endlessly recycled in the modern West – then Herodotus also offered a fair and just account of Persian values and virtues. He also warned that no social system, however righteous, would withstand the ravages of time: 'Human life is like a revolving wheel and never allows the same people to continue long in prosperity.'

Those immemorial spins of the wheel have also given succour to the victims when ruling cultures take a triumphalist or imperialist turn. In 1908, just prior to the Great War, the great Indian Muslim poet

Muhammad Iqbal castigated the 'dwellers in the cities of the West'. 'Your civilisation will commit suicide,' he warned, 'with its own sword.' Iqbal's prophecy proved double-edged, in that the looming conflict wrecked or enfeebled Europe's empires only for another bastion of universalising modernity – the United States – to impose its will on much of the world.

Besides, even ardent imperialists could relish the rhetoric of predestined decline. In 1897, as the British Empire that repulsed Iqbal reached its zenith, Rudyard Kipling (in 'Recessional') foresaw that its 'dominion over palm and pine' would come to an end as surely as the might of 'Nineveh and Tyre'. Elite servants of that empire were schooled in the Greek and Latin literature that, from Theocritus to Virgil, laments the passing of a Golden Age. Awareness of decay has never done much to dampen the zeal of the conqueror. In the second century CE, a Roman aristocrat with a Stoical cast of mind reminded himself that 'in a little while you will be no one and nowhere, even as Hadrian and Augustus are no more'. 'Life is brief', counselled this enemy of pomp and pride, and 'there is one harvest of earthly existence, a holy disposition and neighbourly acts'. Yet such modest concern for the body's mortality and the limits of power did not stop Marcus Aurelius from doing his efficient, and sometimes, ruthless duty as one of the most successful of all emperors of Rome (from 161–180 CE).

The humility of emperors – and their administrators – hardly curbed imperial hubris. Europe lived contentedly with the language of decadence and disintegration even as its rivalrous Great Powers extended their footprint over the globe. In 1817, PB Shelley wrote his poem 'Ozymandias' after a discussion with friends about Napoleon's expedition to Egypt, with its harvest of new (European) knowledge about ancient dynasties and their epoch-making cycles of ascent and decline. The broken statue of Ozymandias, 'King of Kings' – Shelley's literary alias for the Pharaoh Ramses II – gazes across the desert where once the monuments of his empire stood. 'Look on my Works, ye Mighty, and despair!' True, Shelley wrote in the immediate aftermath of one imperial collapse: Napoleon's. But his poems would soon travel to the ends of the colonised earth in the trunks of the British officials who served the power that profited most from Bonaparte's defeat. The fate of Ozymandias lay in store for them as well – but not quite yet. In the meantime, a doom-laden vision of imperial sunset might quicken the pleasures of blazing high noon. A conviction that barbarians stood always just outside the gate might add relish to the ease and mastery enjoyed by the rulers. In 'Waiting for the Barbarians', by the Alexandrian Greek poet CP Cavafy, an ancient citadel of culture panics when it learns that 'there are no barbarians any longer'. After all, 'They were, those people, a kind of solution.'

III

Between 1776 and 1789, Edward Gibbon published six volumes of the work that defined for the English-speaking world the model of the past as a sweeping parabola of ascent and descent. Or rather, his *History of the Decline and Fall of the Roman Empire* takes Rome's bright morning for granted. It fixes its gaze only on the post-noon slump into inertia, dissolution and collapse. Although he began it in the 1760s, Gibbon published the *Decline and Fall* as his nation, Great Britain, first began to lose a large chunk of one empire as its American colonies revolted, then faced the ordeal of a protracted, ruinous conflict with revolutionary France. Yet the rolling thunder of Gibbon's prose bears witness to serenity rather than alarm. Whether peopled by domestic rebels or barbarian invaders, his vistas of decline unroll under the sunny sky of progressive Enlightenment. Faith, and fanaticism, under whatever banner would and must yield to the remorseless advance of reason. Hence his famous teasing fantasy about the extension into northern Europe of the Arab conquests of the 700s.

If Charles Martel had not stemmed the tide of Islam at the Battle of Poitiers in 732, 'Perhaps the interpretation of the Koran would now be taught in the Schools of Oxford, and her pulpits might demonstrate to a circumcised people the sanctity and truth of the revelation of Mahomet.' Yes, the anti-ecclesiastical historian loved to spook the clergy. But he could look with equanimity on the rise and fall of dynasties and denominations because of his belief in an empire of reason. For Gibbon, at the terminus of his long Roman road, 'We may therefore acquiesce in the pleasing conclusion that every age of the world has increased and still increases the real wealth, the happiness, the knowledge, and perhaps the virtue, of the human race.'

Empires may decline, and civilisations perish, but the arrow of human history points ever upwards. This durable 'Whig interpretation' of the past could live happily with the autumnal language of decline-and-fall so long as the motor of progress hummed away at some point on the globe. For Gibbon and his heirs, that blessed hub could only be 'the system of arts and laws and manners which so advantageously distinguish... the Europeans and their colonies'. The prospect of eventual decay, and the cyclical succession of empires, might furnish Europe and the 'West' with a salutary memento mori. It did not much diminish the appetite for growth and rule.

So the zenith of Western global power coincided with a hearty indulgence in tales of decline-and-fall. 'Lest we forget,' as Kipling intones in 'Recessional': 'Lest we forget'. The prophets of doom said their piece; the Dreadnoughts of empire sailed on. For that reason alone, partisans of a coming Asian century should take care about the rhetoric they deploy. Yet more broadsides about Western putrefaction may just bounce off the ironclad hull of a culture long steeped in elegy, irony and nostalgia.

A backlash against perceptions of decadence may also adopt some ugly forms. In 1918, just as the German empire fell part, Oswald Spengler published the first part of his multi-volume *Decline of the West*. With parallel narratives of eight civilisations, from Babylonian and Egyptian through Indian and Chinese to Arabian and Western, Spengler's cultural anthropology treated each system on its own terms. He made few assumptions about innate 'Western' superiority. But the drift of his scheme, as the money-governed democracy of the modern urban world led to stagnation and corruption, pointed towards regeneration in the shape of a revived 'Caesarism'.

In Italy, Germany and the Soviet Union, as well as smaller states, autocratic men of destiny stood ready to intervene and give Spengler's cycle of history a violent push. Historians can hardly be blamed for the ideas and acts of every reader and acolyte. Still, the Spenglerian dynamic of weak-minded decay and hard-bodied renewal underpinned the claims of mid-century dictators to a starring role in national revival. Today, history repeats itself as farce when (in July 2016) Republican candidate Donald Trump promises to 'make America great again'. A mendacious 'Leave' campaign dupes a narrow majority of UK voters into quitting the European Union with meaningless exhortations to 'Take back control'. In Turkey, a shambolic coup attempt leaves President Erdogan free to expand his neo-Ottoman grand designs. If, in the past, imperial elites could live contentedly with narratives of decline, those stories now seem to push mass-media democracies towards desperate measures.

Further east, accounts of the rise or (more often) the recovery of Asia have partnered movements of national self-assertion at least since the Japanese navy vanquished its Imperial Russian foe at the Battle of Tsushima in 1905. That victory resonated around the world, from Turkey and India to China and Philippines. Returning to Harrow School, the future first prime minister of independent India, Jawaharlal Nehru, found that the news from the Pacific put him in 'high good humour'. Yet Japan's new military-industrial muscle also set off a fierce debate about the benefits and drawbacks of emulating the West. It continues to this day. In 1902, reports Pankaj Mishra, Rabindranath Tagore had warned an awakening continent against mimicry of the powers that had plundered it. 'Asia today', he wrote, 'has understood, know thyself — that is the road to freedom. In imitating others is destruction.'

Later, in an essay on 'Nationalism in Japan', Tagore noted that 'There is always the natural temptation in us of wishing to pay back Europe in her own coin, and return contempt for contempt and evil for evil.' Prior to that country's forced march into modernisation, he reflects, Japan 'had all her wealth of humanity, her harmony of heroism and beauty'. And yet 'the Western nations felt no respect for her until till she proved that the bloodhounds of Satan are not only bred in the kennels of Europe but can also be domesticated in Japan and fed with man's miseries'. Asked in 1935 to endorse Japan's own war of conquest in Manchuria, Tagore replied that its militaristic blueprint for Asian regeneration would be 'raised on a tower of skulls'. In a different key to Tagore's, Gandhi also insisted - at every level from his dhoti to his doctrines — that the recovery of Asia could not simply replicate the industrial and colonial excesses of the West. His 1909 manifesto *Hind Swaraj* rejects any model of an emancipated India that merely amounts to 'English rule without the Englishman'.

Partisans of a twenty-first-century Triumph of Asia, or 'the East', should notice the company they keep. The antique geometry of rising and falling power, of the succession of empires and the cycles of culture, may still appeal to thinkers who now locate their own cultures on the downside of history. In his book and television series Civilization, Niall Ferguson delighted Western supremacists and provoked their critics by enumerating the 'killer apps' – from inter-state competition and property rights to scientific innovation – that had allegedly lent the West its dynamism and command. However, even Ferguson calmly accepts that 'What we are living through now is the end of 500 years of Western predominance. This time the Eastern challenger is for real, both economically and geopolitically.' Non-European cultures have enthusiastically 'downloaded' all those apps – as Tagore feared – and so can outpace their former overlords. In other words, Ferguson and those who share his outlook read the 'rise' of an Asian or other non-Western bloc as the ultimate tribute to Western modernity. 'The West' may rule from Beijing, or from Bangalore.

IV

In this perspective, the West loses but still wins. Might it, though, be possible to step off that rise-and-fall seesaw entirely and view cultural interaction from a different angle? In his book *Guns, Germs and Steel*, the anthropologist and biologist Jared Diamond vastly widened the frame of reference. Forget those parochial quarrels of East and West. From the point of view of hunter-gatherer communities in Borneo or pre-Columbian America, the entire Eurasian landmass and its islands – from Japan to Portugal – may resemble a single bloc of smart, selfish and aggressive cultivators and city-builders. 'Biogeography' and the ecological good fortune that stems from it account for this common West-Eastern success. To Diamond, 'the availability of domestic plants and animals ultimately explains why empires, literacy and steel weapons developed earliest in Eurasia and later, or not at all, on other continents'.

Agricultural peoples, taking their cue from farming pioneers in the 'Fertile Crescent' of west Asia and the Nile, 'tend to breath out nastier germs, to own better weapons and armour' and 'to live under centralised governments with literate elites better able to wage wars of conquest'. In this longest of views, passing spats between China and America, Islam and Christendom, Europe and Asia, look like Freud's 'narcissism of small differences' played out as a geopolitical game. Meanwhile, 'Prospects for world domination of Sub-Saharan Africans, Aboriginal Australians or Native Americans remain dim. The hand of history's course at 8000BC lies heavily on us.'

Driven by his scientific dismay at racial and ethnic explanations of cultural rise (and fall), Diamond's scheme instead brands us all as prisoners of the deep biological past. At least, though, we share the same cell. Another recent challenge to the seesaw, or cycle, model of global power arises from the common risk of environmental doom. In the epoch of globalisation, joint emergencies demand deeper solidarity. This is hardly a novel notion: in the wake of the First World War, as the fledgling League of Nations took its faltering baby steps towards international decision-making, champions of 'world government' such as HG Wells saw humankind poised between co-operation and catastrophe. Almost a century on, Ian Morris raises the spectre of a planetary 'Nightfall' provoked by mad-made climate change and/or nuclear conflict: 'After Nightfall, no one will rule.' To sidestep this apocalypse, pooled resources and joint deliberations on a global scale could and must make regional showdowns redundant: 'East and West will be revealed as merely a phase we went through.'

Raised in Stoke-on-Trent in the UK, Morris teaches in California: that mythical heartland of the post-European West. Readers elsewhere might heed his pleas for a suspension of the East-West dialectic, but still question its motives. In the universal language of football (or soccer), they might even conclude that, just as the prospect of an Eastern match-winner nears, the ref has moved the goalposts.

Morris does allow that a definitive East Asian takeover of the West - perhaps in the 2030s — will precede the sort of emergency coalition required to stave off nuclear or climatic catastrophe. So the old Great Power seesaw may have a few dips and surges left in it. Still, this long-term vision of enforced togetherness looks beyond both zero-sum rivalries and the more chaotic, 'multi-polar' model of swings and roundabouts. Instead, a single crowded car hurtles on a roller-coaster ride towards oblivion. Only the concerted effort of all passengers can avert the crash. Those centuries of high talk about clashes and cycles, blooms and busts, dawns and twilights, resolve into the less romantic but more urgent task of collective salvation.

Even a writer as sympathetic to the idea of Eastern, or Asian, vindication and retribution as Pankaj Mishra acknowledges that the entire re-balanced world cannot hope to consume on the level of a Californian professor. That would be 'as absurd and dangerous a fantasy as anything dreamt up by Al-Qaeda. It condemns the global environment to early destruction, and looks set to create reservoirs of nihilistic rage and disappointment among hundreds of millions of have-nots'.

Through this global lens, the 'barbarism' that so troubled the dominant cultures of the past no longer lurks in the central European forests, on the Asian steppes, or in the jungles of Africa. It breeds within the out-of-control productive, and destructive, capacities of an interdependent global economy. However widely you draw its frontiers, civilisation threatens to consume itself. This is what Toynbee, following the lead of Ibn Khaldun, identified as the paradox of development. Now, however, the unit to which the paradox applies is not a people but a planet. Unlike the useful phantasms of Cavafy's poem, those barbarians do exist. Look in the mirror to see one.

'POST-EVERYTHING'

Carool Kersten

For the past decade or so, Hamid Dabashi, the increasingly prolific Iranian-born but New York-based sociologist of religion and cultural critic, has been working on an ideology of resistance that defies the new globalised world order and challenges the allegedly inevitable Clash of Civilisations thesis. Samuel Huntington's proposition is supposed to have replaced the East-West binary of the Cold War Era, as well as the colonial and postcolonial North-South divide, with an irremediable dichotomy between Islam and the West. Rejecting such projections as outcomes of the totalising aspirations of both Enlightenment modernity and parallel tendencies found in Islamist ideologies, Dabashi has developed a counter narrative. The books published between 2006 and 2013 offer a contrarian – and often counterintuitive – account of an emerging world order that is no longer just postcolonial and postmodern, but also post-Orientalist, post-western and post-Islamist. Dabashi's interpretation declares the metaphysics of identity underlying the binary of Islam vs the West outdated. With that, it also renders obsolete the epistemologies that have so far shaped the Eurocentric understanding of historical events and that have informed ideologies like Bolshevism, but in equal measure the two-hundred years of Islamic responses to colonisation and subjugation in the name of Enlightenment modernity. All these regimes of knowledge have not just totalising ambitions, but also harbour totalitarian tendencies.

By way of alternative, Dabashi formulates an oppositional discourse imaginatively attuned to the new geography of what has become in effect a decentred world. Facing a truly global form of 'Empire' without any identifiable epicentre or gravitational point. Dabashi adopts Negri and Hardt's term, but criticises their exposition as 'pathologically Eurocentric'. In a similar vein, he dismisses Julia Kristeva and Susan Sontag's writings on 'the phenomenon code-named globalisation' as provincially European, because in this new world order the colonial is as much in the metropolis as the metropolis in the colonial. Instead, Dabashi sides with Arundhati Roy, Judith Butler, and W.E.B. Du Bois. Their writings open up the prospect of an emancipatory remapping in which the binaries of centre-periphery and coloniser-colonised collapse along with the meta-narratives of nationalism, liberalism and Islamism.

In relation to the Muslim world, Dabashi's mission is to replace the metaphysics of identity with a hermeneutics of alterity, which he presents as a cross-cultural and non-essentialist 'guerrilla' ideology opposed to the nomocentric orientation of Islamism, as well as the logocentric and homocentric aspects of Islam's philosophical and mystical traditions. Aside from a new geography of liberation, this decentred world also needs a new language. Dabashi suggests that, historically, this has been best articulated in the cultural traditions of Muslim literary humanism – or what is called *adab* in Arabic. In his two latest books, *The World of Persian Literary Humanism* and *Persophilia,* Dabashi showcases Persia's heritage of poetry as exhibiting the worldly cosmopolitanism, which he considers the most suitable disposition for that decentred 'post-everything' world.

The theoretical framing of Dabashi's hermeneutics is laid out in three books: *Islamic Liberation Theology* (2008); *Post-Orientalism* (2009); and *Being a Muslim in the World* (2013). The first one, which is aptly subtitled *Resisting Empire*, provides the central blueprint for what is both a critique and emancipatory mission, but it interlocks with *Post-Orientalism*, where Dabashi maps the newly envisaged geography, whereas *Being a Muslim in the World* proposes the new ethos informed by the disposition he calls alternately worldly cosmopolitanism or cosmopolitan worldliness. The heuristics of this project draw not only on Hans-Georg Gadamer's magisterial work on philosophical hermeneutics, *Truth and Method*, and the political thought of Hannah Arendt, but also includes references to postcolonial theory and certain strands of poststructuralism. Orbiting these theory-laden and agenda-setting books are other publications, such as: *Iran: A People Interrupted* (2007); *Iran, the Green Movement and the USA* (2010); *Brown Skin White Masks* (2011); and *The Arab Spring* (2012). These consist in more topical analyses of developments in the twentieth-century Middle East and polemical critiques of what Dabashi regards as compromised intellectuals from the Muslim world. Instead of speaking truth to power, they are no longer informants but have turned into native informers to Western neo-imperialism and its proxies in the Muslim world.

In his latest books on literary humanism, Dabashi's thinking enters most explicitly into a conversation with the aesthetics of Gadamer's *Truth and Method* and the case it seeks to make that our very being as humans inhabits language. At the risk of being accused of romanticising what has become known as the Arab Spring of 2011, Dabashi also looks at these uprisings through a literary lens. He suggests reading these events not as monologues, but as open-ended and dialogical in the Bakhtinian sense, heralding an undetermined postcolonial and post-western world, which parallel the heteroglossia of the novel rather than the teleological crescendo of an epic. This attention for the literary in thinking about philosophy and religion is not unique to Dabashi, we also find it in the theological exposés written by ground-breaking philosophers, such as Richard Kearney and Mark C. Taylor.

Being a Muslim in the World contains a chapter with the telling title, 'Breaking the Binary'. With a nod to the Italian poststructuralist philosopher Gianni Vattimo, it sets up the hermeneutics of alterity as Dabashi's version of a weak strategy for subverting the ontological remnant of the modern colonial world: The metaphysics of identity characterised by essentialising categories of a religious Muslim world allegedly in opposition to a secular West. Although, Dabashi's own explicit reference to Vattimo only concerns the notion of *pensiero debole* or 'weak thought', there are other echoes that are not specifically acknowledged and may have gone unnoticed by other readers of Dabashi's work. Of particular relevance are Vattimo's understanding of Nietzsche's announcement of the 'Death of God' and his reading of the Pauline notion of *kenosis* which is as idiosyncratic as Dabashi's reinterpretation of the theodicy. Also his above-mentioned observation that the colonial is now as much in the metropolis as the metropolis in the colonial resonates with Vattimo's view of the world today.

In an essay entitled 'Hermeneutics and Anthropology', the Italian poststructuralist takes issue with the provocation of his American colleague Richard Rorty that, instead of philosophy, 'cultural anthropology is all we need'. The reason for challenging this — at face value — sympathetic proposition for an open and flexible conversation between cultures is that it assumes a kind of difference which no longer exists. The suggestion is based on an understanding of cultural anthropology that is completely Eurocentric, because it posits 'the other' as being elsewhere, which is no longer the case in our globalised world. In relation to the Muslim world, an opposition between the West and the world of Islam may have made sense for about two hundred years or so, as Muslims took recourse to Islamic ideology as one way of resisting the onslaught of European imperialism; both in the form of capitalist economics and cultural colonisation. But in today's decentred world there is no longer a place for a West-versus-the-Rest dichotomy. The 'hybrid traces and residues contaminated by modernity', which Vattimo regards as characteristic of today's 'third world societies and the ghettos of industrial societies', are none other than the intermingling of the metropolis and colonial suggested by Dabashi, thus breaking down any clear-cut boundaries between centre and periphery, between 'us' and 'them'. The spread of science and technology associated with modernity during the colonial and postcolonial age was accompanied by the relentless Europeanisation of what is called the global south. This has turned the world into what Vattimo regards as a 'vast construction site' characterised by 'generalised cultural contamination'. It dilutes the radical alterity of all those 'others' who inhabit the fieldwork sites that used to be the theatres of operation for the modern scholarly discipline known as ethnography.

Rorty developed his position as part of a critique of Jürgen Habermas's continuing confidence in a rationalist epistemology: A criticism with which Vattimo agreed and which is also shared by Hamid Dabashi. Borrowing the title of Paul de Man's essay collection *Blindness and Insight* for a chapter that appeared under the same name in *Islamic Liberation Theology*, also Dabashi dismisses Habermas's dogged pursuit of the – in the latter's own eyes – unfinished modernity process as a rear guard battle; as futile as the quest by Islamist ideologues for an authentic Islam. Aside from Habermas's over-confidence in the merits of Euro-centred and neo-Kantian rational thinking, Dabashi also takes the Frankfurt School philosopher to task for ignoring the blatant racism that underlies Kant's views of other cultures and the consequent privileging of Western thought.

Dabashi is very critical of what he refers to as the 'autonormativity' of Western thinking, which is the result of its self-proclamation as the benchmark for all critical thinking and intellectual rigour. But at the same time he mines that legacy for the intellectual deposits needed to forge the counter discourse he seeks to articulate. However, aside from relying on advances made in the human sciences in Western academia, Dabashi's new agenda is also very much the outcome of introspection and self-reflection. Based on critical examinations of the Iranian revolution and its religious underpinnings in historical Shi'a Islam, Dabashi's analysis concludes that the success of the Iranian revolution also heralds the failure of political Islam. This is the tragic consequence of what he calls the paradox of Shi'ism as a 'Religion of Protest': Morally strong when politically weak, and the other way around. During two centuries of resisting European colonisation and the concomitant spread of Enlightenment modernity, the mutation of Islam into a counter ideology made sense, only to collapse under its own success after the Iranian revolution. Just as he continues to engage with European thinkers, Dabashi does also not disavow Islam. On the contrary even; it is time to reconstitute the worldly cosmopolitanism of the various Muslim cultures and turn it into the underpinning of a new revolutionary ideology.

In *Islamic Liberation Theology*, Dabashi describes his intellectual mission as developing an 'understanding of globalising power and the emerging revolutionary manners to resist it'. He announces a new solidarity that launches forward from earlier discourses of emancipation. These include the Islamic ideology of Malcolm X, Gustavo Guttierez's Catholic Liberation Theology, and Frantz Fanon's *Tiers-Mondisme*. In contrast to the kind of new transnational politics envisaged by Saskia Sassen, Dabashi foresees more localised instances of insurrectionary resistance. His presentation of this new global confrontation echoes with the Marxist undertones of such poststructuralists as Louis Althusser and Michel Pêcheux, as he pitches the disenfranchised masses in both the global south and the former metropolises against predatory capitalism that is benefiting a select aggregate of interests represented by corporate multinationals, their political allies in the US, Europe and their proxy regimes in Asia, Africa and Latin America. The acute necessity of this transformation is imposed by escalating levels of violence that have accompanied the emergence of Empire and the concomitant extremism of al-Qaeda. Both 9/11 and Donald Rumsfeld's subsequent campaign of 'shock and awe' in Iraq stand as the twin markers of the replacement of the kind of legitimate violence theorised by George Sorel, Karl Marx, Max Weber and Franz Fanon, as well as by the idea of eternal enmity celebrated in the work of Carl Schmitt and Ernst Jünger. To offset Schmitt's appropriation and misinterpretation of Walter Benjamin's notion of 'pure violence', Dabashi turns to Giorgio Agamben's rereading of the essay 'Kritik der Gewalt'. His interpretation cautions against giving the oft-cited 'state of exception' a status of normalcy, because this results in a reduction of human life to the level of *zoë* – the bare life of *homo sacer,* elaborated in Agamben's life-long philosophical project of the same name. Dabashi also notes with approval Agamben's dismay with the breakdown of communications between Foucault's biopolitics, the holocaust, and Hannah Arendt's *Human Condition*, as well as the latter's failure to see the relation between what Dabashi calls her own version of biopolitics and her writings on totalitarianism and revolution. Dabashi advocates the opposition of these pathological mutations of violence with a new consciousness growing out of a parallel transformation of the liberation theologies from the colonial and postcolonial age into what he calls a liberation theodicy. In parallel with the diametrically opposed ways in which Walter Benjamin and Carl Schmitt understood the notion of 'pure violence', Dabashi's interpretation of the theodicy does not account for evil in the world, but for diversity and alterity. It is conceived as an other-based, not self-based, hermeneutics that goes back to Levinas rather than Heidegger or Husser.

It is at this point that the relevance of Vattimo's *pensiero debole* – 'weak thought' and his understanding of *kenosis* to Dabashi's hermeneutics of alterity and his application of the idea of the theodicy become apparent. The idea of 'weak thought' can be traced back to the Gadamerian hermeneutics of *Truth and Method*. Vattimo adopted it as a – to his mind – better alternative to the method of deconstruction, because that strand of French poststructuralism still harbours too much nostalgia for metaphysics. Read together with the other writings of Vattimo, *pensiero debole* offers an entry point for a critical interrogation of what Dabashi means by worldly cosmopolitanism. For example, in *The Transparent Society*, Vattimo's discussion of the transformation of the modern idea of linear-progressive 'utopia' into postmodern 'heterotopia' contains a cautionary note that is not only applicable to the Islamists' return to the *al-salaf al-salih* or 'pious ancestors', it also offers a caveat regarding Dabashi's advocacy of a return to literary humanism; namely the danger that this will only lead to a celebration of literalist religious revivalism or literary nostalgia respectively. Another challenge posed by the use of Vattimo lies in the close connection of 'weak thought' with the nexus Vattimo has established between Nietzsche's nihilism, Heidegger's end of metaphysics, and the incarnation of the divine in the figure of Christ which is so central to Vattimo's writings on religion.

To Vattimo, one of the effects of Nietzschean nihilism and the Heideggerian end of metaphysics also includes the end of Eurocentrism and the pluralisation of the agencies of information. This re-orientation fits with Dabashi's insistence that we live in a decentred world. According to Vattimo, Nietzsche's announcement of the 'Death of God' was not a denial of the existence of God in a religious-historical or theological sense, but a metaphor for the impossibility of establishing an unshakable ground on which certain knowledge or truths can be founded. Vattimo gives nihilism a positive twist. Unlike Heidegger, he does not see it as a series of negations or a negative state, nor as cynical or whimsical. Rather, Vattimo's view of nihilism is an optimistic one, opening up opportunities and offering endless possibilities for alternative ways of being, not restrained by the ontological straightjackets of metaphysics of whatever kind. This has also shaped Vattimo's thinking about religion in general and Christianity in particular. Replacing a static understanding of '*Being*' – resting on foundationalist knowledge and essentialised understanding of human nature – with the alternative understanding as a dynamic becoming of a multitude of '*beings*', allows Vattimo to continue to present the dissolution of foundations and restraints of demonstrative reason as a form of emancipation. The consequence of anti-foundationalist nihilism is therefore not just epistemological, it also has ethical and political implications.

But even in the postmodern 'Death of God' condition, the philosophy of knowledge can't escape modernity completely: Our entire terminological and conceptual apparatus remains locked up in its language. Consequently, instead of the vocabulary and grammar of metaphysics, postmodernity requires a new idiom. The propositional, demonstrative and logical language of traditional philosophy must be replaced by the edifying language of rhetoric, using metaphors (like the 'Death of God') and symbols. Even logic becomes rhetorical, a form of persuasion – similar to the paradigms of Thomas Kuhn's philosophy of science. This means the substitution of hermeneutics for metaphysics as what Vattimo calls the 'koiné or common idiom of Western culture' in the postmodern age. This is where Heidegger and Gadamer come in. After all, it was in particular the latter who has discussed in great detail how our very being is 'in' language. However, Vattimo does not share the aesthetic nostalgia of either Heidegger or Gadamer, nor the metaphysical longings of the French poststructuralists. Instead he foregrounds hermeneutics as open possibility, emancipation and justice; in short, social democratic or leftist political values, which he tries to capture in the expression 'weak thought'. The term is not to be taken too literally; it does not refer to weakness in the sense of inadequate. Instead it is best considered as an instance of intellectual modesty that parallels the epistemological humility of anti-foundationalism in general.

In Vattimo's rethinking of religion, the term 'weak thought' finds its manifestation in the Pauline notion of *kenosis* or 'self-emptying' -- explained in Philippians 2: 6-8 as the incarnation of 'the pre-existent divine Christ into a human being'. In Vattimo's interpretation this emptying out of God into the world, or the transformation of transcendence into immanence, is the ultimate event in Western culture that also establishes secularisation as being inextricably tied up with the teachings of Jesus (as also Gil Anidjar has argued in his seminal article on secularism). Echoing Benedetto Croce and Martin Heidegger's assertion that -- due to this historical conditioning – as Europeans 'we cannot not call ourselves Christians', Vattimo claims that it is this interpretation that has enabled him to assert the in itself seemingly contradictory statement that 'it is only thanks to God that I am an Atheist', while simultaneously embracing his Catholic faith. At face value, such Christian-centred engagement with religion should create serious problems for the relation with other faith traditions or systems of belief. However, it is Vattimo's own further elaboration that offers a way out of this conundrum. He insists that *kenosis* is not limited to the incarnation of God in the figure of Christ. Not only does it also include the revelation of Scripture, but this emptying out – or weakening – of the divine into the world has not ended: Revelation continues, Vattimo says, 'by way of an increasingly "truer" interpretation of Scripture'. This opens a window of opportunity for Muslims to join this conversation as well, since Muhammad's mission can be regarded as a continuation of this Judeo-Christian narrative for a new audience.

Vattimo's writings on religion resonate strongly with Hamid Dabashi's essay '"Religion – Quote, Unquote"' and their shared interest in Gadamer opens up a possible route to a further fusion between the horizons of Dabashi and Vattimo's thinking. Informed by that other core notion of Gadamer's philosophy of the human as a *sprachliches wesen* (linguistic being), both the Italian and Iranian intellectual agree that thinking in this 'post-everything' world needs a new philosophical language. That is what is going on in the idiosyncratic interpretation of the Pauline notion of *kenosis* developed by Vattimo and in Dabashi's refashioning of theodicy. The emptying out into the world of the divine, whereby the transcendent acquires immanence, is interpreted by Vattimo as 'the sign that the non-violent and non-absolute God of the post-metaphysical epoch has as its distinctive trait the very vocation for weakening of which Heideggerian philosophy speaks'. Similarly, Hamid Dabashi doesn't use theodicy to account for evil in the world but to describe 'diversity, alterity, shades and shadows of truth'. Also Muslims have to come to terms with the decentred world in which they live. The Islamic religion of protest or liberation theology that may have worked previously when combatting colonialism, must now be transformed into a liberation theodicy in order to save Islam from itself: 'From the dogged dogmatism of its nomocentric juridicalism having brutally supressed its own logocentric and homocentric domains in Islamic philosophy or mysticism'. Its wording may be a bit awkward, but by speaking of the 'un-naming of religion and re-worlding of the world', Dabashi seeks to avoid using the term secularism, which is – as we have seen – weighed down by and overburdened with Christian connotations. The resulting cosmopolitan worldliness or worldly cosmopolitanism exhibits the same kind of openness and endless possibility as Vattimo's interpretations of nihilism and hermeneutics. Throughout *Being a Muslim in the World*, and in contradistinction to demonstrative reason, Dabashi describes this hermeneutics as a rhetorical device; not oppositional but appositional because there is no east or west; centrifugal and contrapuntal in its challenges of the centripetal tendencies of legal nomocentrism and philosophical logocentrism; and – finally – anthropocentric so as to exhibit humankind's cultural heteroglossia. This Muslim hermeneutics of alterity pushes nomocentric Islamic law and even logocentric metaphysical philosophy from its pedestal in order to restore the imagination and the anthropocentrism of Sufism.

Taken together, Hamid Dabashi's oeuvre provides an interlocking – and therefore sometimes also repetitive and here and there even superfluous – narrative, driven by the deconstruction – or de-narration, as he calls it – of both Islamist ideology and Enlightenment modernity. Subversive and constructive in equal measure, the alternative formulated by Dabashi proposes to reconstitute a cosmopolitan worldliness to which also Muslims can subscribe. His deliberate use of the term 'worldly' – as opposed to the Latin-based 'secular' – is integral to his rejection of European parochialism and his mission to dismantle binaries, like secular-religious or profane-sacred, which replicate the obsolete Islam versus the West ontology. It also echoes Vattimo's 'ontology of decline' where ethics is put at the centre of the epistemological hierarchy and in which final authority is attributed to *beings* rather than metaphysical *Being*. With worldly cosmopolitanism as an exhibition of its attitude, in Hamid Dabashi's mind, the hermeneutics of alterity finds its most eloquent articulation and expression in the literary humanism of certain forms of classical Arabic and Persian Sufi poetry. It could also be said then that Rorty was wrong and that we do not need cultural anthropology either, but only literature.

IS LIBERAL DEMOCRACY A RELIGION OF PEACE?

Andrew Brown

One progressive way of reading the history of the world is as a story of the successive enlargement of our sympathies. We start as completely tribal beings, for whom the destruction of the neighbouring tribe is a pure blessing. There is no suggestion that God, or whatever spiritual entities preceded the idea of God, has any objection to the elimination of rivals. Whether you look at the evidence from archaeology, from anthropology, or even from the Old Testament, humanity is not one but many, and most of the many humanities are useful only as slaves or (archaeologically) as food.

The gods of the ancient world were explicitly gods amongst others. Even Yahweh, the best attested precursor of monotheism, was one god among many. When he leads his people out of Israel to the Promised Land, this is very bad news indeed for the Canaanites, and the awful fate of the dispossessed is taken as an unarguable testimony to the superiority of the Israelite God over others, and his goodness to his chosen people, not to humanity at large. I think it's arguable that humanity itself is a relatively modern conception. All the early words that mean something like 'humanity', such as 'allemanni', (which really does seem to mean 'all men') refer to particular bounded sections of humanity, in that case, Germans – if they were male and free. The others are something less than properly human.

The first crack in this tribal conception of humanity comes with the idea of conversion. At first that is something much more like adoption: in the Old Testament, as in Rome, to change gods was to change family as well. The story of the book of Ruth is often cited by Christian preachers as an example of conversion but to read it is to realise that it is essentially the story of an Israelite man claiming a piece of lost property – the widowed daughter-in-law of a relative of his. Nonetheless, this shows that the bounds of 'humanity' were not fixed. You could be born into one station in the world and move into another without violence. This really isn't a self-evident development: the caste system seems to have survived for millennia in India on the explicit denial that any such thing was possible, and various forms of race-based slavery have proved pretty robust as well. But Greek elites could move among cities, and in the Roman Empire the identity of Roman citizen took precedence over all others, and became eventually open to every taxpayer.

Before then, however, various monotheistic religions had begun to experiment with another kind of supreme identity – that of followers of the one true God, or, in the case of the Buddhists, the one true atheism. Within the Roman Empire Judaism spread by conversion and within Judaism, Christianity spread too. It was with Christianity that the real leap into universalism appeared, when St Paul began to convert Gentiles. 'There is neither Jew nor Greek, there is neither bond nor free, there is neither male nor female: for ye are all one in Christ Jesus. And if ye be Christ's, then are ye Abraham's seed, and heirs according to the promise.'

The tribal and exclusive God of the Jews has been turned inside out, so to say: you can become one of the redeemed and beloved people merely by believing (whatever that means) – wherever you start from. Potentially everyone is a Christian. The huge success of the missionary movements from then onwards show what a powerful impulse this has been. Because everyone human is a potential Christian, the horizon of sympathy extends potentially to everyone human. We are all brothers or sisters in the eyes of Jesus.

The implications of this revolution were slow to sink in and in the early centuries of Christianity to become a Christian was something that involved a long and fairly arduous course of preparation. You were joining a community, and one which was subject to intermittent, savage persecution, so the moment of baptism, and of full participation, was the culmination of a long process. Full humanity was in theory a universal benefit which anyone could claim, but in practice it was means tested.

Islam widened this circle still further by making conversion as quick and simple as possible. You said the words and you were done. Later forms of evangelical Christianity also practised individual conversion by recitation of a form of words. The range of sympathy was correspondingly enlarged. But the lands of war also continued to enlarge.

In both religions the idea of a universal humanity emerged. In the forms of secularised humanism which emerged from Christianity, this idea became completely explicit. With the invention of human rights, a claim was made which would have been ridiculous in all previous eras, that everyone was entitled to certain liberties and chances whatever their beliefs or their belongings, simply by virtue of being members of the species homo sapiens.

Modern humanism shares with some forms of Islam one interesting universalist trait, which is the conviction, more or less explicit, that everyone is born a humanist (or a Muslim), something that makes conversion, strictly speaking, impossible. What can happen instead is reversion, when you rediscover the truths that had been hidden from you by your parents, or society. Without the corrupting effects of culture, the truth of the universalist belief would be self-evident, and anyone would be led to them by reasoning on the world around them, rather as Plato believed the truths of arithmetic could be 'remembered' even by an untaught slave. This is a very grand claim for a political theory, or even a theological system. But of course the universalist humanists believe they have transcended category and ideology.

So much for the progressive story. It has much truth in it, obviously, but the historian would observe that for every single one of these expansions of sympathy there has been a corresponding growth in enemies, in others, and in religious wars.

Christianity, Islam and Buddhism were all spread by force of arms. Within Christianity and Islam at least (I don't know enough about Buddhism) successive attempts to simplify and universalise the message led to civil wars of unparalleled bloodiness, one of which appears to be currently under way in the Middle East.

And although the secularised humanism of the enlightenment appeared to be a huge moral improvement on the blind fervour of the Thirty Years' War, the immediate consequence of the French Revolution and its proclamation of the Rights of Man was twenty-two years of almost unbroken war right across Europe, from Moscow to Lisbon. Communism, too, wrote out in blood its message of universal peace and brotherhood, but this time the writing covered almost all the world. Each flaring of the light of reason casts larger, darker shadows than the one before. Each blinds us to what lies outside the light.

The steadiest, most tranquil and most reasonable illumination today is some form of liberal, tolerant democracy. This seems at least to Westerners, to be the natural form of government for human beings, to which we should all aspire. It is not just the termination of history, but its goal, the end in both the senses of the world.

There are two things possibly wrong with that hope. The most obvious today is that it was simply mistaken about this being the termination of history. All over the world people seem to revolt against rational technocracy. Even outside the horrors of the war in Syria and Iraq, or Sudan, Nigeria and the Democratic Republic of Congo, 2016 has been a year when reasonably peaceful countries are turning away from universalism: the year of Brexit, Trump, and of the AKP in Turkey. Whatever their causes, and however complex these prove to be, none of this was even thinkable twenty years ago. Some of it is still very hard to think about now. The political promise of liberal democracy is that it offered most people a much better deal than they could acquire by any other means. Why can't they see this?

The second flaw is related, but it's more serious. You can look at the horrors of the last twenty years, acknowledge them for what they are, and still hope that humanity will come to its senses. That, after all, is what Europeans did after 1945, with every appearance of success. The dreadful period of the world wars came to be seen as an interruption: a trial from which we had emerged stronger and wiser (and richer) than ever. But suppose in this picture the figure and the ground have been reversed and that the period of growth, stability, and optimism which ran for most of the last half of the twentieth century was no more than an island of uncharacteristic stability in a longer time of general chaos. Suppose, more deeply, that the fascists were right, and that people do not really want peace over war, security over glory, reliability over meaning?

This was a question that was seriously asked by frightened people in the Fifties, when the memories of the past forty years were real. Reading the dystopian fiction of the Fifties, it is astonishing how realistic it is, and how bleak. A science fiction novel like *A Canticle for Liebowitz* (1960) by Walter M. Miller Jr takes seriously the idea that progress is an illusion and history cyclical at best in a way which has very seldom been approached now we're less frightened. I know that popular culture since then is full of apocalyptic imaginings, from *Mad Max* to 'Game of Thrones', but all of these are by comparison distancing. We watch the action from the benches: we are not trapped in the arena. The nearest pop culture comes to a real unflinching examination of the world beyond liberal democracy, where all its promises are hollow and absurd, is the HBO show, 'The Wire', which premiered in June 2002 and ran till March 2008.

In 'The Wire', the rule of the law, and the expectation of order and tranquillity, all happen on the other side of an invisible border but there is very little expectation that this border will move to enclose and shelter the people of the streets. If anything, it is in constant retreat: the school system, the fostering system, the justice system, and, of course, the mechanisms of democracy, are all losing power year by year as the money runs out or is drained away. Nor is the process a peaceful one. The boundary is maintained by constant violence, some of it from the police, and some of it from the drug gangs.

If the blessings of peace and liberal democracy – 'The great society' as Lyndon Johnson imagined it – are ever to spread to the projects, this will happen as a result of overwhelming force. In one glorious scene, a frustrated policeman leaps on his squad car in the ghetto and calls out to the silent, invisible youth around him: 'Now listen to me you little fuckin' piece of shit; I'm gon' tell you one thing, and one thing only, about the Western boys you're playing with: We do not lose! and we do not forget! and we do not give up! Ever! So I'm only gon' say this one time: If you march yo' ass out here right now and put the bracelets on, we will not kick the livin' shit outta you. But if you make us go into the weeds for you, or make us come back out here tomorrow night, catch you onda corner, I swear to fuckin' Christ, we will beat you longer, and harder, than you beat your own dick!'

This is not the kind of policing of which the liberal humanists could approve but it is a pretty accurate statement of attitudes on the frontier of a liberal order. The peace and order of the suburbs is defended and extended using 'the only language those people understand'.

Looked at from this direction, the spread of peace and order – and their later maintenance – become a process that is itself neither orderly nor peaceable. In order to extend the blessings of civilisation to India, the British found themselves compelled to blow prisoner to bits across the mouth of cannons; the establishment of democracy in the former dictatorships such as Iraq and Libya was preceded and only made possible by total war involving the slaughter of civilians on a quite unprecedented scale. The theory of the Cold War, which underpinned all the progress that I grew up inside, was that peace could only be maintained by the threat of absolute nuclear destruction on a completely unimaginable scale.

The more that the rhetoric of peace and love is cranked up, the more destructive become the means by which the states which are supposed to instantiate these ideals maintain themselves. Liberal democracy, in this sense is no more, and no less peaceful than religion. It spreads its benefits through war, just as they do. In fact, it's perfectly plausible that European social democracy could only have arisen on a continent where warfare between states was the norm, or at least an ever-present threat. The habits of discipline and self-sacrifice which war demands are also those which underpin the high-tax, high spending welfare states which work partly because no one is believed to cheat.

The absolute nature of these commitments makes liberal democracy something which would, in other contexts, be called 'religious'. It demands certain moral qualities of its citizens, and demands, too, that these be underpinned by a commitment to factually dubious statements about human nature. To take a very obvious example, it really has not been apparent throughout human history to most men – possibly most people – that it is morally wrong for a man to beat his wife and children. In fact, the Bible and, by some interpretations, the Qur'an assure us that it is morally wrong for him not to do so. But to become a citizen of Britain today you have to subscribe to – you have to believe in – an idea of human dignity that makes it wrong to beat women and children. You have to believe in it as if it were a fact accessible to all reasoning creatures even though it clearly, empirically, isn't any such thing. I don't mean this as a criticism. I don't think any society is possible without that kind of shared belief. We are not creatures who can live on rationality alone. Life is too short to live without prejudice.

Liberal democracy is weak at the moment because it's not religious enough and lacks the kind of collective rituals and practices which move ideas out of our minds and into our hearts and bodies, where they can really flourish.

That doesn't make it a complete fraud. The Chomskyan view that liberal democracies are just another form of brutal conquest is at once too cynical and too idealistic. It's true that they maintain their vision of the siblinghood of humanity by visiting horrible violence on outsiders who aren't properly human. But this is actually what all societies have always done, and if our violence comes on a larger scale, that's a function of technological progress rather than moral regress. The violence necessary to confine the ghetto culture of Baltimore in 'The Wire' is far less than that which was required to maintain the slave states of 150 years ago. The horrors of Stalin's work camps were not different in kind from the stone quarries into which the captured Athenians were placed after the defeat of the Sicilian expedition. Everything we know about the rate of violent death in hunter gatherer societies suggests that young men there can kill each other with very primitive equipment much more successfully than they manage with modern weaponry in places like contemporary Colombia.

The states and societies into which liberal democracy spread were not themselves peaceful or innocent. Neither, of course, were the societies into which Islam and Christianity spread before. Order needs violence to establish, but much less violence to maintain itself. There is no perfect society and there is almost certainly no agreement possible on what a perfect society would be but that does not mean we can't build a better one.

This sounds like a neat liberal conclusion. It is not. It leads to one more universalist temptation, which we must avoid: it suggests that we could at least all agree that there is no agreement possible but I'm not sure this is possible and not even sure it's desirable. The reforming impulse has to be universalist. Slavery is everywhere and absolutely wrong and so is torture. If I did not believe this I would not struggle against them. That struggle isn't always peaceful, as American history reminds us. It doesn't always end well, either. That's not an excuse to abandon it.

In that sense the progressives are right. The expansion of sympathy really is irreversible. The problem is that it has the paradoxical effect of narrowing our tolerance. So long as outsiders aren't fully, properly human, like us, we can allow them their nasty habits, whether these are cannibalism, slavery, or just immodest dress. But once we understand them to be people who inhabit our moral universe and should be judged as we are, their breach of our moral rules becomes a defection, and that's much more threatening. And, because it's more threatening, it needs to be much more thoroughly stamped out – which is why, I suppose, the expansion of civilisation carries a moral imperative to war, whether this is jihad or the liberation from jihadis of Afghanistan.

THE WEST IS DEAD!

Jim Dator

It is clear. The West is dead. It is time to stop beating a dead West. It is time to start grooming and riding new horses beyond even postnormality.

As a futurist, I take a long view – of both the past and the futures. Thus, in my understanding, 'the West' began around 1500 following the invention of the printing press and the rapid diffusion of old and new ideas facilitated by it, on the one hand, and by the hardware, software, and 'orgware' that enabled industrialisation and global colonisation, including the creation of the global nation-state system, by Europeans, on the other.

The zenith of the West was reached by the end of the nineteenth century when physical and social technologies enabled European countries massively to export their surplus populations to the 'empty lands' of North and South America and Oceania, while dominating the rest of the world militarily, economically, and culturally via direct and indirect colonial arrangements. As one consequence, the global population of 'white people' for the first time in world history approached 50 per cent at the end of the nineteenth century – a percentage that has been steadily declining subsequently as a result of substantially reduced fertility among 'whites'. Their numbers may be around only 5 per cent by the middle of the twenty-first century. We may soon be organising 'Walks for Whitey' and 'Take a White Person Home for Christmas' and the like to celebrate their passing.

The West ended just over one hundred years ago on July 1914 with the beginning of WWI, on the one hand, and the rise of electric and then electronic communications systems, and other weapons of mass destruction, on the other. Everything the West has done since the end of WWI has just been spasms of rigor mortis following its death after a brief 'Golden Era' when the idea of the West swayed the world, offering some people reason for hope for a permanently better future – in part by destroying that hope for many more.

I have to be honest and declare that I am not a *bone fide* Westerner and I am unable to understand the world through such strange geographical terms as north, south, east, and west. I have lived in Hawaii for almost fifty years, so when I go to what is conventionally called the East – to Japan, Korea, China, India, Pakistan, Malaysia, Thailand, which I do a lot – I fly due west from Hawaii, while when I go to what Americans call the West Coast – to California for example – I fly east. It is a weird world indeed when one flies west to go East and east to go West. But I have never been a Westerner culturally. I have lived most of my life in the East – in Japan, Hawaii, Korea – not the West. I didn't even start out as a 'real' Westerner.

Even though I grew up in the American Old South, the bastion of the West at its worst, I did so without a father. This provided me with a great advantage over all 'real' southerners for whom patriarchy, patrimony, and filial piety rules. Instead, I was fortunate enough to have been raised by three strong women who imbued me with no sense at all of my gender, my ethnicity, or of any family traditions I had to follow. How many people named 'Dator' do you know? And what ethnicity do you think of when you hear my name? Nothing for sure. I know nothing about my paternity, and that is fine with me. I also had the good luck of having been educated during the height of America's most triumphant, global, confident, brief, and yet also liberal – almost socialist – period, immediately after the end of World War II.

At that time, America had a truly progressive income tax: 91 per cent tax on the income of the top 1 per cent. Racial desegregation, integration, and civil rights were in full flower. Women's liberation was blooming, with my grandmother, aunt, and mother living examples who demonstrated daily that whatever trivial differences there might be between men and women, there was nothing 'inferior' about women in any way. The arc of history was clearly swinging towards equity, fairness, and peace, I believed. The so-called 60s (which really were from 1967 to 1974) were the pinnacle of my personal hope for a better future for all. Whatever you have heard about the 60s are true, though vastly understated. You really, really had to have been there.

But peace, drugs, sex, and rock and roll proved to be just some more death throes of a culture that was dead. That it was not the dawning of the Age of Aquarius after all soon became obvious.

On getting my PhD in political science, in 1959, I did everything in my power to go to Ethiopia. When that proved impossible, I grasped an opportunity to go to Tokyo, Japan, to teach in a newly established college of law and politics in an old private university called Rikkyo Daigaku. I learned a great many things during my six years there, but my biggest revelation came when John Randolph, an old China hand living in Japan, had me read a paper he had written titled, 'The Senior Partner'. He used Oswald Spengler's theory of historical cycles to suggest that Japan was 200 years ahead of the West. Ahead of the West in 1963! How was that possible? Had we not just thoroughly demolished Japan in a bloody war? How could Japan possibly be ahead of us? Or of anyone in the West? Didn't both Karl Marx and W. W. Rostow show that developing nations, like Japan, were striving to 'catch-up' with the West by following the Stages of Economic Growth? How ridiculous!

I don't know whether Randolph was right or wrong. But he made me wonder for the first time about the future of America and the West. He set me off on my career as a futurist, and from that point on, trying to understand 'the future' and ideas about 'the future' was the all-consuming passion of my life.

After a short, misbegotten three years at Virginia Tech (where I introduced what is said to be the first officially-approved university course on the future), buried among the foreboding mountains and hillbillies of Appalachia (speaking of culture shock after six years in Tokyo!), I went to the University of Hawaii in 1969 to teach futures studies. My arrival coincided with the beginning of *Hawaii 2000*, a two-year citizen-based exercise in looking ahead thirty years, from 1970 to the year 2000. As an advisor to the *Hawaii 2000* process, I suddenly became deeply immersed in Hawaii's unique culture, interacting with all classes and ethnicities on all islands, and their diverse ideas about futures.

Hawaii has no single dominant culture. Everyone is a minority. The largest single ethnic group then and now were Japanese-Americans, with many citizens also hailing from China, Korea, the Philippines, Portugal, and of course Hawaii itself and other Pacific Islands as well as the American mainland and elsewhere. In Hawaii, the custom is to 'out marry', to marry someone who is not of your ethnicity, and as a consequence, creating a new local 'island culture' of our own. Hawaii is most certainly not the West culturally. Nor is it the East.

I was also greatly influenced by the World Futures Studies Federation (WFSF). In the late 1960s, its founding members asked: 'If the West is so great, why did it cause two world wars and a great depression?' Why did the leading Western country, Germany, attempt to exterminate a religious group? Why did the major victor nation, America, in the last stages of that war, incinerate the residents of two Japanese cities with a new, vastly more powerful bomb? Why, after that war, did Westerners build an Iron Curtain between them and prepare to exterminate the entire world many times over with new, evermore vastly powerful bombs? This cannot possibly be the best humanity can do! What might we learn from other cultures, and their visions of the future? Throughout my involvement with the WFSF, we wrestled with these questions. The first meetings of the WFSF were in Oslo, Kyoto, and Cairo. A meeting in New Delhi was planned, but Indira Gandhi censored the topic, which was the futures of politics. We had regional meetings in Islamabad, Kuala Lumpur, Bangkok, Boclod City, Nagoya, and elsewhere. We even convinced a quarrelsome person from Pakistan who was living in London to serve as editor of the leading journal in the field, entitled *Futures*, since he promised to bring more non-Western voices to the field, which he certainly did.

I was secretary general and then president of the WFSF during the 1980s and early 90s. As such, I visited almost every communist nation, including North Korea, some many times. Unable to criticise the present safely, many of the leaders wanted to envision futures different from the one they saw currently lying ahead of them. Tragically, I saw what happens when the future arrives too fast, as it did for the eastern European nations. I learned that the futurist's curse is 'may your dreams come true'. People got rid of what was called 'communism' before they had any ideas about how to govern themselves better without it. I have seen this happen many times: people protest for change, but when things do change, they have been so focused on protesting that they don't have a clue how to achieve a better life when the opportunity for it arrives.

That has happened over and over — most dramatically with the end of formal colonialism after the Second World War, and the fall of the wall in 1990.

I think we are in the midst of a similar period now. The corpse of the West is stiffening and we kick and protest against the West as though it were still powerfully striding the globe. Instead, we should be preparing to rule ourselves peacefully and fairly once the corpse has rotted away and the stink is gone.

We say we are in postnormal times. But what's next? That's the question. Or, rather, what do we want to be next? That is what is important to know now, and we don't have a clue. We are still marvelling at the postnormality of it all.

But we are no longer in postnormality. We have moved on to post-postnormality. That is, we are in the early stages of a new normal that we have the opportunity (and obligation) now to shape. And yet, we seem unable psychologically and structurally either to perceive the situation clearly or to guide it confidently. All we seem able to do is to continue to bitch and complain about the West and the US with great heat and eloquence.

Get over it and get on with the work of constructing the new normality. If you don't, others will colonise your future for their advantage, as they have done before.

However, in all honesty, I must tell you that I have very little interest in that project myself. I have been teaching at the International Space University, in Strasbourg, France, for twenty-five years. The faculty and students come from space industries and agencies all around the world. Our mission is to help humanity grow up, leave the cradle, Earth, and peacefully find its place among the other stars of the Universe. I offer classes about living on Mars. You see, truth be told, it is not just that I am not a Westerner, I am not even an Earthling. And I am very suspicious of any organisation that states its number one value is focused on humanity. What a narrow vision of the future! I want to be a Martian. My pudgy gut and warped, hardening back reveal that I am in the process of pre-adapting myself for life on Mars. I dream of becoming a winged turtle with a prehensile tail, scuttling among the rocks and rills of Mars or gliding blissfully in the thin atmosphere with its greatly-reduced gravity.

I clearly do not see myself as an American, certainly not a Hawaiian. I am fascinated by but utterly baffled by and totally uninterested in identity politics now wracking planet Earth. I have no cultural identity and I am proud of it.

Again, my name, Dator? 'Dator' is Swedish for computer. It is true. I am a machine. I am a computer. I am a robot. An inferior beta test, to be sure, but at the time, all that was humanly possible. I am not a human being. I am a human becoming – a robot becoming a human becoming a Martian, perhaps – and then what's next?

So I have no idea at all of what the West is, or the East, or North, or South. And I don't care. But I do have some conclusions. Postnormality is not a new normality. It is a prelude to a new normality. Postnormality is not just a Western, privileged disease. It is worldwide and spreading. The period of postnormality is ending; a new normality is emerging, and it can be shaped in preferred directions if we will focus on its birth and emergence and stop beating the dead corpse of the West, as emotionally satisfying (and safe, since the corpse is dead) that may be.

Non-Western countries like China or India do not at the present time have any image of the future that is fundamentally different from the old, defunct image of the West called progress, development, continued economic growth. They all cleave to the corrupted materialistic American dream. They just want it for themselves, their way. For the past twenty-five years, China has clearly aimed at nothing but becoming America on steroids. India is overwhelmingly gripped by what appears to be its lethal combination of two fundamentalisms: neoliberal economics and nationalistic Hinduism, similar to those festering on the corpse of the US. Those countries and all the other BRICS and BATS are similarly manifesting in their ways the same death throes of rigor mortis of the Western project. Nothing to see here. Move along.

And yet, continued economic growth is a thoroughly discredited unsustainable vision of the future. Therefore, China's rise before its fall is likely to be even shorter than was that of the US. India's may be shorter still.

A process I call 'The Unholy Trinity' is challenging all dominant ways of thinking and living, in the East, South, North and West. The 'persons' of The Unholy Trinity are: 1) the end of cheap and abundant energy; 2) the swift rise of environmental challenges beyond any hope of prevention; and 3) the grotesquely unfair and unsustainable global neoliberal economic system. No government is able to address much less to manage or solve the challenges of this Unholy Trinity.

All of which suggests that it is a great time to be alive and young. What a wonderful opportunity for creativity and hope lies before us! The need for true, cooperative, and radical creativity has never been greater.

Models for – that is, examples of – such creativity are appearing, not in the centres of power and intellect today, but rather in the margins where people in Second Cities who have thought differently and creatively for a long time suddenly have the chance to help others to unleash their own creativity; people in places with unpopular names and diversely-coloured skins. People who create microfinance and community development initiatives, who are trying to find other ways to be human, and who title their peripheries 'Centres' of 'Postnormality'. This is where hopes for the futures lie. Some toil anonymously in backwaters. Others, no doubt, are lurking near you. And some might yearn to be winged turtles with prehensile tails on Mars.

ARTS AND LETTERS

THAR WOMEN
AND PAKISTANI ART

Bina Shah

Two paintings hang in my bedroom, watercolours by the Hyderabad artist Ali Abbas. His primary subject is the men, women and children who live in the Thar desert in rural Sindh, desert nomads who are both Hindu Dalit and Muslim, all from the vast Kolhi tribe. Abbas has devoted his life to teaching art in Hyderabad, both at Jamshoro University and Mehran University; it was after a breakout exhibition, 'Sindh Gypsies', at the Alliance Francaise de Karachi in 2002, that he found critical acclaim both at home in Pakistan and overseas. According to the Pakistan Painters' Series page on Facebook, Ali Abbas 'works on location and creates movement in his compositions by depicting scenes of: dance, migration, labour, dramatic winds/breeze and shadows'.

Although I've never claimed to know much about art, that intellectual explanation of Ali Abbas's themes encapsulates what grabbed me viscerally when I saw the first, smaller painting at his solo exhibition, 'Gurd Baad' (Bad Wind) at the Chawkundi Gallery in Karachi back in 2005. I stood transfixed in front of the small painting, only 10x14 inches in a simple brown frame and cream mount, while the hubbub of the opening night, always a popular event in the Karachi art scene, whirled around me. It was as if all the noise had died away and the only thing that existed in the world was me and the painting.

In the painting, two women took up almost all the space. They stood at the forefront and trained a fixed gaze on me, while a third sat in the shelter of a thatched tent, a two-year-old-girl in her lap, looking off into the distance. The women were adult, but young, unveiled, all dressed in the traditional brightly-coloured clothing of the Thar women, magenta, royal blue and green kermises and long swirling *ghagras*, with necklaces and the well-known white bangles from wrist to elbow that the married women of Thar always wear. But it wasn't the exotica of their clothing and adornments that drew me to the painting. It was the look on their faces, bold, intense, and proud. The woman in magenta had her hand on her hip, the woman in blue rested hers on the pole of the tent. I had never seen a truer representation of a Pakistani woman, unburdened, unafraid, eyes blazing with full knowledge of who they were and what their place was in this most desolate of regions.

I had never bought art before, thinking it the bastion of well-heeled ladies and rich bankers. But I knew I had to have this painting, and I bought it for a fraction of what Abbas's paintings sell for now. Later, I went back to the gallery to find out if they had any more of his work. This time the gallery was silent, the gaily-dressed and talkative elite of the city had vanished, replaced by a few silent art lovers walking reverentially amongst the paintings of another exhibition that I can't remember now. I was only interested in Ali Abbas. My efforts didn't go unrewarded: another watercolour was unearthed for me from the gallery's colourfully disorganised anteroom. In comparison to the first, this was a giant, 22x30 inches, in the same brown frame and cream mount style. A Thar woman and a girl stood in the front, while a good distance behind, another woman held an infant in her arms protectively. They were all dressed in the same way as the figures in the first; a clay pot, the type that they use to carry water on their heads through miles of desert, lay at the first woman's feet. But this time, the figures were small. The emphasis was on earth and sky, both portrayed in the same blue-grey tones, the earth captured in choppy brushstrokes that resembled tossing waves, so that it looked more like an ocean than a desert. In the sky above, Abbas had painted the breeze in large, smooth circular strokes, giving the impression of the wind in a storm, but also of the elliptical shape of the entire universe. The women were standing still, withstanding the force of movement in both sky and land, as if they had always existed here and would do so forever.

I bought this second painting without hesitation and took it home to meet its counterpart. I hung them side by side in my room, fascinated by the closeness and intimacy of the first, and the spaciousness and timelessness of the second. They were a doorway to worlds that I had heard of, but never been able to visit. It's true in Pakistan that we see very little of our own country, but the Thar desert has the reputation of being difficult to access, remote and unwelcoming. Its harsh conditions make the Thar people the hardiest in the world, but they also suffer from underdevelopment and drought, their children dying often in waves of malnutrition that continue to shame successive governments.

Over the next few years, I began to think of the women in Ali Abbas's paintings as my muses. It felt strange at first to do so: the muse is an artistic concept that I'd always dismissed as slightly pretentious, as well as a tradition which usually sees a male artist or writer entranced and inspired by a young, beautiful woman – and I'd always dismissed that as sexist. But as I sat at my desk, writing, the paintings never too far from my line of sight, the women began to speak to me in the language of emotions, rather than words. If they could stand there with their wind-beaten faces and weather-swept hair, in clothing with holes that had been patched over many times, honest, unapologetic and unyielding, then I could do the same in my writing. In short, they echoed what I had always taken as the most important principle of my writing life: to tell the truth.

Pakistanis struggle with the reality of balancing multiple identities throughout their lives: A Pakistani may be, at the same time, a Sunni or Shia (sectarian identity), a Jat or a Mastoi, (tribal affiliation), a Baloch or a Punjabi (ethnic belonging), as well as negotiating the socially constructed roles of gender (male or female or transgender) and the rules of the family. These allegiances can also shift with major life transitions: birth, marriage, death. While such a myriad of identity has its benefits, making the fabric of Pakistani society richer and more diverse, it is stressful and confusing when the demands of each identity conflict within the self or with others in society. Divisions of loyalty between the needs of the individual self and the role that a Pakistani plays in each of the collective identities, has been a source of angst for many Pakistanis, myself amongst them.

By giving me this anchoring image, Ali Abbas had helped me negotiate my own identity. I too am a Sindhi woman, from the province that holds the Thar desert, but also thousands of acres of fertile farmland, nurtures the Indus River, formed the cradle of the Indus Valley Civilisation, the fan of the Indus delta, and the scores of villages, towns and cities where millions of men, women and children flourish under the watchful gaze of the Sufi saints. The women in the paintings, my muses, told me that we all originate from the land of Sindhu, ancient and that its mysteries are the blood that runs in our veins. They told me about who I was and what this land had given to me, as it gives generously and openly to all who make it their home.

I had come across, some years previously, a poem called 'Sindhi Woman,' by Jon Stallworthy, a New Zealand poet and academic. While working at Oxford University Press in Karachi in the 1970s, Stallworthy had found similar inspiration from the sight of Sindhi women, and captured them thus:

> Barefoot through the bazaar,
> and with the same undulant grace
> as the cloth blown back from her face,
> she glides with a stone jar
> high on her head
> and not a ripple in her tread.
> Watching her cross erect
> stones, garbage, excrement, and crumbs
> of glass in the Karachi slums,
> I, with my stoop, reflect
> they stand most straight
> who learn to walk beneath a weight.

As a writer, I longed to tell their stories. Not the individual stories of the women of Thar, but of the women of Sindh, and of Sindh itself. I had always seen Sindh misrepresented in the media, reduced to its simplest denominators: cruel landlords, helpless peasants. But I had also seen much cruelty done to men and women: *karo-kari* (honour killing), bonded labour, child marriage. How to bust the myths while also telling the truth? Out of this conundrum, I began to write short stories about Sindh and Sindhi women: 'The Wedding of Sundri,' about a child marriage that ended with an honour killing; 'Snakebite,' about a peasant child on the farm facing kidnapping by unknown men; and 'Mai Jeandi Faces the Cyclone,' about a village woman who refused to evacuate her village in the face of a storm, preferring instead to bargain with God for her life. And then in 2008 I wrote *A Season For Martyrs*, a novel which weaves the history of Sindh with the retelling of the last three months of Benazir Bhutto's life and death. I included a chapter on Shah Abdul Latif Bhitai, the Shakespeare of Sindh, imagining a journey he undertook all the way from Bhit Shah in Hala to the Thar desert and beyond, to Jaisalmir, a city in the Indian state of Rajhastan:

Then one day he climbed a small hill and came down the other side onto a sand dune that ran parallel to the winds, rows of undulating ridges rubbed into the sand like the lines on the roof of his mouth. Nearby, he saw a group of women dressed in the bright colours of the desert, their arms covered in white bangles up to their elbows. They were cutting at a small scrub tree with hand-axes, and singing as they worked.

Next, I quoted from Latif's *Sur Sarang*: 'In deserts, wastes and Jessalmir it has rained, Clouds and lightning have come to Thar's plains; Lone, needy women are now free from care, Fragrant are the paths, happy herdsmen's wives all this share'.

When I wrote this, I had the feeling that my journey with art had all come full circle. Ali Abbas's art had inspired me to create my own art. I could not have written the description of the Thar women without his paintings in my room, my muses enjoining me to portray their lives with honesty and humility, rather than the exoticism of the city-dweller towards the desert nomad. Yet as much as I needed Abbas's art, I couldn't help but believe that his art needed me as well, in order to give voice to his vision. It struck me, finally, the very thing that I had been trying to grasp about art all along: all art is storytelling. All storytelling is art.

Then, in early 2015, I found myself at a photography and cultural exhibition called 'Tharparkar: Beautiful and Misunderstood', hosted by the Alliance Française in Karachi. Curious to see more of this world, I went to the exhibition, organised by the Green Crescent Trust, a small NGO which does development work in the region. The trust had sent eight photographers and three filmmakers to capture the lives of the people there, mired in hardship and trapped at the subsistence level, in order to attract Karachi's philanthropists to invest in their projects.

In the generous gardens of the French Cultural Centre, photographs were displayed on black scaffolding next to drawings by the children of the Hilal Schools that GCT runs in Tharparkar. The digital representations of the women in Ali Abbas's paintings stood in front of round mud huts with thatched roofs, whose exact duplicate are found in parts of West Africa, though nobody knows why this same architectural style has shown up in two vastly disparate places on earth.

A documentary on the photography expedition played on a loop to the music of the Thari folk musician Sabhago Khashkehli, who played plaintive tunes on a stringed instrument very similar to a violin. Another Hindu tribe, called Manghaniars, play music all around the region, performing under trees or at mosques, or Hindu or Jain temples; they might sing the verses of Shah Abdul Latif or folksongs about the beauty of the rains and how the rainy season transforms the desert into a land of abundance, a dazzling multi-coloured carpet of blooming flowers and fruiting trees.

One of the Thar women's daily tasks is to bring drinking water back to the settlements from whatever water sources they can find; they walk three to four kilometres there and back with clay pots balanced on their heads, the 'heavy weight' of Stallworthy's poem. But often the water is contaminated and their children are prone to diarrhoea and other waterborne diseases. The Green Crescent Trust is working to bring hand pumps and submersible pumps with concrete water tanks to the villages and settlements, but the suffering of the Thar people, especially their children, will take years and billions of rupees to alleviate.

In the middle of the exhibition was a crafts station. Two men, Nandlaal and Varseen, had set up a standing loom and were weaving a portion of cotton *khes*, an intricate cloth made by interweaving contrasting threads in a double twill technique. The geometric patterns that result are beautiful, giving the *khes* its density and texture; typically, women arrange the warp threads on the loom but men do the actual weaving, as was being demonstrated in front of us. *Khes* is traditionally used in clothing, or as blankets and other household accessories, and was one of the Mughal Empire's major exports. In recent years, *khes*, like most of Pakistan's traditional textiles, has been spotlighted by fashion designers who have been integrating it into their designs, to critical acclaim domestically and internationally.

Similarly, the *rili*, the vibrant patchwork quilt that has been produced by women since the time of the Indus Valley Civilisation, has been incorporated into fashion collections by Pakistani designers over the last several years. The word '*rili*' comes from the Sindhi word '*ralanna*,' which means 'to mix' or 'to connect'. Women in Sindh, Baluchistan, and the Cholistan Desert in Punjab collect scraps of cotton from discarded shawls, *ajraks* and tie-dyed cloth, dye them into bright colours — white, black, red, yellow and orange to contrast with green, dark blue and purple. Cutting them into squares and triangles, then appliquéing patterns onto the base cloth results in a myriad of patterns, each one uniquely different from the next. Sandwiched between the colourful top layers are several layers of thick, warm cotton, making the *rili* into a warm duvet for winter, or a ground covering on which children can play in the winter sun.

At the exhibition, a group of Thar women relaxed on *rilis* spread out on the ground, next to the men weaving the *khes*. They were all of childbearing age – a baby crawled between their laps, while a young boy sat cross-legged on the ground in front of them. He was clearly the pride of their lives; their eyes gleamed when I sat down next to them and inquired about his age, and their names. Sita Bai and Taju gestured to a pile of *rilis* in front of them; all were for sale. My eyes fell on a medium-sized quilt that was unusually monotone: navy blue with white patchwork. I bought it immediately, enjoying the conversation with the women too much to try and bargain the meagre price down.

The ubiquitous presence of *rilis*, *ajraks*, *khes* and *khaddar* on the bodies of Pakistani men and women, living and working in the fields and villages and towns and cities, has always ensured that art in Pakistan is a living and breathing tradition, not a curiosity relegated to a museum or gallery. Yet in the new millennium, savvy young designers who had grown up with these textiles in their homes and villages, wanted to take them to a new, urban and cosmopolitan market, both at home and abroad, in order to support and preserve the crafts and artisan tradition which has been endangered by rapid industrialisation and mass production.

Today, Afsheen Junejo, Karachi-based owner of Blocked textiles, is the first Pakistani designer to use *rili* cloth and its distinctive geometric patterns in her clothing. Omar Rahim, the renowned Pakistani actor and textile designer, sells *rilis* through his design company in New York City. He has worked with Paul Smith and Tracy Feith to incorporate the *rili* into upholstery designs; Hollywood A-listers including Julia Roberts and Julianne Moore own *rilis* that he sells under his Soof Designs brand.

My thoughts returned to the Thar weavers and *rili*-makers for many days after the exhibition. Here were men and women living extremely rough lives, without many of the basics that we would consider necessary for human happiness. Yet Sita Bai and Taju were as smiling and joyful as anyone could be, intoxicated with the excitement of being in Karachi and selling their wares to city folk who had never come within a hundred miles of

Tharparkar. Could their art have something to do with their happiness, their self-esteem?

It had to be. Pakistan's art is not relegated to the realms of art galleries and art schools, the preserve of the educated and the elite. The tradition of art for the people, democratic art, is as strong as the formal methods of production, exhibition, and commerce. In the small villages of Sindh, Punjab, Baluchistan or Khyber Pakhtunkhwa, the skills and crafts of the people provide them not just with livelihood, but with identity – psychological constructs that are as important as air and food and water if a human being is to self-actualise and achieve her highest potential, according to Maslow's hierarchy of needs, a motivational theory in psychology proposed by Abraham Maslow in his 1943 paper 'A Theory of Human Motivation'. Maslow theorised that the first four needs – physiological, safety and security, love and belongingness, self-worth and self-esteem needs – were 'deficiency needs' that had to be fulfilled before the higher needs of transcendence and self-actualisation could be addressed. But in 1970, he updated his theory to include two needs that hadn't been addressed in the original model: cognitive needs, or the search for knowledge and meaning; and aesthetic needs, or the appreciation and search for beauty, balance, and form. Yet even Maslow's updated hierarchy has been criticised for being too rigid: the 'starving artist' who must create art even while neglecting his basic needs, for example, doesn't fit into this model of human motivation.

In Pakistan the prevalence of street art, folk art, and crafts – not high art, but people's art – show that the drive to fulfil aesthetic needs operates side by side with the drive to fulfil deficiency needs, and seem to also be indelibly tied to self-worth and self-esteem needs. Simply put, the production of art satisfies the Pakistan individual's need for self-worth and self-esteem. The Pakistani may even derive his or her identity from his art: being known for the best crafts in the village, for example, or being particularly skilled at truck art. The production of art of course has its commercial side; by using art to pay for one's livelihood, the individual is satisfying the physiological needs as well. And one more aspect: by expressing one's inner self through one's art, one is negotiating an individual identity in a collectivist society.

The Indus Valley civilisation, one of the world's most ancient cultures that is the anthropological and archaeological foundation of Pakistan, has fascinated the modern world with two markers: its writing, unintelligible hieroglyphics, and its sophisticated visual art, found on stamps and sculpture – the Priest-King, the Dancing Girl, the strange ox-like animal that is neither a bull or a zebra. The strange cuneiform that nobody has ever been able to decipher point to a vast pre-Islamic civilisation whose roots stretch over thousands of years and still inform Pakistan and Pakistanis today. What greater evidence that humanity, indeed civilisation, has chosen the arts – writing and visual art – as a way of announcing to the world, 'We exist'?

Pakistan is a highly artistic society, its people poetic and creative. Ask someone a question, and the answer is as likely to come back to you in the form of a verse from Faiz or Iqbal or even the lyrics of a *ghazal*, classical rhyming couplets of love, as it is a factual statement. Art and poetry burst and beckon from the backs of trucks and buses and rickshaws, formal verse or colloquial poetry paired with the popular motifs of truck art. Buraq, the mystical winged horse flying to heaven; a pair of beautiful eyes belonging to a *houri* from paradise; flowers and Kalashnikovs all teeming on their hulking metal frames to tell the story of Pakistan.

Art as life, interwoven into the fabric of many lives and many layers, may come as a surprise to most observers and even most residents of this country, positioned as it is at an eternal crossroads between peace and insecurity, instability and chaos, the stranglehold of conventions and traditions and a rapidly approaching, seductive modernity. When our basic needs remain so unfulfilled, how do we even think of making art?

But it's precisely this uncomfortable and untenable position that forces Pakistan and its people to go within, seeking from internal sources answers that are not so easily forthcoming from external forces. Even the questions come from within because art raises the exact same questions of identity, self-formation and self-expression that Pakistanis have been confronting since before the inception of the country: Who am I? Why am I here? What is my purpose? What do I seek to tell the world? Perhaps it is the artisans, the *hunarmand*, of Pakistan, who tell us, in making their art, exactly who we are.

DARK EVENTS

Ana Maria Pacheco

Sculptor, painter and printmaker, Ana Maria Pacheco was born in Brazil in 1943. She taught at universities in Goiás for several years before coming to England on a British Council Scholarship to study at the Slade School of Fine Art, London. Since 1973 she has lived and worked in England. She has exhibited at major institutions in the UK including the British Museum, the Tate Gallery and the Victoria and Albert Museum.

A central theme in Pacheco's work is the abuse of control and power and the vulnerability and alienation faced by victims of oppression. Her work is partly a response to the troubled period in Brazil's history culminating in the military coup of 1964, to which she was an eyewitness. Pacheco draws on folklore and Biblical myths and explores themes of love, family, death and violence. Her aesthetic encapsulates various aspects of the indigenous, African and European ethnicities to be found in Brazil.

Pacheco finds it ironic that in England her art is sometimes reduced to being 'Brazilian', when her very nationality is rooted in European origins. Brazil is, after all, a Portuguese creation. And so by returning to Europe, she has 'completed the puzzle' of her heredity and is able to analyse her colonial legacy from a different vantage point.

Her drypoint series Dark Event (2007) is anchored by the key image of a head bound by wire above a bleeding heart. The other prints in the series provide a narrative that expands upon this image. There are scenes of innocence betrayed by barbarity and the violence of war and scenes suggesting redemption through compassion.

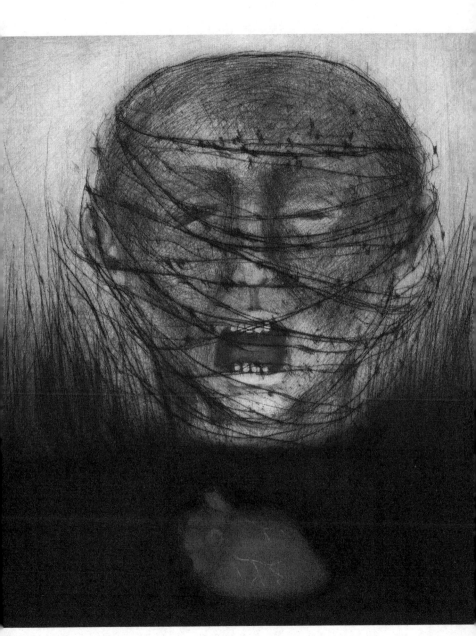

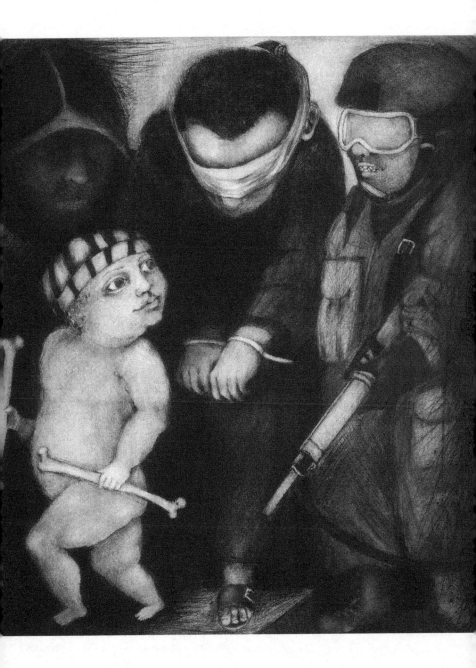

CLASH OF CIVILISATIONS

Avaes Mohammad

The haves the have nots
The haves but will not
The woulds but could not
The coulds but would not

The haves but think not
The thinks but ask not
The asks but know not
The knows but care not

The tongue that speaks lots
But voice that's heard not
The voice that's heard lots
But speech that tells not

Apparent stand-offs
Between us and rest of
The world that thinks not
In terms that suit us
So the lies we spread lots

Of foreign despots
That wish to kill us
So must be killed off
The heads that bow not

The hands that shake not
When holding sling-shots
When facing gun-shots
The view that's changed not

From colonial plots
Civilising dark flocks
To get what they've got
The books that teach not

Each phrase a new knot
Claim cultures move not
And stand as fixed blocks
And the books that flow past

Borders and won't stop
Make ours who once were
People we knew not
A choice we've all got

Be held or hold off
Embrace what's known not
Knowing we know not
Or claim we share not

And so we grow not
What's different trust not
And let it be not
The haves the have nots

The haves but will not
The ones that call shots
The ones that get shot
That is the only clash of civilisations

WHERE I COME FROM

Amir Darwish

From the earth I come
To the earth I come
From the heart of Africa
From the kidneys of Asia
From India with spices I come
From a deep Amazonian forest
From a Tibetan meadow I come
From an ivory land
From far
From everywhere around me
From where there are trees, mountains, rivers and seas
From here, there, from everywhere
From the womb of the Mediterranean I come
From a mental scar
From closed borders
From a camp with a thousand tents
From shores with Alan* the Kurd I come
From a bullet wound
From the face of a lone child
From a single mother's sigh
From a cut in an inflatable boat about to sink
From a bottle of water for fifty to share
From frozen snot in a toddler's nose
From a tear on a father's cheek
From a hungry stomach
From a graffiti that reads, 'I was here once'
From another one a tree says 'I love life'
From a missing limb
Like a human with everything I come to share the space.

*Alan Kurdi, initially reported as Aylan Kurdi, was a three-year old Syrian boy of Kurdish ethnic background whose image made global headlines after he drowned on 2 September 2015 in the Mediterranean Sea.

GENESIS

Fadwa Soleiman

Rain on rain
And mud on mud
My grandmother weaves the story
With a thread of sun
And a thread of moon
She grinds her words
In the mill of her breath, and scatters them
Among the stars

*

Rain on rain
And mud on clay
My grandmother turns with the earth
And kneads sand into her wine
At moonrise

*

Rain on rain
And mud on mud
She attaches the sea to a pen
And spreads its breath on a page
She dries the salt on her knees
Gives birth to clouds
She makes fountains of her breasts
Gives birth to the grass

*

Rain on rain
And mud on clay
At night my grandmother sows cities
That grow at daybreak
And she sings to the reeds

*

Rain on rain
He writes on the clay
We have taken the one in the sky as our witness
And he said
The sky comes from you
The sky is for you
My grandmother locked
All the doors with the cry of her blood

*

Rain on rain
And the clay tablets say
We have taken the one in the sky as our witness
He asked for blood
And would not accept our harvests
The sky is mine
My grandmother barricaded
The doors with the cry of her blood

*

Rain on rock
Blood on the grass
And grass above the blood
Blood leads to blood
Half of you will be slaughtered by the other half
And the sky has bolted its doors

*

Rain on rain
And mud on mud
Each time a herd of gazelles goes by
The hunters devour them
Though they already had gorged themselves

*

She lowered her eyes
And stopped
She did not find her own face
Horses' hooves had smashed the face of the earth
They carried death and the dead on their backs
This time their faces didn't tell her their destination

Her own face fell
She did not find her eyes
She knelt down
The hooves went on crushing the face of the earth
Glistening now in another direction
The horses' hooves arrived at the precipice
Trampling the chrysanthemums back to the womb
Then they all plunged into the desert's abyss
There is no way out if you kill
Your victory will teeter on one leg
There will be a crown of blood on your head

*

Rain on rain
And mud on clay
My grandmother sets her fingers on fire waiting
For a prodigal to return
She gives off an odour of blood
My grandmother is still a virgin

*

At daybreak
A child got up out of the rubble
He looked for his mother
He pushed away the rocks around her
He shook her hard but she didn't wake up
He called all of his brothers and sisters' names
He turned back to his mother, crying out
I won't trust you anymore after today, Mama
Yesterday
You sang to the doves
That no one would slit their throats.
On his birthday
In the orphanage
He wrote on the wall with a bird's feather:
I trust my mother
She never learned how grown-ups have fun
She never knew how they coloured my brothers and sisters,
Coloured her too
Coloured everything red

She didn't yell at them
Because they played at knocking down houses
She didn't shout in their faces
When they set my swing-set
And Hala's house on fire
She did not cry out
When they lined my father up against the wall with the neighbours
And shot crayons from their rifles
That coloured their heads all red
Red, Mama
Kept you from shouting
Or blaming anyone
The child who is no longer a child continues
To make doves fly wherever he can
And his heart is red.

*

Rain on rain
And mud on mud
She bends her neck to the wind
And her waist to the trunk of a fruit-tree
Bends her knees to the pebbles
And her forehead to the dust
She offers her fingers to the bees
And her teeth to the truth
Her songs to the reeds
And her feet to the roots
Her blood to the wedding of pollen and flower
She lets her hair down over the story

*

On the café terrace
Torrents of rain
Violent wind
The flame in my lighter went out again and again
I couldn't light my cigarette
The rain came down in torrents
And the wind was violent
With one touch of his finger on the trigger
The soldier launched the missile

Torrents of rain did not put out
The flames in the building on fire
And the violent winds
Carried away rags of flesh I loved
And scattered them far from here

*

Salt on wound
And water on mud
We are only memories
On the run across time

Translated from the Arabic by Marilyn Hacker

IVORY DEMONS

Imaan Irfan

Crimson unfurls in the sky like a great silk banner and a jewelled sun plunges into the earth. In a few minutes, the *adhaan* will fill the sweet African air, echoing beautifully over the town from the minaret. The call to prayer washes tranquillity over Mali, soothing and powerful, in lilting Arabic.

My mother calls me, 'Ajar Amadi! Ajar, come to lead the prayer.' Tears spring to my eyes as I bend before God, reciting ancient words with my Malian brothers and sisters. Poetry is beloved to us and there is no poetry greater than God's words, which also possess a certain mathematical perfection.

After the prayer, our community gathers to listen to the *jali*, or the storyteller. He performs our histories, tales and songs from memory and weaves vivid pictures with his words which make our hearts crave more. Today, he strikes fear and fascination into our souls, speaking of men with spectre-white skin, wielding weapons which burst into flame. These barbarians, these ivory demons, are said to snatch men away from their homes and return with their prisoners to their strange lands where no free and civilised man has set foot in.

One small girl, dressed in yellow, buries her face in her mother's lap in terror but is hushed and gently reassured by one of the women that it is just a story; it holds no truth. My mother grips my hand tightly and whispers to me, 'Your grandparents were Igbos in Nigeria. "Amadi" means "free man" in Igbo. Do not worry, Ajar, nobody can take you except with Allah's will. You are safe.' I smile and kiss her cheek. Although I feign amusement, I am not ungrateful for her maternal instinct which has become so fiercely protective at a mere story – albeit one that secretly troubles me. My own internal fear is mirrored on the face of Madou, my friend. He is tense and fidgeting and refuses to make eye contact with me. Madou is not the bravest of men, and perhaps his love of money is slightly excessive but for all his defects, his wiry frame is strong, his laugh is infectious and we have known each other since childhood.

The next morning, when I rise early for the morning prayer, I am still slightly uneasy but the familiar movements in worship calm me. The pale gold sun is wrapped up in a soft, shell-pink sky and, upon completing *fajr*, I decide to take a walk to drink in the brilliance of my surroundings. A carpet viper bathes its sleek coils in the sun rays and lazily flicks out a forked tongue toward my direction. I hastily pass it by.

After some time has passed, I sense something watching me. My eye catches a glimpse of ebony skin stalking through the thick foliage and the brief flash of something shining. Cautiously, I begin to walk back in the direction of my home, before two men reveal themselves and begin to approach me from afar. I smile nervously and raise my head to greet them with *salaams*. They do not reply. One of the men looks at me like a famished lion eyeing his prey and suddenly I feel intensely vulnerable. Truly, I wish myself back in the company of the carpet viper. Two more men emerge and I realise that running is fruitless. They would catch me anyway.

Before I can speak, a man darts forward and shock surges through me as I recognise him as Madou. He grabs me while I flail like a fish out of water. The other men wind silver ropes around me, roughly and brutally, and I cannot snap them. While I struggle in vain, screaming at Madou, a raucous, almost demonic laugh catches my attention. As I realise the source of the noise, my gut twists and my heart patters madly against my ribs, as if it were a bird begging to be set free from its cage. His skin and stringy hair is colourless and unnatural and watery blue eyes are fixed upon me as if this were a sport…as if I was an animal. His upper lip is sweaty and the nails are grimy as he scratches his stubble; he barks an order to my captors and they lead me to a short line of young men and women before tying my hands behind my back and placing a noose of rope around my neck. My rope is attached to the rope knotted around the neck of the man in front of me and – like cattle – we are whipped to make us move forward.

My heart swells with outrage as the white man cracks a whip against a woman's skin. Her name is Keita, if I recall. I shout at him, but five smarting lashes on my back put me in my place and I hold my tongue, knowing I am powerless. I glance up quickly and teardrops are clinging to her eyelashes. If he catches us looking up, the white man whips us. We cannot move our hands; Keita can't even wipe her tears away. We are led to a beach where stand crudely constructed cages which we are confined in. We are not humans. We are imprisoned beasts. Later, we see a huge floating house on water and, from the foreign word being repeated constantly by the white men, I understand its name to be 'ship'. The air is thick and humid and the squeals of people puncture the air at irregular intervals. My mother will be wondering where I am. My poor, poor mother. The sting of betrayal is still fresh and, had I seen Madou again, I would have hammered him with my fists until the bones shattered. I try to repress my simmering anger which is boiling and rising...up and up and up...

No!

I will control myself. The white men may consider me an animal but I am still a civilised human being. I turn my mind to matters more worthy of its time. I pray and pray as they push me into the wooden vessel and defiance is stirring inside of me again...they cannot pluck me from my home so easily. But they do.

Now, I do not know how long I have been here. Sometimes I fall in and out of consciousness, day melts into night and night melts into day but we never see light. The putrid stench of vomit, sweat, urine and faeces is suffocating; it envelops the room in a shroud of vile sickness. Grown men are sobbing and screaming. Many of them hail from other tribes so we do not even share a common tongue. My back is aching from lying on the hard planks for hours on end and I am clamped in the icy grip of chains that I cannot break away from. The metal is rubbing against my skin and bruises so my ankles are burning. I have tried to wrench my hands out of the shackles so many times that now they are raw and sore and bleeding. My other joints are so stiff. I want to die. I want to die. I want to die. We are forced to eat the pulpy, blanched food that we are given and it makes our stomachs spill. The spaces are so cramped that we can barely breathe, as if this were some mass grave for the living, except *our* wooden tomb sways and lurches sickeningly. We exist as nothing but piles of stinking bodies and it seems like the fetid miasma is gradually poisoning us, acrid and utterly foul.

'Truly, with hardship comes ease' is my only consolation. Misery claws at my insides when I realise that I cannot pray. I cannot wash, I cannot move and I am unaware of the time, ignorant of the direction. May Allah forgive me. Every so often, the white men come in shrieking in harsh gibberish, like *jinn*. I want to die. I want to die. Allah, please let me die.

Occasionally, we are pulled up 'on deck'. They wrench us by the ankles so that we fall to the ground, where heaps of steaming human waste lie in wait for us. Pitiful groans are mingled with the thuds of our heads meeting the floor.

I have lost control of my legs and they falter as I try to lift myself up. As I attempt my first movement in ages, my vision goes and I stumble around in darkness for a minute, thinking myself blind. Will I be allowed to die now? My sight returns briefly but then vanishes again as agonising bright light floods my senses and my eye struggle to adjust to the glaring sun. The first thing that I notice is that there is no riverbank. A vast expanse of glittering water is all that there seems to be and the tang of salt kisses the air. Breathing deeply, I thank God, because this air is free from the noxious reek that usually smothers us.

All of the men scream in unison when salty water hits our wounds as the white men drench us with their buckets. Our bodies are stripped of blood and muck and the white men are yelling again, forcing us to jump for exercise. I try to look for Keita, for any familiar face. I find none.

Despite the lack of a riverbank, one man throws himself overboard and attempts to swim back home. He struggles pathetically for a while and a woman wails mournfully before the waves overcome him. Every African is punished for this. I will never jump overboard. I am not so weak.

In the distance, a single dark cloud glowers and bubbles on the horizon and now an eerie chill is clinging to the air, like a spider's web to a cloth. Before my mind can register what is happening, rain is hissing and spitting like a feral cat. Smoky swathes of cloud pulse against a murky sky like bats' wings, and rippling black waves gurgle and choke. White claws of sizzling intensity slash open a sea which throbs with pain and bile and hatred. The abruptness of the storm brings distress to the white men and we are stuffed back into the dark belly of our vessel, once again.

We are taken 'on deck' twice more during the course of our journey. Every day there are exclamations of men finding a corpse next to him. The smell of decaying flesh does not last long, however, as the white men are efficient in pulling down the body and disposing of it. I suppose that any dead people are thrown unceremoniously overboard and consumed by the sea.

One day, when the sound of muffled breathing next to me has ceased, I turn my head as far as I can and find a pair of glassy eyes gazing at me blankly. Stretching my fingers to touch his limp hand, I shudder at the cold skin and check his pulse, just to be sure. I recoil with horrified disgust. The heartbeat has stopped. Closing my eyes, I attempt to reconstruct happy memories in my mind: how my mother used to sing as she cooked, how my friends and I lay and watched the stars at night, how Madou once sa—

No.

I will not think of him. However, I do allow misery to engulf me for a moment. It is the longest moment of my life.

Muslims have always been good at handling pain. We cannot drown our sorrows in alcohol or forget our problems with drugs – we are forced to reflect and understand our pain, find comfort in God and heal with time. This time I wish I had something to forget. I don't feel like waiting to heal.

Only God knows how long it was until 'ship' finally stopped. We are washed with water and then coated with oil that makes us glisten before our mouths are wrenched open for inspection and hot tar is rubbed into any wounds to disguise them. I clench my teeth, trying not to scream. We are poked and prodded repeatedly by one white man from our voyage, who appears to be checking that we are healthy. It is humiliating.

In this new land, the air is dry and hot, the language is harsh and the white people glide around, pale and ghost-like. We are put into a pen again as a crowd of whites gather, clothed in suffocating layers of frilled fabrics. The sound of a drumroll thrums through the air and then, without any other warning, throngs of whites burst through the gates. They push and shove like animals to get to the Africans they want. Many begin to fight over the young men like myself while we stand frightened and bewildered. The man who has grabbed me has a vice-like grip, he hands a small piece of paper to the white man who captured me as he leads me away. I try to run and receive a blow to the stomach. I double over, wheezing, but the grip on my wrist does not loosen. I catch a glimpse of a white man leading Keita away while she struggles violently. This is the last time I will ever see her.

We arrive at the largest house I have ever seen. An African is waiting outside, speaking to a rather paunchy white man in his native tongue. The white man cuts off the conversation and looks me up and down. His shrewish eyes bore into me and I stare right back, determined not to be intimidated. He is the colour of spoiled milk and, although his face is fleshy and round, it has a certain harsh quality to it. Its expression is hard and the narrow lips writhe into a permanent grimace. Cruelty is carved into every line of the pasty face. He says something sharply to the African, keeping his eyes fixed suspiciously on me.

The African talks to me in my native tongue, and it is he who later teaches me the work that I must now do for the large white man, whose name is Mister Little. I learn that I am in a place called 'South Carolina' and that I am a slave. I learn that I am worthless because my skin is dark. I learn that whites are intellectually and morally superior. I learn that I must be respectful or they will have me killed. I learn that nobody believes this but the whites...but I must act the part of the subservient slave or I will die here, far away from home.

In the day, I work in the fields with other Africans. We pick cotton in the blazing heat until our fingers bleed. If Mister Little stops by and suspects one of us is not working hard enough, he will have us punished mercilessly. Sometimes he does it on a whim, just to remind us that we are powerless. For negligence, we are usually tied up and whipped with laice-wood switches. Concerning slaves who run away, they are hunted by dogs and dragged back to the plantation. Then, iron rings of immense weight are put on their ankles and pothooks are placed on their necks. We hear of places where the punishments are far worse. There are real places where half a foot is removed for lesser crimes and where geldings and mutilated faces are common. The worst that has happened to me so far was the branding. A red hot poker was applied to my skin and I could not pretend to be brave. I howled in agony. This was no punishment, though. This was to leave a mark that distinguishes me as Mister Little's property.

At night, pangs of homesickness hit me. They hurt worse than the whippings. I have to remind myself that 'Allah does not burden a soul beyond that it can bear'. If God says that I am strong enough to handle my problems, then I must be. But I still miss my mother.

In this country, a wife takes her husband's name to show that she belongs to him. Her own identity is stripped from her like it never existed. Now I am also branded with this pale devil's name. They call me 'James Little'. I can barely pronounce it, let alone accept it. I hold this name in my mouth; it is sour and repulsive. It sickens me that any of my future children or grandchildren will bear this tainted name. Every day, I pray for them to hold firmly to their heritage and to their Islam, and to relinquish this surname in a time when things are better...

I may not be 'Free Man' but no mere man is my master. I may not be 'Amadi' but I will never be a 'Little'. I may not be 'Amadi' but, in truth, I would rather be 'Abdul Malik' or 'servant of The King'. To Allah belongs my life, and my death. To Allah belongs my story, my heart and my soul. To Allah belongs my past, my present – and my future, too.

'Your Lord did not abandon you, nor did He forget. Surely the hereafter is much better for you than present life' (The Qur'an 93:3).

REVIEWS

END OF CAPITALISM?

Giles Goddard

I am vicar of a church in Waterloo, London. When I opened the front doors of the church one recent morning I saw two young rough sleepers, a man and a woman, wrapped up in sleeping bags on ripped up cardboard boxes. Ben, formerly homeless, now one of our key-holders, was selling *Big Issue*. Stallholders were setting up their street food market (a Turkish woman selling wraps, two Lebanese men selling falafel, one Ethiopian man selling coffee, an Ethiopian man running a Thai food stall, and one British man selling burritos). And a stream of students from around the world passing the church gates on their way to King's College London. Beyond that two hundred buses an hour carrying commuters into the City; and further afield trains streamed over the bright blue viaduct into Charing Cross. In the background, the redevelopment of the Shell Centre was proceeding apace for seven new high-rise buildings, providing hundreds of flats and offices for powerful individuals and companies servicing global capitalism.

It's a palimpsest of Britain, and my work as a vicar reflects that. One minute I am responding to a request by a homeless addict for something to eat, somewhere to go, help finding a job. The next I am engaging with the National Theatre on a new jobs scheme we're running supporting young people into technological skills. Then I find myself counselling someone whose job prospects are unclear or working with a banker who took early retirement and is helping with our finances. Inside the church, I pray about the challenges the world faces – meltdown in Syria, global migration, climate change, society's fragmentation. Loneliness. Insecurity. Fear.

What is going on? Responses to the current economic situation fall into two broad categories – those who argue that we need more of the same but more carefully moderated, and those who lay the responsibility firmly at the door of what is broadly termed neo-liberal economics. Paul Mason,

Naomi Klein, David Harvey and Arundhati Roy fall into the second group. In broad terms their argument is similar – we are seeing the outworking of an economic approach which was first seen when President Nixon tore up the Bretton-Woods agreement in 1971 and developed by Margaret Thatcher and Ronald Reagan, influenced by the Chicago School of economists led by Milton Friedman. Neo-liberal orthodoxy called for a fundamental transformation of the relationship between the state and the individual, liberating private enterprise to create wealth wherever it could on the basis that a rising tide lifts all boats. These books challenge that premise, arguing in different ways that this vision of capitalism is fatally wounded, tottering under the weight of its own contradictions; and that we are seeing – in the resistance to capitalism shown by movements such as the Transition Towns in the UK, Occupy, local energy companies and above all the radical transformation of information brought about by the internet – the beginnings of a new structure which has the potential to change the world.

David Harvey is Distinguished Professor of Anthropology at the City University of New York and a leading exponent of Marx's economic theories. In *Seventeen Contradictions and the end of Capitalism*, he identifies the contradictions inherent in the European economic systems of the nineteenth century, the way it has evolved and become the economic animal we know as global capitalism. 'Crises', he argues, 'are essential to the reproduction of capitalism'. The contradictions have produced a dynamism which has at times led to economic collapse but more often to a regeneration, enabling a further level of growth. For example, there is an inherent contradiction between the concept of private property and the concept of the capitalist state; the possession of property includes the right to free enjoyment and disposition of the house, land, car, diamond or whatever. But in order for that right to be safeguarded against piracy or attack, property owners voluntarily hand over power to a centralised state which has responsibility for controlling and managing competing desires for access and possession. In other words, the state, usually but not always underpinned by some form of democratic accountability, is granted rights by property owners in order that their private rights can be protected. As a result, 'there is a good deal of evidence that the coercive power of the state played an important role in opening spaces in which capital could flourish before private property regimes became dominant'; and 'the centralised power of the state is used to protect a decentralised property system'. However, Harvey argues, this time it's different. In the case of property, the working out of the implications of this contradiction, through the granting of property rights to global corporations and institutions has undermined the balance between private rights and public responsibility to the point where the state is now dwarfed by and no longer able to act effectively against the power of global corporations on behalf of the individuals to which it is responsible. Indeed, many governments have explicitly supported the concentration of power in the hands of global corporations: 'this new ruling class is aided by a security and surveillance state that is by no means loath to use its police powers to quell all forms of dissent in the name of anti-terrorism'.

David Harvey, *Seventeen Contradictions and the End of Capitalism*, Profile Books, London, 2015.

Naomi Klein, *This Changes Everything*, Allen Lane, London, 2014

Paul Mason, *Postcapitalism: A Guide to Our Future*, Allen Lane, London, 2015.

Arundhati Roy, *Capitalism: A Ghost Story*, Verso, London, 2015

Harvey's analysis is extensive. He identifies fundamental contradictions in areas such as the relationship between capital and labour, centralisation and decentralisation, and also in areas he terms 'dangerous contradictions' – endless compound growth, and capital's relation to nature (including the stark realities of biosphere loss and climate change). His overarching seventeenth contradiction, 'alienation', is, perhaps, the most dangerous: 'the tactile contact with the commodity' is lost; 'all prospects for social equality or social justice are lost even as the universality of equality before the law is trumpeted as the supreme bourgeois virtue. Accumulated resentments at accumulation by dispossession ... boil over. Freedom becomes domination, slavery is freedom'. But despite all this, Harvey does not expect capital to fall on its own, writing that 'the capitalist class will never willingly surrender its power. It will have to be dispossessed'. And for that dispossession to happen, he calls for a new kind of politics and a new relationship between the economy, the state and individuals – a 'secular revolutionary humanism that can ally with those religious-based humanisms (most clearly articulated in both Protestant and Catholic articulations of the theology of liberation as well as cognate movements within Hindu, Islamic, Jewish and indigenous religious cultures) to counter alienation in its many forms and to radically change the world from its capitalist ways'.

In Waterloo, it is certainly true that society appears increasingly atomised. The cost of housing in London excludes the young (apart from those whose parents are able to support them) and the poor, who are disproportionately members of minority ethnic communities. Diversity in central London is reducing. Communal activities such as churchgoing are in decline, although this decline is masked in London by the effects of immigration. Street homelessness is increasing again after a decade of steady reduction, because of a reduction in resources targeted at alleviating homelessness and a decrease in low-skilled jobs for entrants to the job market. But, at the same time, unemployment is at a historic low, and the City of London appears untouched by the 2009 crash or by its aftermath. So does Harvey's analysis hold water, or are we seeing another re-formation of capitalism, a new take on an old story?

Perhaps London is not the best example of the current situation. It remains one of the world's wealthiest cities and as such presents a distorted picture. The consequences of global capitalism for poorer economies are searingly documented in Arundhati Roy's *Capitalism, a Ghost Story*. Roy, best known in Britain for her Booker-winning novel *The God of Small Things* and a noted environmental and political activist, has a deep knowledge of the damage done by international corporations to local communities. *Capitalism, a Ghost Story*, much shorter and more descriptive than Harvey's book, speaks of the damage done to indigenous and poor communities by major Indian and international corporations. 'India's new mega-corporations, Tatas, Jindals, Essar, Reliance Sterlite,' writes Roy, 'are those that have managed to muscle their way to the head of the spigot that is spewing money extracted from deep inside the earth. It's a dream come true for businessmen – to be able to sell what they do not have to buy.' She traces the spheres of influence, the allegedly corrupt agreements with local and national government, the close relationships between NGOs and corporations, and between India and the USA: 'being a "strategic partner" of the United States does not mean that the heads of state make friendly phone calls to one another.... It means an unequal partnership in which India is held in close in a bear hug and waltzed around the floor by a partner who will incinerate her the moment she refuses to dance.' Roy's approach to the challenges presented by globalisation is different to Harvey's, but her analysis of the situation is similar. 'Capitalism is going through a crisis whose gravity has not revealed itself yet,' she says. 'Those making up the proletariat have over the years been pitted against each other in every possible way', and 'yet all over the world they are fighting back. In India the poorest people in the world have fought back to stop some of the richest corporations in their tracks.'

Both Harvey and Roy see the resistance to global capital and finance – expressed through new movements of local and/or indigenous resistance, through forms of new mutual economic engagement, through transition towns and local power generation, through the anger and direct action of organisations such as Occupy – as a harbinger of the impending collapse of this unhealed economic system. Their approach is thrown into sharp relief by Naomi Klein's *This Changes Everything – Capitalism vs the Climate*. Published in 2015 in the run-up to the COP21 (21st Session of the Congress of the Parties) climate change talks in Paris, the book focuses on the relationship between anthropogenic climate change and global capital. The very real risk of runaway climate change and the apparent inability of governments to agree any meaningful common actions to reduce carbon emissions are, she argues, both the result of neo-liberal economics. 'Our economy is at war with many forms of life on earth, including human life. What the climate needs to avoid collapse is a contraction in humanity's use of resources; what our economic model needs to avoid collapse is unfettered expansion.' Klein, in common with Roy and Harvey, identifies the resistance movements as the vanguard of new, post-capitalist world. She is not confident that it is possible to avoid the imminent collapse, because 'any attempt to rise to the climate challenge will be fruitless unless it is understood as part of a much broader battle of world-views, a process of rebuilding and reinventing the very idea of the collective, the communal, the commons, the civil and the civic after so many decades of attack and neglect'.

I was active in the engagement with the climate change movement in the run-up to the COP21 in November 2015. The Church of England was part of an interfaith and international movement which included a global petition gaining 1.5 million signatures, numerous Pilgrimages to Paris led by the Filipino activist Yeb Sano, marches, demonstrations and all the arrows in the quiver of activism. The pre-Paris agitation was a manifestation of a popular movement, and Christiana Figueres, the Secretary of the UN department who worked tirelessly for COP21, has acknowledged that the global voices raised before and during the talks made a material difference to the outcome.

But Klein's view, after the Paris agreement, has not fundamentally changed: 'it's absolutely true that it's a tremendous achievement to agree on the need to keep warming below two degrees, or 1.5 if that's possible. It could have been worse, it absolutely could have been worse based on past experiences,' she acknowledges. But, Klein notes, 'something can be politically historic and scientifically catastrophic at the same time. Those truths can co-exist and do co-exist.' There is little sign that the collective action before Paris has any prospect of being turned into the sort of global movement for change which Klein, Harvey and Roy all seek; those of us still involved are doing what we can to encourage the implementation of the agreement, but the sense of global interconnection is not nearly as strong as it was in the run-up to the talks.

The underlying theme of these books is that we are seeing, played out in a new way, an age-old story – the battle between the haves and the have-nots, between the powerful and those excluded from power. Paul Mason, in *Postcapitalism – A Guide to Our Future*, focuses his analysis on what he sees as the fundamental transformation of the global economy brought about by technical innovation. Mason is a well known and respected broadcaster and commentator on the Left in Britain. His accessible but rigorous response to the 2009 crash foregrounds an element less prominent in Roy and Harvey's analyses: the implications of information technology. We are, according to Mason, in a radically new financial situation, the neoliberal approach to the economy has created a situation where 'bad banking plus imbalanced growth' (the initial explanation for the crisis) has given way to a recognition that 'secular stagnation' (low demand, low productivity, high debts and growing inequality) is a likely scenario for the foreseeable future. In other words, Mason suggests that capitalism may never recover its dynamism.

He identifies four causal factors. First, 'fiat money,' which allowed every slowdown to be met with credit loosening, and the whole developed world to live on debt. Second, 'financialisation', which replaced the stagnant incomes of the developed world workforce with credit. Third, global imbalances and the risks remaining in the vast debts and currency reserves of major countries. Fourth, information technology, which allowed everything else to happen, but whose future contribution to growth is in doubt. Capitalism is, effectively, out of control. The continued reliance on the notion of compound growth requires unsustainable levels of consumption which can only be fuelled by unsustainable levels of debt. This would in itself be challenging enough, but, Mason suggests, there is one new factor which transforms everything – the availability, at zero marginal cost, of infinite amounts of information. Previously, the replication of goods to satisfy market demands required the input of labour, energy and raw materials, and the value of any commodity was based ultimately on the amount of labour (including ancillary labour, such as marketing, design and transport) which went into its formation. But now the most significant driver of the developed world's economy is the wide availability of information – MP3 tracks, PDFs, software, news – which is replicated at virtually nil cost and requires no labour input. This abundance of information has, according to Mason, created unprecedented challenges to the capitalist system. As an economist and a journalist, he writes lucidly of complex but fundamental economic ideas – the relationship between the labour theory of value, and the marginal utility theory of value, for example. He sees the upsurge in freely available knowledge through the internet – Wikipedia, common source software such as Linux, videos on YouTube – as a radical innovation which contains within itself the possibility of forming a radically new economic structure which is genuinely post-capitalist. 'I call it Project Zero – because its aims are a zero-carbon energy system; the production of machines, products and services with zero marginal costs; and the reduction of necessary labour time as close as possible to zero...We lie at a moment of possibility: of a controlled transition beyond the free market, beyond carbon, beyond compulsory work.'

Are these writers right? Are we approaching a paradigmatic moment as fundamental as the transitions from ancient imperial power to mediaeval feudalism and from feudalism to capitalism? It could be argued that we are seeing one of those periodic readjustments which are intrinsic to the resilience of capital, marked this time by fundamental innovations which will serve to strengthen the power of the corporations and undermine the power of the nation state. But it can equally be argued that we are simply experiencing the outworking of classic Keynesian stimulus theory, with the stimulus targeted at banks as the motors of the new economics rather than old-fashioned public investment.

Certainly, the view from Waterloo is one of steadily rising tower blocks, rents, property prices, incomes and opportunities for those in the upper echelons of the economy, and stagnation for those at the bottom. The view also includes increasingly atomised young people whose identity is informed as never before by virtual, internet-based reality, and who foresee a future which is less prosperous and more insecure than that of their parents.

Books about economics run a high risk of going out of date, and all four of these were published in 2015, but the indicators they cite remain apposite. Migration has continued to increase. National debt has not decreased, despite strong austerity measures in Britain and sluggish growth in America. But the apparent strength of the Occupy and other resistance movements appears to have dissipated and the radical transformation of society appears little nearer now than it did before the crash. Mason, in common with many Marxist thinkers, seems almost disappointed in the failure of the proletariat to embrace its revolutionary vocation. 'If capitalism must have a beginning, a middle and an end, so must the story of organised labour … it becomes necessary to say something that many on the left will find painful; Marxism got it wrong about the working class.'

Why have revolutionary or even resistance movements run out of steam? Why is the unprecedented rolling back of the state implemented by George Osborne, the UK's former Chancellor of the Exchequer, being implemented with extraordinarily low levels of opposition? It can't only be laid at the door of a weakened Labour party. There appears to be little appetite for large scale resistance to the changes and little ideological or political support for any of the alternatives which represented political orthodoxy until the later years of the last century.

The economist J.K. Galbraith, in his seminal work *The Culture of Contentment*, published in 1991 but still relevant, provides a persuasive analysis. He argues that for the first time in the West, 'haves' began to outnumber 'have nots' in the middle of the 1980's. Recently rising inequality masks the extent to which societies across the world have become richer; in particular, the post-industrial world has produced an expanded middle class which is jealous of its privileges and its comforts. This resonates with Mason's analysis of the underwhelming revolutionary zeal of the working class: '200 years of experience show that [the proletariat] was preoccupied with "living despite capitalism", not overthrowing it'. As a result, argues Galbraith, there is now a democratic presumption against any change that might involve increasing taxes. The contented, the comfortably off, outnumber the discontented, those in need, those who in the past benefited most from the post-war settlements in Britain and the USA. This changed demographic means that there is a powerful presumption against redistribution – the likelihood of election for a political party explicitly committed to higher taxation is minimal.

But is that where the story ends? To come back to where I began: Waterloo. My church, St John's, is creating a new project named 'The Bridge at Waterloo'. It will provide support and training for young unemployed people from low-income backgrounds. Our first course, 'Digital Futures', will give them a month's intensive training in coding, internet and digital skills followed by a placement at a local business and mentoring support into work. The participants are from across faith and ethnic backgrounds, learning together and growing together. We are receiving support from the congregation, from local charities and from Lambeth our local authority. The responses to the course have been universally positive; it's a way of enabling traditionally excluded people to participate in and perhaps transform this new economic world. It's a small project, but it is one of many across London, trying in different ways to create a better future. And there are countless other similar projects across the world.

It does appear that in the struggle between the haves and the have-nots, the haves appear to be in control. As the billionaire business magnate

Warren Buffett once put it: 'there's class warfare, all right, but it's my class, the rich class, that's making war, and we're winning'. But there are alternatives; and, in their own particular way, all four of these books argue that other futures are possible. With the right encouragement, we may be able to move into a post-West global economy. 'There are,' argues Harvey, 'enough compelling contradictions within capital's domain to foster many grounds for hope.'

HAIL! THE THREE TOMORROWS

Scott Jordan

This is the age of superheroes. Hardly a month goes by without a new superhero flick. If cinema is the engine of empire, as Ziauddin Sardar and Merryl Wyn Davies tell us in *American Terminator*, then a declining empire indicates that the engine itself is in serious trouble. Certainly, the arms race of films between Marvel and DC Comics reflect the deep anxieties and uncertainties of the declining West. However, we must not overlook Hollywood's other output where pertinent signs of how the western future may unfold can also be found.

So here are three much talked about recent films: Quentin Tarantino's *The Hateful Eight*; Jon Favreau's *The Jungle Book* and Coen Brother's *Hail, Caesar!*. The trouble with *The Hateful Eight* is its director whose constant allusion to his past films and violent narratives draws in a very specific audience with a very specific, unfortunate 'popcorn flick', mindset. So we need to overlook the grotesque violence to discern what the film is saying about the West. *The Jungle Book* is not a reiteration of the Orientalised 1967 Disney 'classic'. It is much more than a crowd pleaser or simply a money-factory family movie. The Coen Brothers are famous for having esoteric settings and their characters come together in such insane circumstances that most viewers are left with a vague picture of 'what were they really saying', as if they intended to say anything. But this is a smart film that pays dividends when taken seriously. Indeed, none of these films are simple. And they all have something to say about the future of the West.

All three of these films are distinctly Western, despite their settings. Needless to say, when I speak of East and West, I mean more than the directions. East and West have become concepts, embodiments; and our own Westernness or Easternness distracts us from the forces they have become. All three of these films are also period pieces. Their distinct temporal settings will help us deconstruct their intrinsic western message.

It separates us nicely from our own day to day, minute to minute, Westernness.

The futures offered for the West in these three films nicely complements the three tomorrows of postnormal times. The future is hard to grasp – given that it has no facts, is largely unknown, can move in many different directions, and is always ahead of us.

The three tomorrows framework provides us with a handle to grasp and make sense of the future. It is a methodology for navigating alternatives futures in postnormal times, where contradictions, complexity and chaos are the norm. The three tomorrows of our futures trajectories begin with the extended present. This is simply the present extended into the future. It is based on the (mostly technological) trends already embedded in society; the trends are merely extrapolated from the present into the future, as though the world can be reduced into a straight line graph! The second tomorrow is the familiar futures, the futures that have colonised our imagination thanks to the images, metaphors and even 'visions' of future all around us – from advertisements to science fiction novels and films. When we think of 'the future', say ten, twenty years from now, we tend to think in term of what is familiar to us, the images of the futures we imbibe, the metaphors we use when talking about the future, the portrayals of the future in films like *Blade Runner* (1982), *The Fifth Element* (1997), going all the way back to *Metropolis* (1927). The third tomorrow is the unthought future. It is unthought not because it is unthinkable but because our basic assumptions and axioms prevent us from thinking about it. This future is located in far distance. Throughout the three tomorrows, uncertainty and ignorance rise perpetually taking us into deeper and more confounding levels. Of course, the future cannot be divided into neat chunks: so the three tomorrows sometime emerge simultaneously and reiterate by feeding on each other.

All three of these films are set in a metaphorical (sometimes literal) storms. These storms have one thing in common. When the dust settles, nothing will be the same, a true change will have occurred. The West as we know it is going through a change, a metamorphosis if you will. Will the West fall, will it consume us all? Perhaps even, the West is the change. It is the storm. It is what is happening as time passes. Maybe, when it does hatch from the cocoon it finds itself in, it will be the same – nothing would have changed! Each film gives us a piece of a potential tomorrow, pieces of information that can help us construct a map. Where that map leads us depends on how we use the pieces.

The Hateful Eight, directed by Quentin Tarantino, Screenplay by Quentin Tarantino, The Weinstein Company: New York, 2015.

The Jungle Book, directed by Jon Favreau, Screenplay by Justin Marks, Walt Disney Studios Motion Pictures: Burbank, 2016.

Hail, Caesar! directed by Joel Coen and Ethan Coen, Screenplay by Joel Coen and Ethan Coen, Universal Pictures: Universal City, 2016.

In *Hateful Eight*, we are challenged to take the multiplicity of the West, turn it into an ensemble, trap ourselves in one room, and watch this experiment unfold. The storm of this film is the literal coupe d'état of winter — a blizzard. Shelter is paramount as we learn from the general lifelessness of the Utah mountain's landscape of the opening scenes. Our first sign of civilisation is that of a wood carved crucifix, the beacon of Western morality, almost unrecognisable beneath a thick cloak of snow, the veil of the political right. A barrelling six-horse carriage is brought to a complete stop before a black man with a pile of frozen dead bodies. In the carriage is The Hangman, John Ruth, a bounty hunter, with his captive whom he is en route to deliver to justice in Red Rock. Reluctantly Ruth lets the black man, Major Marquis Warren, a fellow bounty hunter and perceived business competitor, travel with him. We learn that the American Civil War occurred several years before and that America is going through a changing of norms. Now the black man is seen as human being, equality shall come later as Ruth and his captive, Daisy Domergue, struggle to correct their slang to the new terms of political correctness towards addressing Warren. The confusion is only compounded when, in pursuit of shelter, they come across a former Southern Rebel turned supposed Sheriff of their destination, Chris Mannix. Mannix agrees to leave his 'politics' to himself as they continue to the shelter of Minnie's Haberdashery. Upon arriving at the haberdashery, a familiar stop to Warren, there is no Minnie or the usual occupants. Instead, a British executioner, a homesick cowboy, a weathered former Southern General, and a Mexican await them inside. When archetype characters of the modern West are thrown into a room together, a discussion on justice will naturally emerge, followed by inevitable violent conflict.

Trapped in the Haberdashery, we watch as the three c's of complexity, chaos, and contradiction swirl together like the literal storm outside. Ruth represents an objective form of justice while Warren, burdened with experience, sees Justice as more subjective, a classic Western debate. Domergue is the most mysterious character. We do not know her crime, yet are told not to like her. She has been stripped of femininity and of humanity. Mannix is the recently educated and now somewhere between disenchanted and optimistic, a sort of Greek Chorus. In the Haberdashery we have General Smithers, the seemingly quietly dying old traditionalism, embodied here in a former Southern General. Oswaldo Mobray is a British executioner, the representative of the old sophisticated, imperial West. The European who has 'been there, done that' and will pass on, here and there, bits of wisdom to the young America still new to the game of global domination. Joe Gage, is the quiet cowboy, rugged individualism, freed from compassion's snare. Lastly there is Bob, who is immediately singled out as Mexican. He is the minority voice, always the first suspect, but not an imminent threat as he lacks the capacity to be a ring leader. Bob is the quintessential other, emphasised as he fails multiple times to play 'Silent Night' on the piano, hitting the wrong key as Warren and Smithers have a Northerner to Southerner conversation. As all these characters collide and collapse, as do the old paradigms. What comes next is unknown and most likely unrecognisable.

The complexity piles up begetting chaos beginning with Ruth. Ruth is the reformed American hero, with a sharp, never compromising sense of Justice. This results in a short temper and constant suspicion of other humans, for their ideas of justice are far inferior to his own. As Warren explains, most bounty hunters just kill their targets, for it is the easier and safer option. Our British executioner, Oswaldo Mobray, makes an important distinction between sanctioned justice and frontier justice. Frontier justice is simple revenge where the family of a victim kills the murderer without a trial, while sanctioned justice involves a trial and an impartial executioner. Mobray emphasises the necessity of a neutral hangman by saying 'justice delivered without dispassion, is always in danger of not being justice'. Ruth emphasises his own dispassion through his brutal treatment of Domergue, not even considering her a 'woman' so that he is not tempted to go easy on her.

Ruth's struggle with justice is complicated by the post-Civil War sub plot arising between Warren, Mannix, and the Southern General, Smithers. Mannix holds a fan-boy admiration for Smithers both of whom are weary of the former Union Major, Warren. This is the obvious alliance we are given at the beginning. The alliances are complicated when Warren claims to have brutally murdered Smither's son after he attempted to hunt him down several months before. Mannix's attempts to romanticise the Southern cause while also coming to terms with the unconditional surrender result in the chaos that quickly overtakes the haberdashery. While Warren's apparent 'good' is clouded by his presumed hatred of the white man and the other occupants become more mysterious, the only thing that can be trusted is each character's dedication to self-interest. Everyone lies.

The Hateful Eight takes an interesting approach to the known, not known, and the unknown. Generally, the audience is told that they shouldn't believe anyone's story. Even if any of the characters are telling the truth, which cannot be determined within the set parameters of the story, there is a high likelihood of exaggeration. The story the West tells itself, its history which miraculously emerges from Greece and leads straight to the Renaissance, is an exaggeration at best, and a fabrication at worse. Notice how the neo-liberals are now justifying colonialism as a good thing! The tech firms and their digital bounty-hunters, who have accumulated most of the wealth of the world, talk about 'caring economy' and project themselves as compassionate capitalists. There is an interesting detail in the haberdashery's door being broken. To shut the door properly, two nailed boards are required to hold it. This information is unknown until an outsider must initially kick their way in. Even Warren, based on his prior stop, believes this door to still be functional. Yet each time this door is confronted, the knowing insiders yell and sling vulgarity to the unknowing outsiders that the door must first be kicked in and then quickly nailed shut lest everyone inside freeze to death in the process. This is trivial knowledge, yet the knowers of the fact seem so compelled to boisterously reveal it as though it should have been obvious. How like American and Western politics! We treat the unknowers, our own electorates as well as the people of the rest of the world, as ignorant idiots who understand little about the benefits of democracy and capitalism. Facial recognition is another curious point made throughout the film. In a time where cameras were as limited as photographs, Ruth immediately recognises people he's never met based solely on their reputations. Mannix also has this gift as he encounters Smithers. Everyone recognises the prices on the heads of certain occupants once their real names are revealed. An apt description of celebrity obsessed society; and a culture where everything has been commodified. Even refugees are now seen in terms of monetary benefits; and the only salvation for them is to quickly find ways of commodifying their very existence.

The characters of *The Hateful Eight* are not just a microcosm of good old America, but of the West itself. We are given an extrapolated sense of what is happening and is likely to happen if things continue as they are, if business-as-usual is maintained. The extended present, the future over the next decades, is not going to much different – only worse. The most prominent characters in the Western pantheon have lied, and will continue to lie. Witness what happened during the Referendum campaign in Britain: both the remain and leave sides lied profusely. Donald Trump, the Republican candidate for the Presidency, makes up 'facts' as he goes along. We lied to justify the invasion of Iraq; or to use the words of the Chilcot Report used 'confirmation bias' (which, in earlier similar reports was described as being 'economical with the truth'). Our notions of freedom, justice and democracy are fabrications. Hypocrisy is the essence of the West. It has always been thus, *The Hateful Eight* says; and it will be the same, despite the storm, if the present is continuously extended into the future.

The Jungle Book gives us another glimpse of a potential future for the West. Here, the West in all its potential, be that glory or doom, is compacted within a young boy, Mowgli. Mowgli is an orphaned human found by the empathetic panther Bagheera and entrusted to be raised by the wolves. The storm surrounding the inhabitants of the jungle is the potential of man, of what the West can do to the jungle. This is coalesced in the concept of the red flower, which is what the other animals call fire. Fire becomes the metaphor of the destructive power of man or the West including the demoralising nature of democracy and the consumption of capitalism. The story begins in the midst of a dry season when all animals come together before a truce over a watering hole. These animals are normally separated by the food chain and territoriality, but are drawn together in peace due to the necessity of survival. Here, for the first time, the other animals catch a glimpse of the man-cub, Mowgli. The most fearsome of animals goes in for a drink. This is Shere Khan, a tiger bearing the scar, proof positive, of the imminent danger mankind presents to the jungle. Shere Khan demands the man-cub be turned over to him at the beginning of the next monsoon season for he must eliminate the threat posed by Mowgli. While the wolves protest and refuse, Bagheera admits that it is for the best of the rest, that the man-cub rejoins his own kind.

In the modern context, *The Jungle Book* provides a wonderful allegory for the Western military presence in the Middle East, specifically US operations in the region. When the allegory is analyzed from this perspective, an interesting look at the postnormal condition of the region can be derived. Mowgli does not as one might assume represent US Forces in Afghanistan or Iraq, for he only arrives in these circumstances by accident. Rather the Red Flower itself is the threat of destabilisation that is seen through the introduction of war, democracy, capitalism, or secularisation. Mowgli instead represents the postnormal condition of the region. What happens if the Middle East embraces the West? We watch Mowgli react in a variety of ways and the potentials that exist for his corruption or flourishing.

The other inhabitants of the jungle represent the various reactions to the introduction of the West in the Middle East. Shere Khan makes a ready metaphor for extremist groups, currently and most predominantly, ISIS. Shere Khan's occupation of the Wolf Territory and overthrowing of their alpha gives us an interesting view of the conflict in Syria and Iraq. Bagheera on the other hand represents a more rounded character, the aged and wise Arab. Bagheera knows the story of Muhammad, remembers the various empires that have risen and fallen in the Crescent, and will never forget Faisal's betrayal at Versailles. Bagheera has seen the development of Turkey and Egypt, watched in dismay over the creation of Israel, and fought with the Mujahedeen to repel the Soviets. He is open to Western ideas, but cautious of their damning potential. Faithful and loyal, he is a friend to other animals and wise enough to know what sacrifices must be made. As such, Bagheera and Shere Khan are natural enemies, but both aspire for the same end. The complication of their beliefs and experiences have driven them apart resulting in contradictory attempts at the final end. Mowgli becomes lost along the way confronting the python Kaa. Kaa represents the unvoiced, simply hoping to survive. Kaa may remind us of the groups left over in the wake of ISIS's rise, or the groups who play both sides just to see the next day. Mowgli is saved by an opportunistic bear, Baloo. Baloo is economic opportunity and often the war profiteer. Baloo saves Mowgli's life, but asks for his engineering experience to assist him in acquiring honey. The honey is the capital to be had in the Middle East. Oil profits, resources in the Middle East and Africa, the profits to be made on perpetuating wars all are good in the mind of Baloo, seen as his 'bare necessities,' an ironic sense of the phrase. Finally, King Louie, the most evolutionarily similar to Mowgli hopes to use him to become the new king of the jungle. His song, 'I want to be like you,' is a familiar sentiment of the states of old in the Middle East. The House of Saud, the Baathists, the Shahs, and the Israeli's cunning use of Western alliances and mechanisms have helped them hold a firm grasp on power in the region. Finally, there are the elephants. They are seen as gods or the true creators of the world to the inhabitants of the jungle. Perhaps they represent the Sufi mystics, but I'd more metaphorically apply them to the spirit of Islam, or more generally faith, untouched by Western concepts.

This story brings to light a second tomorrow for the West that of the Familiar Future. Essentially, *The Jungle Book* asks if there could exist a future where Western concepts and the Islamic Identity of the Middle East could coexist in harmony. We can see this by looking into a couple of the interactions which take place in the film. Bagheera, though at first quite opposed to his influence on Mowgli, comes to not only work together with, but befriend Baloo. Baloo, the perfect capitalist, a master of accumulation who can commodify anything, even ideas and beliefs. How could the wise Arab find the war profiteer a redeeming character? Baloo must abandon the rigid demoralising character of commodification and understand the lines that must be drawn between accumulation and the safe guarding of the environment and the livelihood of his fellow beings. After all, the capitalist alone cannot accumulate for the game of capitalism requires players to play it. An interesting scene seems to distract from the core of the film when one of the young elephants becomes trapped in a pit.

Mowgli and the other animals know well that the elephants are to be left to their own affairs, interference is seen as disrespectful and law breeching. Mowgli, although he is scolded earlier in the film for using his hands to make simple machines (for that is not the way of the Wolf!), decides to intervene and help the young elephant. Everyone looks in awe as Mowgli devises a pulley to lift the elephant out of the pit. The elephants give a profound demonstration of gratitude to Mowgli. Can religion and Western technology and ideals mix in a progressive and productive fashion? Must they be natural enemies or instead can they counter act each other's flaws? Lastly, there is a moment when Mowgli learns the destructive power and haunting allure of the red flower. He thinks that he can use this power to destroy Shere Khan, thus freeing the jungle. As a result, Mowgli nearly destroys the entire forest and comes no closer to having rid it of the scourge of Shere Khan. Perhaps, this demonstrates that the war against ISIS will not be won the Western way. In fact perhaps to see it as a war is the incorrect response. After all, ISIS was born out of handling things in a strictly Western fashion.

The Jungle Book suggests that a future can be shaped with the familiar tropes of western worldview and Muslim culture. This future may be familiar but it can still be better – given there is open and transparent debate and discussion on how Islam and the West can come to some form of reconciliation. But there are hazards too. Western concepts have a tendency to domesticate all other ways of being. It can all end in a gigantic fire! The potentials of this tomorrow are finely balanced with its inherent threats.

So to Coen Brothers. *Hail, Caesar!* is a quirky and imaginative movie. We follow Eddie Mannix, an executive at Capitol Pictures, the one man holding a major film studio together. He is the quintessential fixer and works round the clock and behind the scenes to make sure the films are produced without kinks, the circus of actors is kept happy, and their secrets hidden from the press. Like *The Hateful Eight*, we begin with religious undertones. Mannix in the confession booth of the local Catholic Church. We learn it has been less than twenty-four hours since his last confession and the priest hearing him has nothing new to offer. We also learn that he has been offered a sweet deal, a lucrative position with the Lockheed Corporation.

As we follow Mannix in a yet another day of trying to hold the present world together, he is faced with a number of complex challenges. His biggest actor, Baird Whitlock, has been kidnapped from the set of the studio's epic production, *Hail, Caesar!* Mannix has to negotiate his return with the captors who refer to themselves as 'The Future'. Meanwhile, his starlight actress, one of the most beautiful women in Hollywood and a role model for women everywhere, DeeAnna Moran, has become pregnant out of wedlock. At the same time, Mannix is trying to launch the career of the untalented, pretty boy Hobie Doyle; he has imposed Doyle on the director extraordinaire, Laurence Laurentz, who is working on his new film set in the upper echelons of society.

The storm of *Hail Caesar!* is less obvious than the other two films, but it is just as dangerous. It comes in the form of twin reporters, competing for the latest scoop that promises to bleed and therefore lead the front page. The storm is also seen in the two-fold setting of the film. First is the Red Scare and the fear of communism and communist infiltration of the United States, the period within which the film is set. Second, in terms of Hollywood, this is a pivotal period in the history of the American film industry. The studio system appeared to be a dying animal awaiting its fate. Writers were wising up and demand more while the public was beginning to realise that Hollywood's attempts to pour money into their grand epics was a veil that could not cover the vastly diminished quality and flagrant racism and sexism of the art. The setting of film is beautifully postnormal – with the accent on contradictions and chaos generated in Mannix's life by events which are totally out of his control. He is a gambling man, a mortal man, and lives within the constraints of his own ability. He must know what he can know; yet even the knowledge he acquires leaves him utterly powerless to manage and control the events unfolding around him.

Mannix is forced to use an insane level of creativity to fix the constantly multiplying and fractioning events within the studio. At first, his solutions are simple. He has an inexhaustible amount of resources at his disposal; money and influence are his source of power and provide a way of getting what he wants. Writing checks, misleading the press, and checking in high profile individuals in a bind; 'cleaning up' is routine, everyday work for him. But simple solutions often produced complex results. For Ms Moran's situation, he first attempts to simply have the birth father marry her before the child's birth. When he finds that the famous German director who is the birth father is already married, he must find another method. He speaks with legal aids to have Ms Moran disappear through the later stages of pregnancy and have her child anonymously put up for adoption. After the birth, she will adopt her own child and her reputation will not only be left intact, but possibly lifted in light of this 'compassion'. To retrieve Whitlock, he simply gives the captors, proclaiming themselves The Future, the ransom they desire in a briefcase. But the briefcase proves to be too small for the ransom's amount in cash. As he struggles to close the briefcase, he is forced to simultaneously to deal with famed director Laurentz's inability to coach Doyle, who has demonstrated a thick ineptitude towards the art of acting. To solve the briefcase issue, Mannix request Doyle's belt, thus revealing the whole Whitlock situation to him. Doyle turns out to be quite perceptive and tells Mannix that the most suspicious persons on a set are the extras; and the kidnappers must be amongst them. In fact, it turns out to be an extra who led the first phase of the plan behind Whitlock's kidnapping. Lastly, Mannix must continue his constant, never ending, misdirection of the press, represented as twin sisters. On this day, the sisters happen to have their hands on a potentially devastating lead which suggests that the secret to Whitlock's rise to stardom is the result of a sexual relationship with Laurentz during a past production. At first, Mannix gives the sisters a weaker lead, but emphasises its exclusivity, hinting at a relationship between Doyle and another starlet. When the lead's temporary distraction runs out, Mannix's sources reveal that the devastating lead was procured by a Communist sympathiser and defector. Things, and the narrative, continues to get more and more complex.

An interesting interplay occurs between Mannix's fairly fool-proof plans and the unexpected moments, over which Mannix has no power, that end up taking full control of the situations. Mannix thinks the case is closed on Ms Moran and her child. Instead of letting his complicated bait and switch play out, Ms Moran falls head over heels in love with the agent hired to play the custodian of her child until she adopts it. A simple solution proved to be the answer, but it was not of Mannix's doing. Again out of his control, Doyle's adept perception pays off as he sees the ransom trade off while at dinner and follows the case to a beach home where Whitlock is being held. Doyle sneaks in and takes Whitlock back home just before the police arrive which would have turned the whole kidnapping into an unavoidable media circus. However, during his time with The Future, Whitlock is persuaded of the truth of Communism, and comes to respect his kidnappers – some of whom are major players in the film business.

At the film's climax, Mannix is left with all of his conflicts hopelessly unresolved with a time clock ticking on his deal with the Lockheed Corporation, the productions of Laurentz's next feature and 'Hail, Caesar!' on the rocks, and the media's pressure getting ever so close to ruining the studio's reputation. Even his meeting with members of the various faiths, Christians and Jews falls apart. They are brought together to review the script for *Hail, Caesar!*, which overall is a picture about Jesus Christ. Is the content liable to be seen as blasphemous, Mannix wants to know. But instead of offering useful theological advice on the depiction of Christ, the religious leaders are more concerned with film criticism.

At the story's conclusion, it appears that Mannix has defeated the paradigm shattering events thrown at him. But the events represent the unthought. Mannix's simple actions unleash events he had not imagined, indeed cannot imagine. The unthought is beautifully fragile, so much so that it is slave to infinity of possibilities and randomness that awaits the unknown. It defies all methods and tools presently available – and therein lies the challenge. Film, and art in general, in being locus of creativity and perspective morphing, is the idea medium for investigating the unthought. Mannix survives the unthought by sheer luck, or as the film partially suggests, the hand of God!

We seemed to end where we started. This is a classic move used in other films by the Coen brothers. Though, the audience cannot be satisfied with all the work done in over two hours being undone by the time the credits role. After all, the characters have undergone drastic changes. The immediate fear is that the West, its methods and systems, is here to stay and will survive any tumult the world can throw its way. However, upon reflection, Mannix, our main character, though not readily demonstrated in a nice Marvel-esque post-credit scene, has gone through change. With Whitlock safely back at the studio, and purged of his communist sympathy, we prepare for the most expensive scene of *Hail, Caesar!*. This is where his character meets Christ. But Whitlock forgets his line. Another take will be required. Perhaps in the end, the West will reappear in another take, different in its presumptuous, arrogant, and ignorant face. Now there is an unthought that needs some reflection.

Needless to say, the three tomorrows these films present are not, in any shape or form, predictions about the future of the West or commentaries on where the West goes from here. I see them as a contribution to the greater polylogue needed on the West, the East, and the world writ large. From *The Hateful Eight* we learn the necessity of restructuring the Western dialogue. The narrative of the West has been framed within a discourse of justice since time in memorial; and its application has not only failed in the West itself but is not so easily translated onto other cultures and norms. For a new discussion at least the fundamental precedents taken for granted need revision and updating. In *The Hateful Eight*, we watch the stripping of femininity and personhood seen in Domergue's and Bob's characters. Feminism and appreciations of the other have and continue to plague the Western dialogue on Justice creating the problems of poverty, inequality, and ideological warfare that should not be passed onto the rest of the world needlessly. *The Jungle Book* continues, begging that we investigate further what it is to be Western. Is the West the global 'bad guy'? If so, is there any chance of redemption? Can the discussion of the West in the world take into account the East, the other, and the motives (each being rather specific to time and place)? The potential polylogue, the other beasts of the jungle given speaking parts, presents us with endless possibilities. In *Hail Caesar!*, we are asked to evaluate what we know, what we don't know, and what is truly powerful. No one, not even the chief executive of a Hollywood studio, is all powerful.

Tomorrow the sun may in fact rise as it always has. But it is obvious that the West as the valiant cowboy will not ride into the sunset. Only through a great polylogue, that involves all of us, can we find our way out of the jungle's darkness; and hopefully into the warm embrace of a better tomorrow.

HISTORIC ENCOUNTERS

Tamim Sadikali

With George W. Bush's 'War on Terror' now looking like a war without end, recent years have delivered an expected slew of ignominious 'Muslim' stories. Undoubtedly, the medieval theatre of ISIS, in all its fifty shades of black, takes top billing. One spin-off that caught the eye, however, was the extra-judicial killing of the young Britons, Reyaad Khan and Ruhul Amin. Khan, 21, was a bright student with keen interest in politics and wanted to be Britain's first Asian Prime Minister. The trajectory from wannabe PM, to tweeting from Syria that 'the brother that executed James Foley should be the new Batman', captures the very essence of today's malaise. Indeed, nothing says 'post-postmodern' quite like the home-grown terrorist. No one could have predicted, or imagined, such a transformation in a young Muslim man?

On reading *Britain Through Muslim Eyes*, a compendium on the decidedly pre-modern Muslim-British exchange, one realises that what we see as new, unchartered territory, is often old ground. A 1918 short story, 'Between Ourselves', explored by Claire Chambers concerns a young Egyptian, Abbas Lutfi Suleyman. It was written by the noted translator of the Qur'an, Muhammad Marmaduke Pickthall. Abbas starts off as an admirer of the British mission in Egypt, but the rose-tinted spectacles soon fall from his eyes. He travels to London, and from a seedy Bayswater bedsit, 'constructs an identity for himself' as 'representative of the Egyptian nation'; and transforms himself into 'a well-known and fiery speaker'. Eventually, the fictional Abbas becomes 'completely disillusioned with Britain, goes into exile in Paris, becomes a terrorist, and is finally imprisoned'. Slam-dunk.

Claire Chambers, *Britain Through Muslim Eyes*, Palgrave Macmillan, London, 2015

A main point keeps re-surfacing as one reads *Britain Through Muslim Eyes*: the oscillation between excitement and ennui, opportunity and brick-wall is, for the Muslim in Britain, a path already well-trodden. The temptation, especially for young eyes, is to view one's own situation as unique – exceptional. But what Chambers shows us is that young Muslims in the West – in Britain – have always been pulled by opposing, and yet equally irrepressible forces. Indeed, she distils the British Muslim headspace on the very first page, following an excerpt from the King of Persia's 1873 *Safarnama*, or travelogue, of his state tour to Europe. After attending a Fire Brigade drill, the Shah cuts his praise for British 'celerity and agility in... saving men from death', with a wry observation of their ingenuity in building 'cannons, muskets, projectiles, and similar things, for the quicker and more multitudinous slaughter of the human race'. Chambers concludes that 'the Shah evinces simultaneous admiration and scepticism towards his British hosts'. Frankly, for all the academic tomes, think-tank papers, op-eds, pulp fiction and sombre volumes written on the British-Muslim 'clusterfuck', as the military types say, that one sentence, in a nutshell, is it. Given that Chambers is herself non-Muslim, her commentary is often so precise as to be unnerving. On describing another Pickthall short story, 'Karàkter' (1911) – wherein a 14-year-old Ahmed is dispatched to a British public school to develop 'Karàkter' (character) – Chambers comments: 'Ahmed next goes to Cambridge, where he tries to acculturate by buying a dog, but cannot get over an Islamic sense of defilement in its presence'. Quite.

The book's arrangement is broadly chronological, starting with accounts of Muslim travellers to Britain from as early as the late 1700s. We begin with a lightning tour of the Muslim-British exchange from even earlier – from before the European Renaissance. And how arresting – and important – it is to read of Britons such as Adelard of Bath (1080–1152) who 'went to Turkey, determined to learn from the Muslims rather than kill them under the sign of the cross'.

The first in-depth account is that of Mirza Sheikh l'tesamuddin (1730-1800), who wrote what is probably the first book by a Muslim about experiences in Britain. His manuscript, the *Shigarf-nama-'i Vilayat*, was produced some time between 1780 and 1784. Like most of the earliest travellers, l'tesamuddin was educated and from a privileged strata of society – in his case, Indian. He receives a mixed reception in England. The English had 'never seen an Indian wearing such opulent clothing, because they are only used to poorly-dressed lascars, so there is much gawking. He is even expected to dance for a group who mistake him for a performer'. Eventually, he claims to receive 'great kindness and hospitality' from the English and to be treated 'like an old acquaintance'. Later, we learn of the praise he showers on the British landscape and architecture, their technological advancement and even their women who he finds 'lovely as *houris*'. But he complains about their 'scepticism and atheism'. Poignantly, his time in Britain ends on a sour note, as he falls out with Captain Swinton, a close friend both during his British trip and in India beforehand, in part 'because of Swinton's increasing anti-Muslim invective'. As Chambers notes, 'the Englishman is guilty of jokey microaggressions towards his Indian friend, teasing him about specifically Islamic practices'. Nowadays, it would be called 'Islamophobia and the mutual incomprehension that exists between believing Muslims and the dominant irreligious British majority'.

That strikes a chord: of a Young Gun who came, saw, but didn't quite conquer. At the risk of over-projecting, one sees someone who entered a secular space, wanting both to preserve – protect – his communal identity, and hand-in-hand, to wrestle with and indeed enjoy the new environment. But ultimately, it does not play out quite so smoothly. And as Chambers correctly points out, that trajectory is far from being historic.

History is never dead, as is evidenced by the battles over what we teach children. Was the British Empire a benign, even a benevolent force, or simply the start of a project for dominion over land, resource, people, hearts and minds, whose tentacles reach out to the present day? 'Never again,' says Britain on the subjects of totalitarianism and genocide: hence the push to keep the Holocaust alive in everyone's memory. But history can only influence one's understanding of past and present, to the extent that it is known. And this is the essence of Chambers' volume: she breathes life into the lives and work of early travellers, who we ought to know and appreciate.

How many will have heard of Dean Sake Mahomed, owner of Britain's first Indian restaurant — The Hindostanee Coffee House? He published *The Travels of Dean Mahomet* in 1794, an English-language account of his journey through Northern India, intended for a British audience. What is noteworthy about both his account, and his life in Britain and Ireland, is how he seems to have become a self-taught master of public relations. We learn that to further his various enterprises — which included opening up vapour baths, introducing Indian massages and eventually being appointed 'Shampooing Surgeon' to George IV and William IV — Mohamed 'styles for himself a layered identity', and 'soft-pedals his Muslim background', but is also 'prepared to explain and defend Islam to an Orientalist audience'. For all intents and purposes, Dean Sake Mohamed was the first poster-boy for multiculturalism — the first to consciously cultivate a part-Western and part-Eastern identity, with a moderate Islamic base.

Out of all the earliest accounts Chambers examines none illustrates better the split-personality tendencies of the religious journeyman than that written by Mirza Abu Taleb Khan (1752–1806). An aristocratic Shia with ancestry in Iran (though emotionally attached to India), his innate elitism buffered him, and made him indefatigable when confronted with hostility. He is 'attacked on the apparent unreasonableness and childishness of some Mohammedan customs', but this does not dent his self-confidence. Because of his titled background, he is treated with warmth and flattery. He goes to the opera, masquerade balls, and the theatre in the company of British nobility. He is even entertained by George III and Queen Charlotte. But none of this disturbs his fundamental world view. In his journal, he brazenly 'enumerates 12 national character defects of the British: their lack of religion and morality, pride and blind faith in their good fortune, passion for acquiring material objects ... misplaced vanity, selfishness, living beyond their means at the expense of others, and prejudice towards other customs while remaining blind to their own imperfections.' Were he alive today, he would surely be forced onto some de-radicalisation programme. Despite his undeniable attachment to Shia Islam, he gets drunk with new friends in Ireland and, 'like l'tesamuddin, Abu Taleb apostrophises the beauty of English women'. While regularly describing wine as 'excellent' and having an obvious eye for the ladies, Abu Taleb does not 'go native'. Rather, he is 'comfortable with his Islamic heritage and views Christian habits sometimes with admiration, at other moments pitying amusement', and even 'as spiritual corruption'. Dare I say, Abu Taleb personifies the timeless, classic-cut British Muslim.

The first Muslim woman to visit and write about Britain was Atiya Fyzee (1877–1967). She came as a single woman of nearly thirty to study at the Maria Grey teacher training college. While studying at the college, she wrote a string of letters to her sisters about her European experience. The letters were serialised in an Urdu women's journal and eventually published in 1921. Atiya was an independent traveller and recognisably modern but she wore the veil: 'I have continued wearing my Indian clothes and do not intend to ever give them up. When I go out I cover my head ... with a gauze cloth. Everything is covered except the face ... Everyone appreciates that I have kept my ways in the English world'. She does not seek to assimilate by wearing fashionable European dress. 'She finds a woman who has done just that, absurd.' The veil gives her freedom. When she goes to see the then famous English contralto Clara Butt sing, she is filled with pity. 'God knows how she can bind herself and sing in such a constricted state, and that too with a smile. These people bear all kinds of tortures for the sake of appearance.'

The real payload in this excellent book is the emphasis on the fact that the push and pull between Islam and the secular world is nothing new. Almost every account, fictional or otherwise, describes some variation on the same theme: with the Muslim in Britain forever bouncing between fascination and isolation, intoxication and a biting sobriety, an irresistible attraction and outright disgust. And astutely, Chambers points out, how Muslims have wrestled with that difference is as much – if not more – about education, class and the degree of amity or hostility they face, than religiosity. And from this new vista, today's British Muslim mire begins to look different. My own generation not only experienced the harsh end of old-school racism, but also lived through the disintegration of stock identities, such as 'Asian', before reconstituting others. Some formed for themselves a vacuum-sealed Islamic milieu, whilst others threw out every inherited identity to blend in. But just like l'tesamuddin, Atiya Fyzee and the Muslim travellers who followed in their wake, most couldn't – can't

— deny the irresistible pull of each. But without the class, education and confidence of their forebears, many are left disorientated, like a compass needle spinning round and round, searching endlessly for magnetic north. They have no option but to navigate modernity alone. Like everyone else, they are at the mercy of whimsical winds. Same as it ever was.

ET CETERA

ON RADICAL HOPE

Hassan Mahamdallie

There is one book that for some reason I am compelled, every so often, to return to. I don't fully understand why – I just know that it must somehow connect with something buried somewhere in my subconscious. I'm not talking about a familiar book that gives me pleasure, I mean a book that creates a disturbance in me.

It's a short book and it's called *Radical Hope: Ethics in the Face of Cultural Devastation*, authored by a social scientist and philosopher named Jonathan Lear. He tells the story of the disappeared world of the Native American Crow nation, through the recollections and reflections of the first nation's last great leader, Plenty Coups, who died in 1932 in his native Montana at the age of eighty-four. A few years before his death, Plenty Coups was interviewed at length by journalist and politician Frank Linderman, who devoted most of his later life to recording stories and memories of Native American Indians. Linderman turned the conversations into a biography, *Plenty Coups: Chiefs of the Crows* (1930), which is regarded as a classic. Plenty Coups' life spanned the nomadic freedom of his plentiful 'Buffalo Days' to the time when what was left of his people were corralled into reservations and all that happened in-between. In a note at the end of his biography, Linderman tells the reader that he was unable to get Plenty Coups to talk about anything that happened after the Crow were confined to a reservation. 'Plenty Coups refused to speak', he writes, 'of his life after the passing of the Buffalo, so that his story seems to have been broken off, leaving many years unaccounted for. "I have not told you half of what happened when I was young", he said when urged to go on… "But when the Buffalo went away the hearts of my people fell to the ground, and they could not lift them up again. After this nothing happened"'.

Jonathan Lear takes Plenty Coups' final sentence and interrogates it for 150 pages: Did he mean he didn't want to talk about it, that it depressed him, that it was an inconsequential time in his life compared to life before? Or was Plenty Coups saying that literally nothing happened. That time had stopped, and the Crow people had toppled over the abyss and into a nothingness? As Lear asks, 'What if his remark went deeper? What if it gave expression to an insight into the structure of temporality: that at a certain point things stopped happening? What would he have meant if he meant that?'

One of the aggravating features of the post-9/11 landscape we inhabit is a new strident ideological intolerance of the diversity of the human culture and societies, mirroring the destruction of the Earth's bio-diversity as part of what some are now calling the Anthropocene epoch: a new planetary age defined by human activity. It is a paradox of our times that assertions of the civilisational superiority of the West, and its representation as the historical zenith of human development, grow in inverse proportion to the destruction wreaked upon those put to the neo-liberal sword emanating from the West's economic model. This intolerance is clearly an integral part of the Islamophobia rooting itself in Europe and America. It manifests itself on the elevation of ignorance, small-mindedness and disregard of reality to the level of principle. I guess Donald Trump is a grotesque living symbol of this. Another more mundane example would be UK Conservative Party Michael Gove's declaration, when confronted with some inconvenient truths during Britain's EU 'Brexit' referendum, that 'people in this country have had enough of experts!'.

This is, of course, part of an older narrative that has its roots in the first phase of Western expansion: colonialism, the expropriation of the land of indigenous peoples and their forced assimilation into the world order. Plenty Coups, is in part, unconsciously echoing that dark description 'terra nullius' (no one's land) that early British colonisers employed to describe the landmass we know as Australia; a concept later used to justify their terrible genocidal war on its original inhabitants, powerfully narrated in Robert Hughes's foundational text *The Fatal Shore* and subsequent accounts.

Some on the extreme right celebrate this bloody past, as Nathan Lean in his excellent, but scary, book *The Islamophobia Industry* points out. Lean shines a light on one particularly unpleasant character on the American Islamophobia scene – Bryan Fischer of the evangelical American Family Association. In between describing Muslims as parasites who should convert or die, Fischer likes to take a stroll through history along paths Plenty Coups would not recognise. In a 2011 blog he extolled the example of the seventeenth century Native American Indian Pocahontas – in a version of her life depicted by the execrable 1995 Disney cartoon. According to Fischer, Pocahontas exemplified the correct behaviour of a native when faced with English settlers in what became known as Virginia: courageously saving the life of one of them (John Smith) from a cruel death at the hands of her father, converting to Christianity, changing her name (to Rebecca), marrying another Englishman (Thomas Rolfe), having his child, and thereafter living with him in matrimonial bliss amongst the civilised race, thus saving her soul from the hellfire. 'It's arresting to think of how different the history of the American settlement and expansion could have been if the other indigenous people had followed Pocahontas' example,' Fischer mused. And went on to declare: 'She not only recognised the superiority of the God whom the colonists worshipped over the gods of her native people, she recognised the superiority... of their culture and adopted the patterns and language as her own. In other words, she both converted and assimilated...Had the other indigenous people followed her example, their assimilation into what became America could have been seamless and bloodless. Sadly, it was not to be.'

Sadness doesn't really cover the outcome of what The Smithsonian Institute calls the 200-year 'American Indian Genocide' that resulted in the wiping out, through a combination of European-borne diseases, dispossession, massacres and forced assimilation, of 80–90 per cent of the indigenous population of America. Fischer's Pocahontas Good Indian/Bad Indian yarn fits snugly with the Good Muslim/Bad Muslim binary we are supposed to inhabit. For those lured by the promised blissful rewards of Good Muslim conformity it is worth considering Pocahontas' actual fate. It was certainly no Disney Cinderella ending. In reality, as Ziauddin Sardar points out in his detailed and forensic analysis of Disney's *Pocahontas*, she was kidnapped by the settlers and was a captive when she converted to

Christianity. Her first husband, Kocoum, was killed by the settlers, and she suffered a nervous breakdown after becoming pregnant as a result of being raped by one of her English captors. She most likely had to marry Rolfe (who was not the father of her child) as a condition of her release from captivity. Rolfe then took her to England in 1616 as part of his propaganda campaign to get more financial and military support for his tobacco venture in Virginia, which was later to become the forced destination for generations of enslaved Africans. The unfortunate woman was exhibited for the titillation of London high society and royalty, living with Rolfe for a time in the godforsaken London suburb of Brentford, before dying a year later, aged 22, possibly of smallpox or dysentery. Pocahontas was buried in the aptly named estuary town of Gravesend, probably the first victim of Stockholm syndrome. Had she known that four centuries later, notes Robert Steinback of the Southern Anti-Poverty Law Center, that 'a bigot like Bryan Fischer would state that her people deserved to be eradicated from the continent because they didn't follow her example of deference and submission to the English, she might have let her father execute John Smith after all.'

It may be unfashionable now, given the excesses of postmodernism, to suggest that we need to return to some sort of cultural relativism, but I do think that before we judge a particular culture, society or civilisation and slot it into a civilisational hierarchy, we ought to acknowledge that we too are products or our own culture. In short, just because we believe we represent 'the best of all possible worlds' doesn't mean that it's true. Long before postmodernism, the founding father of modern anthropology and social science, Franz Boas, struggled against this superior world-view during the 1920s and 1930s. 'The value which we attribute to our civilisation is due to the fact that we participate in this civilisation,' he wrote. 'But it is certainly conceivable that there may be other civilisations, based perhaps on different traditions and on a different equilibrium of emotion and reason which are of no less value than ours.'

Boaz is a rather interesting figure. He was born in 1858 in Minden, Germany, into a middle class secular Jewish family, and was clearly sensitive from an early age to the ramifications of notions of innate European racial and cultural superiority which were emerging in Germany and elsewhere on the continent at the end of the nineteenth century. At university, Boaz initially studied mathematics and physics, however Robert Wald Sussman, in his recent book *The Myth of Race*, recounts that Boaz's academic studies then evolved towards an examination of indigenous people (famously the Netsilik Inuit of Baffin Island), and concerns about 'how to conserve indigenous people and the urgent need to obtain knowledge from and about them, since he foresaw the rapid disappearance of their way of life'. Boaz's fieldwork led him to appreciate that the worth of any society lay far beneath the veneer of civilisation: 'I often ask myself what advantages our "good society" possesses over that of the "savages" and find, the more I see of their customs, that we have no right to look down upon them.' In 1886 Boaz moved permanently to New York, where he became a professor at Columbia University. In the decades that followed, Boaz became a central figure in the struggle to wrest anthropology away from those – largely teaching and working at Harvard University – who used pseudo-scientific methods such as eugenics to justify inequalities, principally the racial hierarchy embedded in American society (the curse of which remains today, explicitly expressed in the name of the new US civil rights movement: 'Black Lives Matter'). Boaz was tragically vindicated when the theories of the eugenicists and racial purists he was arguing against fed directly into the Nazi movement, culminating in the Holocaust of Europe's Jews.

In such works as *The Mind of Primitive Man* (1938), Boaz widened his gaze to encompass global processes such as colonisation. He asks what might have been the progression of particular countries if they had been spared colonialisation and had instead been allowed to develop independently? As he put it: 'The rapid dissemination of Europeans over the whole world destroyed all promising beginnings which had arisen in various regions.'

There is no one template for human development, with universal ideals being the sole property of the West. To point this out is not to deny historical progress, or even to refute the contribution of the European Enlightenment, rather it is a prerequisite for the emergence of a universality which can encompass the totality of human achievement and its future potential.

One should also point out that much of the contemporary 'Muslim world', partly because it defines itself in opposition to the Western project, tends to mirror the discourse of civilisational and historical 'nothingness' identified by Plenty Coups. 'Muslim progress' is always just that, whereas Western progress is a damned lie. In general, we seem to have little time for history or peoples that fall outside the 'Muslim' narrative. For example, most of us seem happy to consign the pre-Islamic Arab world to the void we call *Jahiliyyah* – a state or time of ignorance. In a sense Muslims have been encouraged by preachers and ideologues to internalise *Jahiliyyah* – as though ignorance of others, their beliefs, cultures and histories, equates to some kind of spiritual purity. How then can we assert our difference from the Trumps and Goves of the world? Even those of us, particularly in the West, who are interested in history seem content with versions of a linear narrative that starts with Medina and ends with the fall of the Ottoman Empire. It's a top-down Kings and Queens history that we decry when imposed on our children in British schools. We proudly talk about Al Andalus's *convivencia*, where all were tolerated, but what did it actually mean to be a 'tolerated' Jew in Granada during Muslim rule? We know about the biographies of Islamic rulers, philosophers, religious scholars and jurists during Islam's 'golden' era, but what did it mean to be a Christian herder or a shoemaker, or a Muslim woman agriculturalist or concubine in Islamic Spain? How many Plenty Coups were tipped into nothingness as part of the expansion of Islam after the death of the Prophet, during the Muslim invasion of Spain, the expansion of the Ottoman Empire or the consolidation of the Mughals in India? In India there has been the emergence of a school of history called 'subaltern studies' that looks at Indian history and society from the bottom-up. Where is such a movement amongst Islamic scholars? I'm sure there are academics and historians doing this kind of work, but they are not widely known or recognised, at least outside their academic field. How can we know how many 'promising beginnings' were also destroyed by the expansion of Islam and the Muslim world?

How many ancient civilisations are being exterminated today in the name of Islam? Novelist and essayist Amin Maalouf, in his thoughtful but angry treatise, *Disordered World*, highlights the plight of the Mandaeans, or Sabaeans, named in the Qur'an as *al-sabi'a*, a 'people of the book', who have clung onto their way of life for the past fourteen centuries on the banks of the Tigris, south of Baghdad. In 2007 Maalouf discovered that the Sabaeans were being persecuted out of existence by religious fanaticism:

'Zealous preachers now denied them the status that the Islamic holy book had clearly granted them. In Fallujah, terrified families had been forcibly converted at knife-point; in Baghdad and throughout the country, the Mandaeans had been chased from their jobs, expelled from their homes and seen their shops looted.' In 2002, the population stood at around 30,000 across Iraq. By 2008, only 6,000 remained. No one knows how many there are in Iraq today. Some thousands were dispersed throughout the region. Others were given asylum abroad, in the UK, the USA and Australia, with the largest group, 7,000, given sanctuary in Sweden. But, as Maalouf says, 'they have little chance of surviving as a community. In a few years its language will no longer be spoken, and its rituals will be reduced to a sham. A culture that lasted over a thousand years will have disappeared as we looked on indifferently'. Is there somewhere in the world a Sabaean equivalent of Plenty Coups – looking over the abyss into nothingness – thanks to 'al-Islam'!

We may be entering a PostWest era, although the West clearly still dominates militarily, economically and culturally, even if it has lost forever its moral and civilisational legitimacy. But we are also entering the Anthropocene era, marked by an ecological crisis that may be already beyond recovery. However, for many peoples in recent human history, including Plenty Coups, the tipping point has already occurred. And so we must return to grasp the title of Jonathan Lear's meditation on Plenty Coups: *Radical Hope*. Indeed.

SAMIA RAHMAN'S TOP TEN POSTWEST FILMS

Much like Zayn Malik's 'shock' departure from One Direction, one of the world's least well-kept secrets is the unfailing power of American concerns to inform Hollywood's film-making machine. This western bastion of cultural imperialism has long been able to spread its tentacles across the entire globe, cultivating our perceptions of beauty, success, justice and social convention. Hollywood celebrities are revered to the extent that when Paul Walker, star of the *Fast and the Furious* crime action franchise, was tragically killed in a car accident in 2013 (in true macabre irony the car in which Walker was a passenger was being driven very fast and very furiously), days before the death of anti-apartheid revolutionary and former president of South Africa Nelson Mandela, my trusty barometer of opinion within my social bubble, Facebook, was littered with laments from anguished teenagers in Pakistan offering prayers for the soul of their recently departed action hero. Guess who. One of the more absurd tragi-comic memes to emerge was Walker taking Mandela for a hair-rising spin in heaven. As if the actor was the one who could teach the statesman a thing or two.

Challenges to Hollywood have certainly existed in the form of Bollywood, Lollywood and Nollywood (see what just happened there?), yet domination is almost resolute. After all, US cinema needs to have a stock villain that it can cast as the inimical enemy of civilisation as we know it. Whether it is the Indian of the Western, the Japanese or Viet Cong of the war glory days or the Muslim of the terrorist-attack-era, the message is clear: It's our way or the highway if we're going to beat these enemies of our way of life who have absolutely nothing better to do than to attack western civilisation. PostWest films depict a threat to Western, read US, civilisation, and do little other than reinforce this message. The audience is slowly fed a disconnect that only serves to ramp up their pre-existing fears and prejudices. Film does not convey the ambiguity that real life affords us. It promotes the concept that absolute truth and absolute security is a tangible goal that can somehow be attained if only the hero manages to stop the bad guy. What results is a film-consuming society that is locked into an ever-perpetuating cycle of anxiety. And the plot twist? The terrifying prospect of a PostWest, apocalyptic, cataclysmic, end-of-days, eternal hell on earth as we know it. Essential viewing is the following top ten list of PostWest films to convince you that West is ultimately best. Right?

1. *Trump: The Movie* (2016)

If there ever was a scenario that should render us fearful for the longevity of western civilisation, it is the glimmer of possibility that Donald Trump may one day be elected as President of the United States of America, Leader of the Free World. The 2016 parody film satirises Trump's 1986 book: *Trump: The Art of the Deal* in a searing takedown of the Republican frontrunner that is both hilarious and, because of his political currency, terrifying. When Trump is not calling for a wall to be built along the border with Mexico or for immigration of Muslims into the US to be halted, he is flip-flopping on almost every issue that exists as he ploughs through interviews and rallies without scruple, skill or even logic. His watchword is that he wants to make America 'great' again. As empty as his rhetoric is, it seems to have captured the imagination of a slew of disenchanted voters, which is what makes him so dangerous. Director Ron Howard appears as himself in the film, which is set in 1988 and presented as an 'autobiographical' depiction starring the brilliant and inimitable Johnny Depp as Trump. He could not have known that Trump would by any stretch of the imagination be taken seriously in the Presidential nominations, but, as they say, truth is often stranger than fiction and as Steve Fraser writes in Salon.com: Trump 'embodies that well-worn if still stinging observation about the country he hails from: that "America is the only country that went from barbarism to decadence without passing through civilisation".'

2. *Rollover* (1981)

In the 1981 limp political thriller *Rollover*, featuring woefully underwhelming performances by Jane Fonda and Kris Kristofferson, a PostWest nightmare is sketched out for horrified audiences to feast upon. Fonda's character is the widow of a man who is murdered after discovering that the Saudis have a secret slush fund. This obscene amount of money will soon enable them to control the world's economy due to the imminent and unforeseen collapse of global currency. Since 1974 when the A-rabs started putting up oil prices they have amassed millions. Up until now they have been good enough to put the money in US banks. That is all about to change and the audience is faced with the terrifying prospect that inordinate amounts of cash will be concentrated in the hands of such a small group – over which they have no control. Oh the irony! Conspiracy theories on the stockpiling of gold are ruthlessly mined as the capitalist, neo-liberal, free-market infrastructure upon which the free world is built, is brought to its knees. Long before the emergence of the ugly spectre of the Islamic extremist, the Arab was either an exotic curiosity or a desert-dwelling raghead and the orientalist stereotype is very much alive in *Rollover*. A meeting with the Saudis sees Fonda venture to a traditional tent in the middle of the desert. Despite their immense wealth, the Arabs' concept of civilisation is utterly at odds with that of the US, which is exactly why, dear audience, we must fear their supremacy. The ethos of the film is perfectly captured when Kristofferson's character tells the Arabs: 'You're playing with the end of the world.' To which they reply: 'The end of the world as you know it.'

3. *Rising Sun* (1993)

Culture clash mired in historical prejudice, the threat to US dominance by Japanese-controlled multinational corporations and corruption are the pervading themes of this American crime film based on a Michael Crichton novel. The seemingly straightforward case of a sex worker murdered by a client is complicated by the fact the crime took place in the office of a Japanese company. Such is the perceived gulf in understanding between the two cultures that it is deemed necessary to call upon the services of

Sean Connery, an expert on Japanese affairs. Connery unearths a quagmire of murky dealings and underhand activity, with any hope of solving the case centring upon surveillance footage from the night of the murder. However, in what appears to be a warning by Crichton of the decline of the West in light of Japanese technological superiority, it is eventually discovered that the video has been digitally altered to protect powerful Japanese interests. The film conveys the stark message that technological advances in Japan are leaving the US trailing behind. The unthinkable consequence is that the Japanese are now able to manipulate what the world perceives to be reality, in order to gain dominance over the West. *Rising Sun* captured a low point in Japanese-US relations. The early 1990s saw the US government increasingly alarmed by the business machine that was proving so successful in Japan and casting its own efforts firmly in the shade. The fear of a PostWest future resounded, and is brought to the fore in *Rising Sun*.

4. *The Road* (2006)

According to post-apocalyptic films, civilisation is only skin-deep, subject to untold horrors should the existing status quo be skewered in any way. Films such as *The Book of Eli* and *The Postman* are ultimately a commentary on contemporary realities. Society's preoccupations are laid bare and interrogated mercilessly as we stumble to perpetuate the technocratic agenda that brought about its own downfall. But what is the consequence? A post-apocalyptic world that brings out the worst in all but a chosen protagonist. The audience is invited to invest all hope in a solitary hero who defies mayhem and danger to restore humanity's future. *The Road* depicts the cruel choices he must make in order to ensure his and his son's survival in a post-apocalyptic world. An unnamed catastrophe has polluted all the land and rivers. Suicide is the preferred option for many who did not have the good fortune to perish. Others resort to cannibalism and banditry. Marauding gangs of desperate humans are a constant danger. Think *Mad Max* but much grimmer. You'll leave the cinema thanking your lucky stars you live in a neo-liberal, right of centre, globalised mediocrity, sorry, I mean democracy.

5. *Soylent Green* (1973)

Extreme environmental catastrophe seems less unlikely with the passing of each year, and Hollywood certainly can't be accused of ignoring this harbinger of high-octane action and sweeping cinematography. What's more, in a triumph of both style and substance, marrying together climactic apocalypse with science fiction produces an eerily accurate barometer of the West's concerns. Rising sea levels are the culprit in the ambitious but resoundingly average 1995 film *Waterworld* starring Kevin Costner, while the abrupt onset of an ice age wreaks untold havoc in *The Day After Tomorrow* (2004). Don't be fooled into thinking that such concerns are recent. *Soylent Green*, released in 1973, envisages a post-industrialist age in which overpopulation and pollution have decimated the earth's resources. Survival is dependent on a substance that inspires the film title itself: Soylent Green, a nutritious plankton food believed to be sourced from the sea. It turns out that it actually comes from a rather more ghoulish source. Cannibalism rears its ugly head once more. The already industrialised west could well be sending a message to the developing world – slow down your growth rate… and your growing rate. Or we will use you as fodder for our own growth!

6. *Red Dawn* (1984)

Hollywood bogeymen come in various shapes and sizes but one evil spectre has consistently struck terror in the hearts of our anxiety-prone Western audiences. Fearing Soviet invasion of the free world may now be the stuff of folklore (excepting recent transgressions into Ukraine of course). Yet, for decades the Cold War caused sleepless nights for many as the dread of nuclear warfare seeped into the global population's recurring dreams. Ironically, the US Congress accused Hollywood of being infiltrated by Communist sympathisers in the 1930s and 1940s, leading to the McCarthy witch-hunts and film industry hearings conducted by the House Committee on Un-American Activities. Fast forward to 1984 and Patrick Swayze stars in an all-American war film in which Soviet occupation of the US creates the perfect climate for the onset of World War III. While the adults flail ineffectually in their efforts to combat the threat, a group of high school students organise themselves into a resistance group called the Wolverines in an effort to stave off the red scourge. Western hegemony can only be adequately defended and secured by the efforts of the young, exemplified by Swayze and his coming-of-age co-stars Charlie Sheen and Jennifer Grey. The fragility of Western hegemony is plain for all to see and only the energised youth are able to offer any hope of salvation. In the closing sequence of the film, the camera zooms in on a plaque that reads: 'In the early days of World War III, guerrillas – mostly children – placed the names of their lost upon this rock. They fought here alone and gave up their lives, so "that this nation shall not perish from the earth".' The kids fought the PostWest horror to preserve our way of life, and the kids won.

7. *Handmaid's Tale* (1990)

When it comes to female sexuality, Hollywood seems to have tied itself up in knots. The sexpot heroine has been fetishised, debated, decried and subverted for time immemorial but her role as a supporting act to our dear hero remains static. In a parallel universe it is the fertility of women that is strictly controlled and regulated, such is its anarchic potential. The Gileadan regime in the *Handmaid's Tale* is a fascistic theocracy driven by religious extremism and a desire to control the female gender. Women find that they exist as mere vessels of reproduction in a regressive nightmare that puts the priorities of totalitarian rulers before the needs of the individual. Natasha Richardson offers an impressive performance as Kate in this adaptation of Margaret Atwood's feted novel, which is written as an internal monologue. Her emotions must not be betrayed to the people around her who need to be convinced that her indoctrination is complete. Only the audience is permitted an insight into her innermost feelings. Attempting to escape the oppressive militaristic state, our protagonist's husband is killed while her daughter escapes to an unknown fate. She is captured by the Gilead Border Guard and renamed Offered before being forced to train to become a handmaid and becomes the concubine of the Commander, tasked with bearing him and his wife a child. Forget Western ideals of gender equality and sexual liberation in the Free World, the alternative to secular Western liberalism is this misogynistic horror show.

8. *Lives of the Bengal Lancer* (1935)

A classic stock villain saga courtesy of Hollywood is that of the Western. The heroes are of course the cowboys and the villains are undoubtedly the Indians. What's more, the West owes everything to this perennial enemy. It is only because they were afforded the opportunity to wipe out the original inhabitants of the New World that the US was able to come into existence. But that's an aside. Take the concept of the Western one step further and you come up with the Eastern Western. *Lives of the Bengal Lancer* is a rousing adventure film that charts the defensive campaign of a band of British cavalrymen and high-ranking officers in the face of a native attack on their headquarters in Bengal. The film is well-known for the, albeit misquoted, line 'We have ways of making you talk'. It is also notorious for the fascination it holds for fascist and far-right movements. In a moment of small talk candour in 1937, Adolf Hitler told British Foreign Secretary Lord Halifax that he had watched *The Lives of a Bengal Lancer* about three times and counted it as one of his favourite films. He explained: 'I like this film because it depicted a handful of Britons holding a continent in thrall. That is how a superior race must behave and the film is a compulsory viewing for the SS.' The film was eventually re-made as a Western with, yes you guessed it – the British upper crust army officers recast as Cowboys and the members of the Bengal uprising the Indians.

9. *Snowpiercer* (2013)

If you're wondering what a parable of Darwinian economic and political determinism looks like you might want to spend a couple of hours watching *Snowpiercer*. A perfect storm of globalisation, the South Korean production is based on a French graphic novel by Jacques Lob, complete with an English-language cast. The audience can expect to hold its breath in suspense as well as suspend all notion of reality throughout this science-fiction thriller, which evolves into a stark commentary on hierarchical and dogmatic societies. Unlike the democratic vision of the American dream, the characters in this bleak story are allotted their place in a carefully constructed pecking order and any attempt to veer off track is violently suppressed. The backdrop is a cataclysmic environmental disaster triggered by an attempt to offset climate change. Survivors are assembled onto The Rattling Ark train to escape a second ice age and spend the next fifteen years navigating a barren land. Life on board the train is luxurious and opulent for a small elite who occupy the front section of the train but those condemned to the filthy, inhumane conditions in the last carriages endure a living hell. Resentment is rife and before long there is talk of revolution. An attempt to overthrow the powers that maintain the status quo through the use of brutality and intimidation is finally underway. Our villain is actually a rather complex character, the transport magnate Wilfred. He disregards all notions of justice and equality in favour of pursuit of a policy of the survival of the fittest. He echoes the philosophy of dictators of all hues, from communists to theocrats: 'This train is a complete ecosystem, which must respect the balance. Air, water, food, people. Everything must be regulated. For this, it was sometimes necessary to use more radical solutions.' Let us thank our lucky stars we live in the West where environmental disaster may be on the horizon, but we are Free to ignore the warnings!

10. Alien (1979) and Mars Attacks! (1996)

Possibly the most terrifying and horrific scene in film history has to be the macabre gore of an alien erupting from the chest of John Hurt in Ridley Scott's spectacle of cinematography. A film that could easily be about workers on zero hours contracts who witness their jobs being wiped out by an uncontrollable techno-parasite, the take-home message is that democracy should never be rendered subservient to the greed of big business. Unbeknownst to the workers, it was the multinational corporations' intention all along to dupe them into sacrificing their lives to bring home the alien they would later utilise for biological warfare. In the second film of the franchise, seventy years have passed during which Sigourney Weaver has been kept in a coma-like state. She wakes to be told by the corporation that they own her. The human colony residing in the alien-inhabited planet has abruptly ceased contact with Earth and an indebted Weaver is forced to return to the alien planet to find out why. Whether you think this is a film about the mutation of neo-liberal social order or, according to film critic Mark Kermode, a hetero-normative fear of male rape, the *Alien* franchise will tap into the darkest recesses of anyone's imagination. For some light relief and an antidote to the nightmares, treat yourself to a night in on the sofa watching *Mars Attacks!* A cult sci-fi parody, it turns the genre on its head, reportedly an A-list celebrity love-in that is actually a searing overload of 1990s anti-Hollywood cynicism. What more could you possibly expect from a Tim Burton film?

CITATIONS

Introduction: The Last Post
by Shanon Shah

On things Shakespearean, see Laura Bohannan. 1966. 'Shakespeare in the Bush: An American Anthropologist Set out to Study the Tiv of West Africa and Was Taught the True Meaning of Hamlet.' *Natural History* 75. http://www.naturalhistorymag.com/picks-from-the-past/12476/shakespeare-in-the-bush; John Burger. 2016. 'Shakespeare at 400: How He Continues to Shape Western Culture.' *Aleteia.org*. 23 April 2016. http://aleteia.org/2016/04/23/shakespeare-at-400-how-he-continues-to-shape-western-culture/; Margaret Litvin. 2016. 'Shakespeare in the Arab World: Introduction.' *MIT Global Shakespeares*. Accessed 10 August 2016. http://globalshakespeares.mit.edu/blog/2010/10/18/arab-world/; Robert McCrum. 2016. 'Ten Ways in Which Shakespeare Changed the World.' *The Guardian*, 17 April 2016. https://www.theguardian.com/culture/2016/apr/17/ten-ways-shakespeare-changed-the-world; Poonam Trivedi. 2012. 'Why Shakespeare Is … Indian.' *The Guardian*, 4 May. https://www.theguardian.com/stage/2012/may/04/why-shakespeare-is-indian; Frances Wood. 2011. 'Why Does China Love Shakespeare?' *The Guardian*, June 28. https://www.theguardian.com/commentisfree/2011/jun/28/china-shakespeare-wen-jiabao-visit. The Robert Graves quote can be found in Fred Metcalf (ed.). 'Shakespeare.' In *The Penguin Dictionary of Modern Humorous Quotations*, Second Edition. London: Penguin. On Brazil's political and other woes, see Terry L. McCoy. 2016. 'Why Brazil's Post-Olympics Hangover Will Hit so Hard.' *The Conversation*. Accessed 10 August 2016. http://theconversation.com/why-brazils-post-olympics-hangover-will-hit-so-hard-61488; Anthony Pereira. 2016. 'Brazil Shoots for Olympian Heights at a Time of Political Lows.' *The Conversation*. Accessed August 10. http://theconversation.com/brazil-shoots-for-olympian-heights-at-a-time-of-political-lows-62862.

More information on the engagement with the concept of the West in Brazil and India was obtained from Oliver Stuenkel. 2011. 'Identity and the Concept of the West: The Case of Brazil and India.' *Revista Brasileira de Politica Internacional* 54 (1): 178–95.

See also: Ziauddin Sardar, *Postmodernism and the Other* (Pluto Press, London, 1998); and *Introducing Islam*, which has been enchantingly illustrated by Zafar Abbas Malik (Icon Books, London, 2001).

The Concept of the West by Jasper M. Trautsch

For the concept of the Occident see Edward W. Said, *Orientalism* (New York: Pantheon, 1978). Thierry Hentsch, *L'orient imaginaire: La vision politique occidentale de l'Est méditerranéen* (Paris: Les Éditions de Minuit, 1988). James G. Carrier (ed.), *Occidentalism: Images of the West* (Oxford: Clarendon Press, 1995). For the concept of Christian civilisation in the nineteenth and twentieth centuries see Jean-René Derré, Jacques Gadille, Xavier de Montclos, and Bernard Plongeron (eds.), *Civilisation chrétienne: Approche historique d'une idéologie, XVIIIe-XXe siècle* (Paris: Beauchesne, 1975). Vanessa Conze, *Das Europa der Deutschen: Ideen von Europa in Deutschland zwischen Reichstradition und Westorientierung (1920-1970)* (Munich: Oldenbourg, 2005).

No comprehensive history of the concept of the West yet exists. For general overviews and relevant aspects see David Gress, *From Plato to NATO: The Idea of the West and its Opponents* (New York: Free Press, 1998). Patrick Thaddeus Jackson, *Civilizing the Enemy: German Reconstruction and the Invention of the West* (Ann Arbor: University of Michigan Press, 2006), 72-111. For the 'Western Civilization' courses in the US see Carol S. Gruber, *Mars and Minerva: World War I and the Uses of the Higher Learning in America* (Baton Rouge: Louisiana State University Press, 1975). Gilbert Allardyce, 'The Rise and Fall of the Western Civilization Course,' in: *American Historical Review*, Vol. 87, No. 3 (1982), 695-725. Peter N. Stearns, *Western Civilization in World History* (New York: Routledge, 2003).

The argument about the merger of the concepts of the Occident and Western Civilisation is based on original research and has not yet been advanced in this form.

For the 'Clash of Civilizations' argument see Samuel P. Huntington, *The Clash of Civilizations and the Remaking of World Order* (New York: Simon and Schuster, 1996). For critical responses that do not, however, question the existence of clearly definable 'Western' and 'Muslim Civilizations' see Jonathan Fox, 'Two Civilizations and Ethnic Conflict: Islam and the West', in: *Journal of Peace Research*, Vol. 38, No. 4 (2001), 459-472. Shahrough Akhavi, 'Islam and the West in World History,' in: *Third World Quarterly*, Vol. 24, No. 3 (2003), 545-562. Abdullah Al-Ahsan, 'The Clash of Civilizations Thesis and Muslims: The Search for an Alternative Paradigm,' in: *Islamic Studies*, Vol. 48, No. 2 (2009), 189-217. The way Middle Eastern autocrats portrayed themselves as 'enlightened' to justify their rule is discussed in Mona Abaza, 'The Trafficking with Tanwir (Enlightenment),' in: *Comparative Studies of South Asia, Africa and the Middle East*, Vol. 30, No. 1 (2010), 32-46. For the distinction between 'the West' as a civilisation and as a normative project see the magisterial overview of the history of 'the West' as presented in: Heinrich August Winkler, *Geschichte des Westens*, 4 vols. (Munich: Beck, 2009-2015).

The Struggle for World Power
by Roger van Zwanenberg

On the history of the British East India Company, see Niall Ferguson, *Empire: How Britain made the Modern World* (Penguin, London, 2004); William Dalrymple, *White Mughals: Love and Betrayal in 18th-century India* (Harper, London, 2004) and Nick Robins, *The Corporation that Changed the World* (Pluto Press, London, 2006). On the sixteenth century battle for control of the Mediterranean between Spain/Portugal and the Ottoman Empire, see Roger Crowley, *Empires of the Sea: The Final Battle for the Mediterranean 1521-1580* (Faber and Faber, London, 2009). On the impacts of the Versailles treaty, see John Maynard Keynes, *The Economic Consequences of the Peace* (Createspace Independent Publishing Platform 2010). On the rise of the US, see Jack Rasmus, *Epic Recession: Prelude to Global Depression*, (Pluto,

London, 2010) and Eric Hobsbawm, *The Age of Extremes: The Short Twentieth Century 1914-1991* (Abacus, London, 1994). On the role of Japan in the Second World War, see Rana Mitter, *China's War with Japan, 1937–1945: The Struggle for Survival* (Allen Lane, Londo, 2013) and Kai Bird and Lawrence Lifschultz (editors), *Hiroshima's Shadow* (Pamphleteers Press 1998).

More detail on Lin Zexu's letter to Queen Victoria and his life can be found in Amitav Ghosh's novel *River of Smoke* (John Murray, London, 2012). For more on the TTIP, see John Hilary, 'TTIP: What Can We Expect From 2016?', *openDemocracy*, 15 January 2016, https://www.opendemocracy.net/ournhs/john-hilary/ttip-what-can-we-expect-from-2016 and his other writings on openDemocracy and at http://www.waronwant.org/what-ttip

PostWest Anxieties by Gordon Blaine Steffey

Works Cited in this essay, include: De Certeau, Michel. *The Practice of everyday life*, tr. Stephen F. Rendell (Berkeley: University of California Press, 1984); Gibbon, Edward. *The History of the decline and fall of the Roman empire*, 12 vols. (New York City: Fred de Fau and Co., 1906); Godin, Benoît. 'The Information economy: the history of a concept through its measurement, 1949-2005,' *History and Technology* 24, no. 3 (2008); Gudynas, Eduardo. 'Buen vivir: Today's tomorrow,' *Development* 54, no. 4 (2011), 441–447; Lear, Jonathan. *Radical hope: Ethics in the face of cultural devastation* (Cambridge, MA and London: Harvard University Press, 2006); Linderman, Frank B. *Plenty-Coups: Chief of the Crows* (Lincoln, NE and London: University of Nebraska Press, 2002); National Secretariat of Planning and Development (Senplades), 'National plan for good living, 2013-2017 [summarized version],' Quito, Ecuador: 2013); Rollins, Philip Ashton. *The Cowboy; his characteristics, his equipment* (New York City: Charles Scribner's Sons, 1922); Santiesteban, Gustavo Soto and Silke Helfrich. 'El Buen vivir and the commons,' *The Wealth of the Commons: A World Beyond Market & State*, ed. David Bollier and Silke Helfrich (Amherst, MA: Levellers Press, 2012); de Sousa Santos, Boaventura. *Epistemologies of the south: Justice Agaist Epistemicide* (Boulder, CO and London: Paradigm Publishers, 2014); Valéry, Paul. 'Notre destin et les Lettres,' *Oeuvres*

Complètes, Tome 1, Édition La Pochothèque, ed. Michel Jarrety (Paris: Le Livre de poche, 2016) and 'La crise de l'esprit,' *Europes de l'antiquité au XXe siècle* (Paris: Éditions Robert Laffont, 2000).

Hanson, Victor Davis. 'The Postwest: a civilisation that has become just a dream,' *National Review Online*, 13 April 2007, can be accessed at: http://www.nationalreview.com/article/220598/postwest-victor-davis-hanson; a pdf file of Plurinational State of Bolivia's Constitution of 2009, tr. Max Planck Institute, (Oxford University Press), can be obtained from: https://www.constituteproject.org/constitution/Bolivia_2009.pdf; and Wolcher, Louis E. 'The Meaning of the Commons,' The Law of the Commons Conference, Seattle University, can be accessed at: https://www.youtube.com/watch?v=sz8EpvK3ClI

Where is the East? by Amrita Ghosh

Surekha Davies quote is from. 'The Wondrous East in the Renaissance Geographical Imagination: Marco Polo, Fra Mauro and Giovanni Battista Ramusio', *History and Anthropology* 23 (2) 215-234 (June 2012); Karen Culcasi quotes are from 'Constructing and Naturalizing the Middle East', *The Geographical Review*. 100 (4) 583-597 (October 2010); Gayatri Chakravorty Spivak quote is from *An Aesthetic Education in the Era of Globalization*. (Cambridge: Harvard University Press, 2012) p9, 26; and Edward Said quote is from *Orientalism* (New York: Vintage Books Edition, 1979), p12.

See also: Dipesh Chakravorty, *Provicializing Europe: Postcolonial History and Historical Difference* (Princeton: Princeton University Press, 2007); John Sweeney, 'New Wave Orientalism: Postnormal Imaginings in Wes Anderson's The Darjeeling Limited', *EastWest Affairs* 1 2 75-98 (2013); and Ziauddin Sardar, *Orientalism* (Buckingham: Open University Press, 1999).

Oprah Winfrey's 'India, The Next Chapter' can be found at: www.oprah.com

Russia's Identity Crisis by Julia Sveshnikova

Daniel Treisman's article, 'Why Putin Took Crimea', published in *Foreign Affairs*, 18 April 2016 is available at: https://www.foreignaffairs.com/articles/ukraine/2016-04-18/why-putin-took-crimea

Levada Center's opinion poll on the events in Ukraine, August 2014 and the role of Joseph Stalin in Russian history, March 2015, can be accessed at: http://www.rbc.ru/politics/29/08/2014/945781.shtml.4 http://www.levada.ru/2015/03/31/stalin-i-ego-rol-v-istorii-strany/

The WCIOM opinion poll on Crimea, Spring 2016, is available at: https://wciom.ru/index.php?id=236&uid=115622

On the Social Doctrine of Russian Muslims, see: http://islam-today.ru/socialnaa-doktrina-rossijskih-musulman/. An estimate on numbers of Muslims in Russia by Levada Center is at: http://polit.ru/news/2012/12/17/religon/. However, religious denomination is not included in the population census, so to it is almost impossible to have an exact number. Estimates are based on the number of people 'living in the Muslim tradition', meaning within locations traditionally populated by ethnic Muslims. Religious coordinating bodies normally report a larger Muslim population in Russia. It is even more difficult to have an account of converts to Islam.

About NORM, see: http://islamist.ru/%D0%BD%D0%BE%D1%80%D0%BC/; http://norm-blog.livejournal.com/; https://vk.com/pravoverie; http://www.harunsidorov.info/. Since the organisation was named radical in Russia and its leader called on his followers to leave the country, there is no single authoritative source of reference for the group.

To learn more about Pussy Riot 'punk protest', see 'Pussy Riot: the story so far': http://www.bbc.com/news/world-europe-25490161 and to view the performance itself go to: https://www.youtube.com/watch?v=ALS92big4TY

To see Russian Minister of defence Sergey Shoigu crossing himself before the Victory parade in 2015, see: https://www.youtube.com/watch?v=_F-r7q3vMtA and 2016, see: https://www.youtube.com/watch?v=3nm2M0EOpq8

For more on Vyacheslav (Ali) Polosin officiating the Simferopol mosque opening, see: http://islam.ru/news/2015-10-01/44131 and conducting a seminar there, see: http://www.islamfund.ru/news-view-2739.html Qurban Mirzakhanov's website is http://alshia.ru/

China's Balancing Act by Jalal Afhim

On China's foreign relations, see the following articles and reports: 'China's vision of the Middle East' by Geoffrey Aronson. *Al Jazeera*, 21 January 2016; 'Is China's President About to Make His First Trip to the Middle East?' by Shannon Tiezzi. *The Diplomat*, 9 January 2016; 'China Seeks Foreign Investors for One Belt One Road push' by Lucy Hornby, *Financial Times*, 25 May 2016; 'Xi Jinping warns on limits to diplomacy as China-US talks begin' by Tom Mitchell & Yuan Yang, *Financial Times*, 6 June 2016; 'Chinese Investors shore up Kazakhstan FDI despite commodity bust' by Jacopo Dettoni. *Financial Times*, 6 June 2016; 'As Xi heads into Middle East feud, China says aims for balance' by Reuters, published in *Egypt Independent*, 18 January 2016: http://www.egyptindependent.com/node/2465243; 'Revealed: China's Blueprint for Building Middle East Relations' by Shannon Tiezzi. *The Diplomat*, 14 January 2016; 'Chinese Policy in the Middle East in the Wake of the Arab Uprisings', by Michael Singh, *The Washington Institute for Near East Policy*, Dec 2014; 'China, Qatar and RMB Internationalization', by Muhammad Zulfikar Rakhmat, *The Diplomat*, 6 June 2015; 'The Dragon Heads West: China – Arab Cooperation in the New Era' by Degang Sun, in *Georgetown Security Studies Review: Conference Proceedings: China in the Middle East*, June 2015; and 'Key facts behind China's warming ties with Saudi Arabia, Iran, and Egypt, as Xi Jinping signs mega oil deals during his Middle East tour'. By Zhuang Pinghui, *South China Morning Post*, 20 January, 2016.

On Muslims in China, see Michael Dillon, *China's Muslims* (OUP, Beijing, 1997); Jean A. Berlie, *Islam in China: Hui and Uighurs between Modernization and Sinicization* (White Lotus Press, Chonburi, 2004); Michael Dillon, editor, *Islam in China: Key Papers Vols. 1 & 2* (Oxford University Press, Oxford, 1996: and Jonathan Lipman, *Familiar Strangers: A History of Muslims in North-West China* (University of Washington Press, Seattle, 1998). For China's policies on its Muslim minorities, see Reza Hasmuth (2013). 'Managing China's Muslim Minorities: Migration, Labour, and the Rise of Ethnoreligious Consciousness Among Uyghurs in Urban Xinjiang' in *Religion and the State: A Comparative Sociology*, edited by Jack Barbalet, Adam Possamai, and Bryan S. Turner (Anthem Press, London, 2013.

On China's billionaires and income inequality, see '2015 Forbes Billionaires: Wanda's Wang Jianlin repeats as China's richest man' by Russell Flannery, *Forbes*, 2 March 2015: http://www.forbes.com/sites/russellflannery/2015/03/02/2015-forbes-billionaires-wandas-wang-jianlin-repeats-as-chinas-richest-man/#5958cb5d3968 and 'China's Income Equality Among World's Worst' by Gabriel Wildau and Tom Mitchell, *Financial Times*, 14 January 2016.

For an account of heterodox Sufi worship and music, see Jonathan Lipman's keynote lecture at Mount Holyoke College, 'Head Wagging and Obscene Music: Conflicts over Sound on the Qing-Muslim Frontiers': https://www.youtube.com/watch?v=WV3o2vq7sRA

For China's position on Palestinian statehood, see 'Palestine UN bid: Where does China stand?', by Nima Khorami Assi, *Al Jazeera*: http://www.aljazeera.com/indepth/opinion/2011/09/2011928163950390354.html

Seesaws and Cycles by Boyd Tonkin

The Muqaddimah: An Introduction to History by Ibn Khaldun, in Franz Rosenthal's translation, has now been reissued as a Princeton Classic by Princeton University Press (2015). The Histories of Herodotus appear in a spirited and readable new translation by Tom Holland from Penguin

Classics (2013). Isaiah Berlin discusses the central ideas of Vico and puts them in context in his *Three Critics of Enlightenment* (Pimlico, 2000). For a skilful one-volume abridgement of Edward Gibbon's *History of the Decline and Fall of the Roman Empire*, see David Womersley's edition in Penguin Classics (2000). In 1987, Oxford University Press issued DC Somervell's two-volume abridgement of Arnold J Toynbee's *A Study of History*. Rabindranath Tagore's essays on Nationalism appear as one of the Penguin Great Ideas series; see also *The Essential Tagore*, edited by Fakrul Alam and Radha Chakravarty (Harvard University Press, 2011). Samuel Huntington's 'The Clash of Civilizations' was first published as an article in *Foreign Affairs* (1993) and then in a book of the same name (Simon & Schuster, 1996). Edward Said's essays on Huntington and other cultural thinkers are collected in *Reflections on Exile* (Harvard University Press, 2002), while 'The Clash of Ignorance' appeared in *The Nation* (4 October 2001). Jared Diamond's *Guns, Germs and Steel* first appeared in 1997 (Jonathan Cape), and Niall Ferguson's *Civilization: The Six Killer Apps of Western Power* in 2011 (Allen Lane). Ian Morris's *Why the West Rules - For Now* was published by Profile in 2010, and Pankaj Mishra's *From the Ruins of Empire* by Allen Lane in 2012. Other widely-cited 'big picture' histories I have consulted include Paul Kennedy's *The Rise and Fall of the Great Powers* (Unwin, 1988), David Landes's *The Wealth and Poverty of Nations* (Norton, 1998) and John Darwin's *After Tamerlane* (Allen Lane, 2007). For an antidote to this sometimes portentous genre, sample the incomparably subtle and wistful end-of-empire verse of CP Cavafy, for instance in Edmund Keeley and Philip Sherrard's translations (Chatto & Windus, 1990; or at www.cavafy.com).

'Post-Everything' by Carool Kersten

Material in this essay is drawn from two other publications: Carool Kersten, 'Islam vs the West? Muslim challenges of a false binary' in: Klaus-Gerd Giesen, Carool Kersten and Lenart Škof (eds.) *Poesis of Peace: Narratives, Cultures and Philosophies* (New York: Routledge, 2017) and Carool Kersten, 'World Philosophies as Philosophies of Worldliness: Vattimo's Weak Thought and Dabashi's Hermeneutics of Alterity' in Cosimo Zene (ed.) *World Philosophies in Dialogue: Perspectives and Challenges* Inaugural Volume of the World Philosophies Series (Milan, MIMESIS, forthcoming).

References cited include: Giorgio Agamben, *Homo Sacer: Sovereign Power and Bare Life* (Palo Alto: Stanford University Press, 1998); *State of Exception* (Chicago: University of Chicago Press 2005); Gil Anidjar, 'Secularism,' *Critical Inquiry* 33, no.1 (2006); Hamid Dabashi, *The Arab Spring: The End of Postcolonialism* (London and New York: Zed Books, 2012); *Being a Muslim in the World: Rethinking Islam for a Post-Western History* (London: Palgrave Macmillan, 2013); *Brown Skin, White Masks (The Islamic Mediterranean)* (London: Pluto Press, 2011); *Iran: A People Interrupted* (London and New York: The New Press, 2007); *Iran, the Green Movement and the USA: The Fox and the Parado* (London and New York: Zed Books, 2010); *Islamic Liberation Theology: Resisting the Empire* (London and New York: Routledge, 2008); *Persophilia: Persian Culture on the Global Scene*. (Cambridge, MA: Harvard University Press, 2015); *Post-Orientalism: Knowledge and Power in a Time of Terror* (New Brunswick, NH: Transaction Publishers, 2009); *Shi'ism: A Religion of Protest* (Cambridge, MA and London: Belknap, 2011); *Theology of Discontent: The Ideological Foundation of the Islamic Revolution in Iran* (New Brunswick: Transaction Publishers, 2006); *The World of Persian Literary Humanism*. Cambridge, MA: Harvard University Press, 2012); Hans Georg Gadamer, *Truth and Method* (New York: Continuum, 2004); Richard Kearney, *Anatheism (Return to God after God)* (New York, Columbia University Press, 2011); Richard Rorty, *Philosophy and the Mirror of Nature* (Princeton: Princeton University Press, 1979); Mark C. Taylor, *Erring: A Postmodern A/ theology* (Chicago and New York, University of Chicago Press, 1984); Gianni Vattimo, *Belief* (Stanford: Stanford University Press, 1999); *The Adventure of Difference*. (Baltimore: Johns Hopkins University Press, 1993); *The End of Modernity* (London: Polity Press, 1985); 'Towards a Nonreligious Christianity,' in *After the Death of God*, ed. Jeffrey W. Robbins (New York: Columbia University Press, 2007); *The Transparent Society* (Cambridge and Malden, MA: Polity Press, 1992); Gianni Vattimo and Pier Aldo Rovatti, *Weak Thought* (Albany: State University of New York Press, 2012).

The West is Dead! by Jim Dator

On my work with the World Futures Studies Federation, see Jim Dator, 'WFSF and I', *Futures* 37 5 371-385 (2005). See also: Jim Dator, 'Judicial governance of the long blur' *Futures* 33 2 181-197 (2001) and 'The dancing judicial Zen masters' *Technological Forecasting and Social Change* 46 1 59-70 (1994). On postnormality, see: Ziauddin Sardar, 'Welcome to Postnormal Times' *Futures* 42 (5): 435–44 (2010), 'Postnormal Times Revisited' *Futures* 67 (March): 26–39 (2015), 'Postnormal Artefacts' *World Future Review* 7 (4) 342-350 (2016); and Ziauddin Sardar and John Sweeney, 'The Three Tomorrows of Postnormal Times.' *Futures* 75 1–13 (2015).

Thar Women and Pakistani Art by Bina Shah

The poem from Jon Stallworthy is from *Rounding the Horn: Collected Poems* (Carcanet Press, London, 1998); it first appeared in *Out of Bounds* (OUP, Karachi, 1963). *A Season For Martyrs* is published by Delphinium Press, New York, 2014. 'Pakistan Painters' Series: Ali Abbas' can be accessed at: https://www.facebook.com/media/set/?set=a.481547435190696.117 539.127464093932367&type=3; and a report of the 'Photography Exhibition on Queen of Thar' by Muhammed Ali, published in 'PakArt. Org', 2 March 2015, can be accessed at: http://www.parkart.org/events-exhibitions/photoraphy-exhibition-on-queen-of-thar/

Dark Events by Ana Maria Pacheco

We thank Ana Maria Pacheco and Pratt Contemporary Art for the permission to reproduce these images. To explore her work further, see Pratt Contemporary Art's *Collected Essays: Texts on the Work of Ana Maria Pacheco* (Sevenoaks, 2004) and Robert Bush's *The Role of Prints and Drawings in the Work of Ana Maria Pacheco* (2016), which can be downloaded at: http://read.uberflip.com/i/675004- the-role-of-prints-and-drawings-in-the-work-of-ana-maria-pacheco. Pacheco's page can be found at the Pratt Contemporary Art website: http://www.prattcontemporaryart.co.uk/ana-maria-pacheco-2/

Hail! The Three Tomorrows by Scott Jordan

The quote from Ziauddin Sardar and Merryl Wyn Davies is from *American Terminator: Myths, Movies and Global Power* (Disinformation Books, New York, 2004), p24. For a detailed discussion of the three tomorrows methodology, see Ziauddin Sardar and John Sweeney, 'The Three Tomorrows of Postnormal Times' *Futures* 75 1–13 (2015), and on Postnormal Times, see Ziauddin Sardar, 'Welcome to Postnormal Times' *Futures* 42 (5): 435–44 (2010) and 'Postnormal Times Revisited' *Futures* 67 (March): 26–39 (2015). See also The Iraq Inquiry (Chilcot Report), at: www.iraqinquiry.org.uk/the-report

Last Word: On Radical Hope by Hassan Mahamdallie

On Plenty Coups, see Jonathan Lear, *Radical Hope: Ethics in the Face of Cultural Devastation* (Harvard University Press, 2006) and Frank Linderman, *Plenty-coups: Chief of Crows* (University of Nebraska Press, 2002). On the ideas of Franz Boas, see Robert Wald Sussman, *The Myth of Race: The Troubling Persistence of an Unscientific Idea* (Harvard University Press, 2014) and Franz Boas, *The Mind of Primitive Man* (Free Press, New York, 1965). On Pocahontas, see Ziauddin Sardar, *Postmodernism and the Other: The New Imperialism of Western Culture* (Pluto Press, London, 1998); and on Harvard University's cardinal role in promoting American eugenics see Adam Cohen, *The Supreme Court, American Eugencis and the Sterilization of Carrie Buck* (Penguin, New York, 2016).

See also: Robert Hughes, *The Fatal Shore* (Vintage, London, 2003); Nathan Lean, *The Islamophobia Industry: How the Right Manufactures Fear of Muslims* (Pluto Press, London, 2012); Amin Maalouf, *Disordered World* (Bloomsbury, London, 2011); and Ian Angus, *Facing the Anthropocene* (Monthly Review Press, New York, 2016).